International Business

International Business

MARGARET WOODS

palgrave

First published 2001 by
PALGRAVE
Houndmills, Basingstoke, Hampshire RG21 6XS
and 175 Fifth Avenue, New York, N. Y. 10010
Companies and representatives throughout the world

PALGRAVE is the new global academic imprint of
St. Martin's Press LLC Scholarly and Reference Division and
Palgrave Publishers Ltd (formerly Macmillan Press Ltd).

ISBN 0–333–75978–8 paperback
ISBN 0–333–75979–6 hardback

Cataloguing-in-publication data

A catalogue record for this book is available
from the British Library.

A catalogue record for this book is available
from the Library of Congress.

This book is printed on paper suitable for recycling and
made from fully managed and sustained forest sources.

10   9   8   7   6   5   4   3   2   1
10 09 08 07 06 05 04 03 02 01

Printed and bound in Great Britain by
Antony Rowe Ltd, Chippenham, Wiltshire

Contents

Foreword

Learning management is like learning to play a musical instrument: it demands talent, hard work, and the luck to be able to practise. Learning international management demands additional talent, more hard work, and even more luck. It means muddling along in foreign languages, being prepared to travel, even settling abroad.

Effective international management partly calls for different attitudes and skills than effective home-based management. A multicultural perspective implies restraint in passing judgement: the ability to recognise that in different environments, different rules of the game of business may apply. Successful managers at home are often those who have proven themselves by a strong drive and quick and firm opinions. These very qualities may make them less qualified for international management.

International managers need to be context-sensitive. Narrow specialists may be needed at times for solving technical problems abroad, but they should be shipped back as soon as possible. International managers need a broad interest and an eagerness to absorb new information, including from fields like history, geography, religion, literature and art.

International managers export not only their professional lives, but their private and family lives as well. Families are deeply affected by their fathers, more rarely mothers, accepting an international management career. Partners may lose their jobs if they join in expatriation, and each other if they don't. Unmarried couples, commonly in some Western countries, may have to formally marry in order to be admitted into countries with traditional morality laws. Even if the international manager remains home-based, he or she will be away from home more often. Children will be affected by expatriation or by their parent's frequent absences. Expatriations seem to fail more often for family reasons than for job reasons.

This textbook on international business management differs from home-based management. No book can make one an international manager, like no book can teach one to play an instrument. What a book can do is create awareness of what there is to be known, and motivate the user to find out what he or she will need to know in addition to what the book contains.

The student of this book will also discover the complexity of, and some of the value conflicts inherent in, the international business field. If he or she feels comfortable with this amount of intellectual and moral confusion, then maybe this is the first step to a productive international management career.

Newspapers frequently announce international mergers, acquisitions and strategic alliances between companies from different countries, and almost equally frequently their failure and dismantling after a few years. In spite of overwhelming evidence of serious pitfalls, top managers deciding on such ventures are surprised and trapped again and again.

This evidence only stresses the need to educate a new generation of future managers and professionals in the essentials of the International Business field. There is a naïve slogan 'Think globally, act locally'. Its naïveté lies in the arrogant assumption that anybody can think 'globally'. The essence of international management is precisely that we all think 'locally' and have to learn to cooperate with others who think differently because they grew up elsewhere. The slogan should be reversed: 'Think locally, act globally'. Let this be the motto for this book's future users.

Velp, The Netherlands, May 2001
Geert Hofstede

Preface

The aim of this book on of *International Business* is to explain and discuss the issues faced by companies engaged in identifying and developing their overseas operations. The study of international business straddles a variety of different disciplines, and this book deals with the problems of international operations from the perspective of economics and politics as well as the functional disciplines of strategic planning, finance, marketing, human resource management and operations management. Most importantly, it seeks to show how the international economic and political environment serves to act as a very powerful influence over how company policies are set: corporate strategy reflects the managers' understanding of the external environment, and functional policies are fine tuned and adjusted to that environment. The structure of the text is designed to draw out these links.

After many years of teaching international business, I concluded that there was a need for a book which took key theories and illustrated them by the use of detailed examples of company behaviour. There is a danger that texts which have a theoretical emphasis will lie unread because they are difficult to digest and understand. Equally, books which are purely collections of case studies or observations of business practice can be too descriptive in nature, lacking a strong conceptual foundation. The problem for anyone studying a semester length course is that there is not time to read both the theory and the practice, and this book aims to resolve that problem. Each chapter summarises the current thinking and theoretical principles in the relevant field of study, and illustrates them via examples of business behaviour. For readers interested in finding out more, there are end of chapter references to other textbooks, academic journals and web sites. Combined with the end of chapter questions, these references ensure that the book is well suited to distance learning and self tuition packages.

The book is intended for use by both undergraduate and MBA students who are undertaking university courses that have an interdisciplinary and international content. It will be most useful for modules that require a general overview of all of the functional elements of international business, as well as an external 'environmental' orientation. At the same time, individual sections and/or chapters may be used to enrich modules that focus on domestic issues, but which can be enlivened by the introduction of an international dimension. A key feature of the text is its broad geographic scope which includes examples and case studies from around the globe.

Now, students from Western Europe, South East Asia and North America will all find scenarios and examples which discuss familiar products and concepts.

STRUCTURE OF THE BOOK

The theme of the book is that conditions in the broader international environment help to determine corporate and functional strategies. What is more, the combined policies of many individual multinational companies serve to influence and change the broad environment of which they are a part. The book is therefore subdivided into three separate sections, dealing with each of the issues of the broad environment, corporate policy making, and the impact of multinational companies in turn. Each section can be used on a stand alone basis, but the overall text builds on the lessons of the preceding chapters.

Section One of the book is devoted to a discussion of the global context within which international businesses must function in the twenty-first century. The first chapter provides a broad overview of the historic growth of international business operations, and a summary of areas of topical concern in respect of the world economy, political relations, and technological change. The aim is to describe the external framework which exists today, and which will influence company strategies in the international arena.

Although the broad environment is of concern to companies, there are clearly some factors that will be more important than others in determining the likelihood of success in international markets. The state of the world economy, and the rules and regulations governing international trade and investment are critical here. Chapter 2 is therefore devoted to a detailed consideration of trade theory, the historic development of world trade, and the simultaneous and rapid growth of foreign direct investment. Chapter 3 then takes the debate a stage further by looking at the extent to which trade and investment patterns have been matched by the development of regional trading blocs such as the EU and NAFTA. The presence of such blocs, and the growth of the Triad are inevitably going to affect the future patterns of international trade and investment.

The political and social environment also impinges on businesses, and so the final chapter in this first section is devoted to a consideration of the role of culture in international business. A large number of courses and textbooks are devoted solely to the study of comparative management practices in different cultures, and trying to cover the topic in a single chapter is clearly going to result in a relatively brief summary of key theories. Nonetheless it is included here because the author believes that students need to understand the importance of cultural empathy to business success. As the chapters on management functions demonstrate, culture is relevant right across a business, and is not just an issue for the marketing department.

This structure means that on completion of the reading of Section One, students should have a good understanding of the background of international business in the twenty-first century. This is the foundation stone for any international business course. Although the Section is intended as a lead in to discussion of the functional areas of management that are covered in the succeeding chapters, it could alternatively be used as a stand alone element to prepare students for a focused course in international HRM, marketing or any business function. Teachers can 'mix and match' elements of the text to suit their own course requirements.

Section Two moves from away from the broad global picture to address the problems of international business in the context of the individual business. The question being posed in this part of the book is 'what company decisions and management choices are influenced by the conditions in the wider environment, and how does the internationally oriented business react?' The day to day operational practices of any business are predetermined by the overall business and corporate strategy. This section of the book therefore starts with a review of international business strategies, and Chapter 5 covers the reasons why companies may decide to internationalise, alternative theories of internationalisation, and the implications of international involvement for company structures.

Narrowing down from the corporate to the functional level, chapters 6–10 then look at the international management of the various functional processes across the value chain, starting with finance. Company strategies are inevitably restricted to the pursuit of goals for which the capital and cash is available, and so the first of the finance chapters (Chapter 6) looks at sources of funding for international business, and the workings of the international financial markets. Technological developments, particularly in the field of information technology, have led to significant growth in these markets. Chapter 7 goes on to discuss the financial risks of international operations, and how those risks can be managed. The material covered in this chapter is technical in nature, but offers useful insights into how careful application of hedging techniques can significantly reduce the financial risks of trading in foreign currencies. The chapter includes a section on the implications of the European common currency for international business in the region.

Once a company has a strategy, and the funding that is deemed necessary for its fulfilment, managers can turn to answering the question of *where* to trade or invest, *what* to buy/sell, and *how* to maximise the international potential. These are all issues that relate to international marketing, which is the subject of Chapter 8. Methods of market segmentation are discussed, together with techniques that can be used to screen potential markets. In addition, readers are presented with the pros and cons of an array of different routes of entry into foreign markets, and explanations of how decisions on pricing, promotion and distribution policies are established. The impact of technology on promotional methods is also discussed.

Armed with a set of objectives as to exactly what is to be sold where, it is possible for management to devise a plan that details the operational process by which the items will be supplied to the markets. International companies face very specific operational problems in relation to ensuring that they can produce and efficiently serve all of their markets and this branch of management, which is commonly referred to as operations management, is the subject of Chapter 9. In many universities and colleges, operations management is taken only by a small proportion of students as an optional field of study, and so this chapter assumes no prior knowledge of the subject on the part of readers. The reader is taken through an introduction to the subject to a discussion of the main operational decisions that need to be made in an international organisation. Technological change impacts very heavily on this area of management, and so the role of technology as an influence on international competitiveness is also explained. Finally, linking back to the preceding chapter on marketing, the operational implications of different market entry routes are highlighted.

By this stage in the book, we have looked at each of the primary functions within Michael Porter's value chain, as well as the support functions relating to finance, planning and technology. Chapter 10 completes the functional analysis of Section Two, via consideration of international human resource management. Using a contingency approach, the chapter deals with the factors that influence the development of HRM strategy in a multinational company, before linking back to the question of culture (as covered in Chapter 4) and its impact on the level of centralisation of HRM management. This leads into a discussion on variations in employment practice and conditions around the world, and the implications for recruitment and remuneration of staff. This discussion raises issues which were covered in Chapters 2 and 3 at a global level, but draws out the implications at a narrower, corporate level.

Insofar as Section Two deals with each function of management separately, teachers and other readers can pick and mix the chapters that they choose to use. Broad brush courses are likely to make use of most of Section Two, whilst shorter, more focused courses may select out just one or two key areas of interest. For all types of course, however, it is suggested that Chapter 5 provides a foundation for consideration of the corporate perspective of international business.

Section Three, the final part of the book, takes us back to the link between the individual corporation and the global environment. The theme of the book is the interface between global developments in the fields of trade, investment, politics and technology and the evolution of individual corporate policies at both business and functional levels. It is, however, easy to see that the large multinational corporations are now of such a size that they help frame the broad environment, as well as respond to it. In other words there is a need to recognise the existence of a loop which means that companies *react* to global trends but also *make* global trends. Chapter 11 is therefore devoted to a discussion of the impact of multinational companies on both the home and host nations. There are no clear cut arguments either for or against the increased globalisation of business, and so the aim here is simply to outline the economic, social and political effects of the large companies. The reader is then left to reach his/her own conclusions.

The overall structure of the book is strengthened by the inclusion of focused end of chapter case studies which illustrate international business practice. Companies featured in the cases include IKEA, GTE, Philips, Ford and Nissan. The cases detail how businesses have sought to manage the difficulties of their international involvement, with the problem under discussion being directly related to the content of the associated chapter. These cases provide useful material for tutorial work and discussion.

Finally, to help with revision and preparation for examinations, readers will find at the end of each chapter a section which summarises the material covered. The summary is brief, but focuses attention on the key learning points.

Additional Recommended Reading

At the end of all chapters there is a list of references which details all of the information sources used by the author. The list is intended to give readers and lecturers the information needed to access original data sources if required, and help students with an interest in deepening their knowledge of a particular topic. It is not intended to be a general reading list. A separate section is used to identify useful web sites, articles or books which provide good additional sources of information to complement the material covered in the chapter.

The Global Business Environment

CHAPTER ONE

International Business in the Twenty-First Century

INTRODUCTION

The rules are the same world-wide, from Trieste to Tokyo – if a business is to be successful then it needs to be aware of its general environment. Awareness means understanding the environment on two levels: the broad, which is relevant to most companies, and the specific, which is important to the individual business. The Cold War and the Asian Crisis were important to the vast majority of international businesses, but the political climate of Hungary may only be of relevance to a small number of firms. The broad environment includes the economy, the political and technological world, and sociological issues. The specific environment includes customer/supplier relations, investor requirements, workplace issues and individual financial and operational requirements. As explained in the preface, this book seeks to look at how international corporations respond to the external environment at all of these levels.

The purpose of this chapter is to introduce the broader context which faces international businesses at the start of the twenty-first century by discussion of important general trends in the key areas of politics, the economy and technology. One may well ask if companies entering the world of international business in the next decade face challenges that are any different to those which they would have encountered in the 1950s, 70s, or 90s. Given the continual changes in world political and economic trends, the answer is, almost inevitably, yes. In some areas of management, the changes are merely one of degree, but in other areas, such as communications technology, the situation today is almost equivalent to a new era. Consequently, the issues facing international business must be analysed in terms of their historic context, and so it is useful to begin with a brief overview of the historical events and processes which have moulded the world of international business today.

The Role of History

History colours the present and nurtures the future. The distribution of wealth across the world today is a consequence of several thousand years of economic change. The countries which are economically powerful and rich in technology, versus those which are relatively poor, can look to history for an explanation of their current position. Geography and topography also play significant roles, but there is a school of thought which suggests that the merchant venturers of the past, who raided the treasures of the Spice islands and helped to found empires, set in motion an economic tide which has blown inexorably in favour of certain nations. Wealth has been generated by enterprise – collecting together economic resources and exploiting the principle of comparative advantage – so that the few original game players such as the Hudson Bay Company can be viewed as the corporate ancestors of familiar twenty-first-century names such as Daewoo, Sony, Adidas, Akzo Nobel and Nestlé.

Over the course of history we have witnessed an increasing internationalisation of business activity, particularly during the twentieth century. Only 100 years ago, the individual nation state was still the focal point of production and marketing for the vast majority of industries. Dicken[1] points out that few of today's industries are oriented towards local, regional or national markets. Instead, the production and distribution process has become fragmented in a way which cuts across national boundaries. Companies may manufacture components in several different countries, assemble them in another and then sell the finished product globally. In the United Kingdom, for example, two large retail chains – Marks and Spencer and Laura Ashley – have cut back on sourcing products from local (UK) suppliers on the grounds that lower cost products from Asia and other 'cheap' labour regions of the world are vital to maintaining market position in a competitive environment. Simultaneously, the English retail world is cautiously seeking to forecast the consequences of the entry of the US company Walmart, the world's largest retailer, onto the local economic scene. Manufacturing, assembly, distribution and selling are now truly international for a very wide range of goods and services. In the early 1990s it was estimated that there were 37,000 multinational companies, with annual sales in excess of US$5,500 billion, controlling one third of the world's private sector assets. The figures today are bound to be larger – this is the competitive reality facing business in the year 2000.

It is history that has created this scenario, and the events of today are the history of tomorrow, so if we want to try and predict how international business will develop in the future, we must analyse today's issues, as well as those of the past. The major factors influencing business behaviour can be classified under the headings of politics, economics, and technology and the rest of this chapter is devoted to addressing each of these in turn.

THE POLITICAL ENVIRONMENT

A number of political factors stand out as being potentially very significant influences on the international business environment over the course of the next 100 years, including:

- the integration of Less Developed Countries (LDCs) and formally centrally planned economies into the international economy

- the difficulties (and opportunities) raised by economic inequalities across the world

■ the sheer size of the world's largest multinational companies (MNCs) now raises issues of where the centre of control over international business actually resides – in the boardroom or in government. In other words, 'who runs the world?'

■ the role of major world institutions such as the OECD, World Bank, World Trade Organisation (WTO), the European Commission and the IMF in relation to the direction of international trade and investment

■ the twentieth-century division of the world into geographic areas which were the 'home' countries of MNCs and those which were 'host' countries is now disappearing. The political complexities and social and economic consequences for a country which is simultaneously both 'home' and 'host' to a number of MNCs poses interesting challenges for businesses and governments alike

■ environmental concerns. As consumers and governments recognise the direct environmental impact of greater industrial production resulting from higher levels of general consumption, the question of whether market or regulatory mechanisms should be used to limit levels of environmental pollution raises awkward political questions.

In essence, all of these political issues come down to the basic problem of inequalities – of entrepreneurial opportunities, control over decision making, access to markets, the benefits of environmental improvements and basic levels of personal wealth. David Landes[2] states that 'the difference in income per head between the richest industrial nation, say Switzerland, and the poorest non-industrial country, say Mozambique, is about 400 to 1. Two hundred and fifty years ago this gap between richest and poorest was perhaps 5 to 1, and the difference between Europe and, say, East or South Asia (China or India) was around 1.5 or 2 to 1.' It might thus be suggested that the twenty-first century will be the one in which politics is dominated by debate over these economic inequalities. Needless to say, these issues also have an economic dimension.

ECONOMICS

The internationalisation (some would say globalisation) of business over the last 100 years can be said to have re-drafted the world economic map. In particular, over the last thirty to fifty years, we have witnessed international economic agreements which have both liberalised trade and capital flows, and led to the establishment of regional economic groupings which supersede the nation state.

The process of trade liberalisation was set in motion by the General Agreement on Tariff and Trade (GATT), established in 1947. Later, after eight different rounds of multilateral trade negotiations over the course of almost fifty years, the conclusion of the Uruguay Round of GATT in December 1993 marked the end of the GATT achievements in cutting import duties and tariffs and creating a new multilateral framework for world trade. In January 1995 GATT was replaced by the World Trade Organisation, a regulatory body which now defines and enforces rules which cover 90 per cent of world trade. Most of the countries of the world accept the WTO system, which applies core principles of non discrimination and multi-lateralism. More specifically, the WTO (and GATT before it) demands that if two countries agree trade concessions between themselves, then those concessions must be applied equally to all WTO members. The only exception to this occurs if a subgroup of members creates a free trade area/customs union which grants concessions across the subgroup. The European Union would be one example of such a subgroup. At the same time the WTO requires that countries treat imported goods in the same way as domestically produced goods – there is no discrimination against imports. The result is that today's economic environment is one in which free trade is favoured, and international competition is thereby increased.

There are, and will continue to be, issues upon which countries continue to disagree about trading terms. These may relate to particular classes of goods/services, or the WTO's judgements on trade disputes. Two particular issues are of importance for the future, and these are labour standards and environmental issues. In essence, there is a division of thinking between the countries of the developed versus the developing world over the extent to which basic standards of working conditions, wage rates, and environmental controls should be set globally. The poorer countries are arguing that setting standards, such as the banning of use of child labour, or strict controls over industrial effluent at levels which reflect the living standards of the richer world, constitutes a form of protectionism. The opportunity to industrialise and develop their economies will be denied to the poor countries because they will lose the commercial advantage that is currently available because of differences in standards. The question is one of morals and politics as much as it is one of economics, but it poses a problem for future trade and development, and as such it is a matter of concern to all multinational companies.

Running alongside a freer world trading environment, is a trend of rapidly growing international financial markets. The need for international finance arises because of company decisions to invest directly in foreign owned assets, rather than reaching the markets via trading. During the 1980s the level of foreign direct investment grew at a rate five times faster than world trade, and markets have developed to service those financial needs.

The growth of both short- and long-term capital markets is particularly important for companies seeking to raise very large amounts of funding. For example, in 1999 Hyundai Electronics made a single convertible bond issue valued at US$64 million, and Deutsche Telekom raised Euro10.4 billion in an equity issue. Capital market growth and corporate growth therefore go hand in hand. At the same time, institutional and personal investors now have access to international equity markets such as NASDAQ, EASDAQ and EURONM; this latter is a pan European market where stocks are priced in Euros. These developments raise questions about the future role of domestic financial markets, and whether they will disappear under the growth of the large international markets, especially as technology is allowing us to move closer to 24-hour global trading in stocks and bonds.

The increasing movement of goods and capital across the world (as a result of greater trade and investment flows) has led to the emergence of regional trading blocs which operate alongside the multilateral trade encouraged by the WTO. The World Bank Review of 1998 declared that 'nearly every country in the world is a member of

– or in the process of discussing participation in – one or more regional integration agreements', and according to Egan and McKiernan[3], the result has been the convergence of the economic development of nations into the three main trading blocs known as the Triad*, i.e. North America, Europe and East and South East Asia.

The move towards the establishment of such major trading blocs began in the latter half of the twentieth century, and is discussed in detail in Chapter 2, but it has significance for the future because these blocs dominate the world economy. Schiff and Winters[4] estimate that between 55 and 60 per cent of world trade occurs *within* trading blocs. United Nations statistics for 1995 show that the Triad blocs together account for a staggering 87 per cent of the world's manufacturing value added, and it has been suggested that they have resulted in a shift in the world's centre of gravity for manufacturing. In 1995 prior to the 'Asian Crisis', Asia accounted for one quarter of the world's output of manufactured goods.

The interesting question, from an economic perspective, is what this means for the future. There are some who argue that the nineteenth century was dominated by Great Britain and Europe as colonial powers, the twentieth century by the USA as the great economic power, and the twenty-first century will be controlled by Asia, and China in particular. Economic strength brings wealth to a region, and this has implications for business because for most products the markets are largest where the wealth is greatest. Currently, the widely held view is that multinational companies need to have a market share in all three Triad blocs, if they wish to be significant world players. An alternative viewpoint argues that each of the Triad blocs has geographic proximity to low cost manufacturing sites, such as the Central American states, Eastern Europe, Vietnam and Malaysia. Consequently, if the levels of *intra-regional* trade continue to grow more rapidly than *inter-regional* trade, then the need for a corporate *global* presence may be reduced.

For the individual business seeking to survive in this economic environment, one of the clear implications is that firms must be able to manage the increasing global concentration of industries. Strategic planning must adapt to find new ways of dealing with competition, and one of the noticeable trends of the last twenty years has been the evolution of new organisational structures for global businesses. These structures are characterised by the growing use of networks, strategic alliances and joint ventures, and one example of this type of organisation is Nike, the footwear and clothing company. Nike headquarters is responsible for research and development of new products, and the co-ordination of a tiered group of subcontractors responsible for the production of specialised components and standardised footwear; in addition to research and development, the primary role of Nike Head Office is co-ordination of the network. **This type of 'virtual corporation' which produces nothing, but manages a network of inter-linked suppliers and distributors is a relatively new

---

* Triad members are as follows:
   The NAFTA grouping, comprising USA, Canada and Mexico.
   The European Union, comprising Belgium, France, Germany, Italy, Luxemburg, Netherlands, Eire, Britain, Denmark, Greece, Spain, Portugal, Austria, Finland and Sweden.
   East and South East Asia as the third leg of the Triad is the most difficult group to classify, as it does not consist of one single regional trade bloc. The definition used throughout this book includes South Korea, Taiwan, Japan, Hong Kong, Singapore, Malaysia, Thailand, Indonesia, Philippines and China.
** For more detail on this see Donaghu, W. and Barff, R. (1990) 'Nike just did it: international subcontracting and flexibility in athletic footwear production', *Regional Studies*, vol.24, pp.537–552.

phenomenon, and one of the challenges for international businesses over the next fifty years or so will be how to manage such structures effectively, and avoid the threat of trans-national take-over.

Reviewing the economic context within which international business commences this century, we have thus defined a number of challenges which will need to be faced by organisations seeking to expand their international operations:

■ the increased competition arising from a greater freedom of world trade

■ the changing distribution of economic activity across the globe arising from the importance of regional trading blocs

■ the threat created by increased levels of foreign direct investment, made easier by highly efficient international financial markets

■ the need to devise strategies which take maximum advantage of trading and investment opportunities within regional trading blocs

■ acceptance of changes in corporate structures in order to match the strategic changes required to survive the global marketplace.

THE TECHNOLOGICAL ENVIRONMENT

Technological change drove the first industrial revolution in the nineteenth century, and seems set to drive a second one some two centuries later. In fact the link between technology and global economic growth is demonstrated in the work of the economist Kondatriev[5]. Kondatriev suggested that economic cycles of prosperity, recession, depression and recovery tend to operate over fifty-year time scales termed Kondatriev waves, and the waves are linked to phases of technological change. The latest wave cycle, which began in the 1980s/90s is described as the information and communication wave, in which economic growth is driven via networks of firms using computers and technologically based communication, production and control systems. Indeed Brookes and Guile[6] go so far as to argue that 'long-term technology trends and advances are re-configuring the location, ownership and management of various types of productive activity amongst countries and regions.' The impact of technology upon international business can be classified under three separate headings covering organisational issues of transportation and communication, product and process innovation, and sales and marketing, respectively. We will look at each of these in turn.

Transportation has, over the centuries, led to global shrinkage. In the nineteenth century the railways and steamships made it much easier for goods to be transported over long distances relatively quickly. The twentieth-century developments of the jet engine and containerised shipping speeded the process still further. The usefulness of such technology from a business perspective is the extent to which it facilitates geographic specialisation. Production and distribution facilities do not need to be replicated in all of the markets served: a single specialised centre can be used to service a large geographic area. The decision by Toyota and Nissan to locate car production plants in the United Kingdom is one example of this. The plants produce goods for the whole of the European market, not just the country of location.

The impact of transportation technology on international business has therefore been to aid industrial relocation on a global scale. This has had the effect of de-industrialising some nations, and shifting the world's centre of gravity of production. This question of industrial location is discussed in detail in Chapter 9.

International communication technology has been revolutionised over the last fifty years, firstly by satellites and more recently by the use of optic fibre and digital systems. The time period required to send data from one side of the world to the other has shrunk to almost nothing. For example, it is now possible for a multinational company to run its design office at the other side of the world from its production units, because it is simple enough to transmit data for technical drawings and 3D modelling down international telephone lines. Similarly, a factory manager in Dubai can e-mail an end of day stock report to Head Office, in say Philadelphia, and the data can be used in compiling a global stock figure within a matter of minutes. This type of technology is also used to give senior managers a daily update of regional and world-wide sales figures. At the more sophisticated end of the scale, a significant number of multinational companies now centralise their entire global materials requirement planning systems (MRP) in this way, with regional centres sending materials usage and requirement levels on a real time basis to a central co-ordinating point.

From a corporate viewpoint, the benefit of such technological change goes beyond that of the increased control created by speedier information flows, because the actual cost of international communication services is falling. Large organisations use internationally leased telecommunication network systems, which have fixed lease costs, so that the cost per unit of transmitted data falls as they use the network more heavily.

The developments in communications technology have thus served as a catalyst to aid the process of growth of multinational companies. Not surprisingly, however, the global spread of such technology remains uneven, as the companies invest in establishing systems where there is the greatest market potential. This is clearly revealed by Table 1.1 below, which shows the location of the global telecommunications infra structure in terms of the number of connected lines per location. Over half of the lines

Table 1.1   *Geographic Location of Communications Infrastructure 1999*

Location	Percentage of global connections
Western Europe	28%
United States	21%
Eastern Europe	7%
Japan	9%
Rest of the world	35%

Measure is in millions of connections, of which 851 million are fixed lines and 305 million mobile lines

Source: *Financial Times*

are on just two continents, and it is clear that the developed nations dominate in their access to communications technology.

The 1997 World Trade Organisation agreement to liberalise the global telecommunications market will perhaps help to reduce such inequalities by increasing the competition in national markets and driving down prices, thereby increasing the accessibility of the technology. Such changes will, however, take time to have an effect on relative rates of economic growth.

Technology also has an effect on both production processes and product design and specification. Since the mid twentieth century, the key change in production technology has been the progress from traditional automated mass production systems, via numerically controlled methods (CNC) and Computer Aided Design and Manufacturing (CAD–CAM), into flexible manufacturing systems (FMS). The progress is important because it offers the potential to move production away from the old high volume, standardised approach, into an environment in which machines are multipurpose, or 'flexible'. The flexibility means that even small production batches are feasible without massive increases in product costs, but such systems place new demands on staffing because they require a multi-skilled workforce prepared to work in teams. (This topic is discussed in Chapter 10 which covers international human resource management.) Such arrangements can be used to enable a single production plant to manufacture a product range which is easily modified batch by batch to meet the customised requirements of different national markets, and as such it is a great help to multinational companies. Modern car production plants use FMS so that one pressing plant, for example, can be used to press body panels for a number of different car models simultaneously. It costs no more to set the machines to produce ten door panels for a Ford Mondeo, followed by ten for a Fiesta, followed by roof panels for the Mondeo etc., than it does to set the system to produce just Sierra door panels. FMS technology is not, however, cheap and so not surprisingly the geographic distribution of new production technology is uneven.

The use of FMS also offers benefits in terms of product design, because it makes design modification easier and lower cost. As a result, where the competitive environment has created a short product life cycle which demands regular innovation, the firms using the flexible technology are at an advantage. Large-scale multinational producers tend to be the main users, because the cost, risks and complexity of investing in the technology mean that large markets need to be available in order to earn a reasonable return on the investment. The scale of global concentration of the electronics industry is evidence of this, where the cost of research and development for new products is huge, requiring investment levels beyond the reach of the smaller company.

The final way in which technology affects international business is via the impact it has had on the methods use to promote, sell and distribute goods and services. The current debate on the potential significance of e-commerce is evidence of this.

International product promotion has been made much easier by the growth of importance of electronic media. Radio and television advertising, via satellite and cable, offers the potential to simultaneously access huge numbers of potential customers across many different countries. Electronic selling via the Internet or interactive television is still in its relatively early stages, but has revolutionary potential. Furthermore, Internet usage is still dominated by the USA. The *New York Times* of 3rd October 1999 reported that 30 per cent of the personal computers bought by US households over the preceding six months had been purchased direct from the manufacturer via the Internet. Nonetheless, such sales tend to be confined to specific industrial sectors and product groups, and the newspaper forecast that despite the growing number of Internet connections and corporate web pages, such sales would still represent just 7 per cent of US retail sales by 2004. These issues are discussed further in Chapter 8 on international marketing, but the statistics tend to suggest that the use of electronic technology for direct purchasing may turn out to be lower than current media hype is suggesting.

In conclusion then, the technological context in which international business must operate over the next decade is one where technology costs continue to fall, and the speed of change in both communication and production technologies is very rapid. Under such circumstances, it might be suggested that access to, and effective use of technology will be a very important determinant of global business success in the twenty-first century.

SUMMARY

In summary then, we can conclude that the issues which challenge the international business in the twenty-first century are very different from those of the previous century. There is political, economic and technological evidence of increasing inequity, and yet at the same time, communication systems, transport systems and freedom of movement for people, goods and services seems to be making the world 'smaller'. Certainly the threat of foreign competition is much stronger, and the key to success would appear to be long-term vision. To succeed in the international market place, a company needs to devise a detailed long-term strategy, which matches with its internal functional capabilities, and then regularly review and amend its strategy as the political and economic environment changes. If sound strategic thinking is combined with cultural sensitivity of management style, then the future offers great opportunities for new international businesses. This book seeks to address both the broad contextual issues and the narrower company specific issues relating to international business, and will hopefully enable managers to see a way through the maze and ultimately 'manage the world'.

References

1 Dicken, P. (1998) *Global Shift (Transforming the world economy)*, Paul Chapman Publishing, London
2 Landes, D. (1999) *The Wealth and Poverty of Nations*, Abacus, London
3 Egan and McKiernan (1993) *Inside Fortress Europe: Strategies for the Single Market*, Addison Wesley, London
4 Schiff, M. and Winters, L.A. (1998) *Dynamics and politics in regional integration agreements: an introduction*, pp.177–195 in *The World Bank Economic Review* Vol.12, May 1998, No.2
5 See Dicken (Reference 1, pp.146–151) for a useful discussion of Kondatriev waves.
6 Brooks, H.E. and Guile, B.R. (1987) *Technology and Global industry: Companies and nations in the world economy*. National Academy Press, Washington D.C.

Further Reading

The *Financial Times* offers invaluable daily examples of news reports on topics that are of relevance to international business, together with regular supplements on special topics such as Information Technology, Global Telecommunications or special reports on individual nation states.

   If you cannot get access to hard copy versions of the newspaper then you can visit their website www.ft.com which contains archives of their news reports which can be searched by keyword, company name or geographic location. It is recommended that you use the site throughout your course of study to build up a database of examples of national and international policies, and company strategies which can be used to illustrate the theoretical arguments presented throughout this book.

ESSAY QUESTIONS

1   What political and economic disputes might arise in seeking to integrate the Less Developed Countries and the countries of the former communist bloc into the world economy?

2   To what extent does lack of access to leading edge technologies prohibit a company's participation in the international marketplace?

3   Does/can technology lead to a change in consumer tastes? If your answer is 'yes', then explain why and how the change might occur.

CHAPTER TWO

International Trade and Foreign Direct Investment

LEARNING OUTCOMES

On completing this chapter, it is expected that you will be able to:

- Understand and explain international trade theory and the principle of comparative advantage
- Discuss and evaluate the arguments for and against protectionism
- Analyse the role of GATT and the World Trade Organisation, and their impact on world trade and foreign direct investment
- Describe and discuss key changes in the pattern of world trade and production post World War Two
- Discuss the growth of foreign direct investment post World War Two
- Analyse and evaluate the impact of international trade and foreign direct investment on the distribution of wealth across the globe

INTRODUCTION

The aim of this chapter is to look at the reasons why international trade is good for the world economy, and the effect that promotion of free trade and investment is having on national economies around the globe. The scale and direction of international flows of goods, services and capital have important implications for international business in the future.

International business is concerned with the purchase and sale of goods and services across national boundaries. As such, the volume and direction of business transactions impacts directly upon world statistics for international trade and foreign direct investment (FDI). The pattern of international trade and investment is constantly changing and evolving, both in terms of the type of products traded and the countries involved in investment inflows and outflows. One particularly noticeable change in recent years has been the growth of regionalism, and this change is reflected in the statistics on trade and investment.

This chapter seeks to introduce the theoretical and topical issues relating to international trade and FDI, and it concludes that patterns of trade and investment are becoming more regionally focused. The growth of regionalism and its implications for the world economy are then discussed in detail in Chapter 3. We begin with a theoretical background before moving on to look at the historical evolution of trade and investment, and an analysis of current statistics.

INTERNATIONAL TRADE: THE THEORY

Mercantalism

'Free trade between nations is unambiguously good for the world as a whole but by no means necessarily good for all'. Any attempt to understand the drivers of international business activity must start with an appreciation of the tensions inherent in this simple statement.

Nations have traded ever since there were nations to trade and what economists term the 'gains from trade' accrued long before there were economists around to coin such a term. The urge to trade has over the centuries been a major driver not only of commercial policy but also of domestic and international political events. Empires have been created to foster trade and wars fought to defend trading interests.

Yet it was as relatively recently as the early nineteenth century that a coherent body of economic theory started to emerge to provide a compelling rationale for trade as an engine of economic growth. Until then trade, with many of its less desirable by-products, had taken place against the backdrop of an altogether less enlightened doctrine known as mercantilism.

In language with which they would have been unfamiliar, mercantilists saw trade as a zero sum game – a game such as beggar-my-neighbour where one player's gains are another player's losses. A mercantilist nation was one that strove to maximise its exports and minimise its imports. The margin between the two – what would now be termed a surplus on the current account of the country's balance of payments – would be matched by the inflow of gold and foreign currency it received for its net exports and added to its reserves. The larger these reserves, the stronger the nation would feel in its dealings with the rest of the world.

From this brief description, it should be clear that the world today is not exactly free of mercantilist thought. Indeed, there is nothing necessarily wrong with policies which are designed to develop a country's exports or strengthen its import-substituting capabilities. But there is something wrong with policies which are designed simply to maximise a country's current account surplus, especially if those policies incorporate import tariffs, export subsidies or other artificial barriers to trade.

For a start, as every export is somebody else's import it is self-evident that not all countries can be in balance of payments surplus simultaneously – any more than all players of beggar-my-neighbour can end up by winning. The aggregate surplus of all countries in surplus has to equal the aggregate deficit of all countries in deficit in any one period. The larger the aggregate surplus of the former group, the larger the aggregate deficit of the latter.

Does this matter? Yes, if the result of policies designed to maximise individual payments surpluses is a lower level of income and wealth throughout the world than would otherwise be the case. The theoretical advances of the ninteenth century demonstrated that this would indeed be the result of trade designed to promote short-run national interests. The resulting shift in economic and political orthodoxy to a presumption in favour of free trade, and the increased income and wealth which has accrued in the process, is perhaps the best example in history of economists actually having had a beneficial effect on humankind.

The Gains from Trade

The individual economist who deserves most of the credit for this is David Ricardo, who codified the law of comparative advantage which rests at the heart of the case for free trade. To appreciate the force of that law, it is necessary to bear in mind the economic concept of opportunity cost, whereby the cost of producing or acquiring an item is measured in terms of the benefits forgone by doing so. In other words, opportunity cost is a measurement of the best available alternative use to which the producer's or consumer's resources could otherwise have been put.

The concept of opportunity cost is crucial to an understanding of the law of comparative advantage and thus the case for trade. Prior to Ricardo, the costs of producing a particular output were typically measured in terms of the resources they consumed. It followed that a country which was well endowed with raw materials, benign geography, a skilled workforce and so forth might well enjoy an absolute (resource cost) advantage over other nations in the production of many, and conceivably of all, goods. Prior to Ricardo it was far from intuitively obvious why such a nation should not follow a strategy of maximising its exports of all the goods in which it enjoyed such an absolute cost advantage.

Ricardo's intellectual breakthrough can best be illustrated by imagining a simple world economy of two countries, two goods and a single factor of production (labour). Suppose that in the United States it takes one man year to produce a computer and five man years to produce a car, while in the less well-endowed United Kingdom the equivalent figures are two and six man years respectively. Suppose also that labour can be moved freely between the two manufacturing activities with no loss of productivity and that goods can be shipped across the Atlantic free of cost.

Clearly the United States has an absolute advantage in the production of both computers and cars. But the opportunity cost of producing a car in the United States is five computers, whereas in the United Kingdom it is only three computers. That is to say, the labour required to produce a car in the United States could instead have been applied to its best (in this example its only) alternative use of producing five computers, whereas the labour required to produce a car in the United Kingdom could otherwise have produced only three computers.

Let us now consider two scenarios, in one of which each country aims for self-sufficiency in both goods, while in the other each specialises in the production of the good in which it enjoys a comparative advantage. If each country had a workforce of a million, divided equally between the two industries, the United States could produce 500,000 computers and 100,000 cars and the United Kingdom could produce 250,000 computers and 83,333 cars – a total of 750,000 computers and 183,333 cars.

Now let us suppose that each country specialised in the activity in which it enjoyed a comparative advantage. The United States could produce 1,000,000 computers and the United Kingdom could produce 166,667 cars – a lower total number of cars than before since there is no getting away from the fact that the United Kingdom is less efficient in car production than the United States. But, as Figure 2.1 shows, if the two countries agreed to engage in trade at a rate of exchange of, say, four computers to one car (dotted lines), it can be easily seen that each country could be better off than under its former policy of self-sufficiency.

Figure 2.1   *The Gains from Trade*

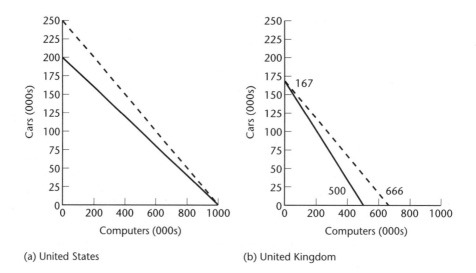

(a) United States   (b) United Kingdom

The USA, for example, could elect to exchange half of its computer output for 125,000 cars, leaving it with the same number of computers as previously and 25,000 more cars. Or the United Kingdom might seek to exchange half of its cars for 333,333 computers, leaving it with the same number of cars and 83,333 more computers. A vast range of actual trading outcomes is possible, but in every case the two countries would each end up with a combination of cars and computers that it could not have produced on a basis of self-sufficiency.

Indeed, this will be true not only at the assumed rate of exchange of 4:1 but at any rate of exchange between 5:1 and 3:1, though the closer the rate is to 5:1 (reflecting the opportunity costs of the two goods in the United States) the more the rate of exchange (in economic parlance, the 'terms of trade') will favour the car-producing United Kingdom, while the closer it is to 3:1 the more it will favour the computer-producing United States.

Outside these trading limits, one or other of the countries would indeed be better off splitting its production between both goods rather than importing one of them, since the cost of importing the good in which it lacks comparative advantage would now be higher than the opportunity cost of switching production into that good – an important consideration when it comes to predicting how far up or down a country's actual exchange rate might move.

In the real world, decisions to export and import are made not by nations but by individual producers and consumers. Many goods and services are traded multilaterally between many countries. Costs (including opportunity costs) are measured in money terms and switching the resources of production (not just labour) between different activities can be a complex and costly process: rates of productivity change over time and with the scale of production. Goods and services are generally paid for in money rather than bartered for other goods; rates of exchange between nations are expressed in terms of the values of their respective currencies and it does generally cost more to sell your output abroad than at home. Firms wishing to do business internationally have many strategic options open to them other than those of exporting or importing.

International trade theory and policy, and international business strategy, have to take account of all of these real world considerations. Yet nothing in this recital detracts from the essential truth of the doctrine of comparative advantage, which is that a world in which nations concentrate on producing goods in which they enjoy such an advantage, trading their surpluses for goods in which they do not, will generate more output than one in which each aims for self-sufficiency.

The Sources of Comparative Advantage

The sources of comparative advantage are many and varied, and received their earliest systematic treatment by the Swedish economists Eli Heckscher[1] and Bertil Ohlin[2]. They emphasised the importance of the factor endowments – the availability of land, raw materials, capital or labour – which give rise to inherent cost advantages. Self-evidently, countries where (productive) land is plentiful are likely to have a comparative advantage in agriculture; those where labour is plentiful are likely to have an advantage in labour-intensive industries; and those where capital is plentiful are likely to have an advantage in capital-intensive industries.

Heckscher and Ohlin went an important stage further, however, in pointing out that trade between such nations will not only allow higher levels of aggregate output, as per Ricardo, but also tend to reduce the initial differentials in the prices of the countries' respective factors of production. Thus if a country with a plentiful supply of labour is able to sell its labour-intensive products internationally, the demand for those products will tend to bid up the price of labour on the home labour market and help to close the gap between wage rates there and elsewhere.

Indeed, in some countries international trade is essential if any meaningful market is to be created for the product in which it enjoys a factor endowment, the most obvious example being small countries well endowed with specific raw materials. However low the oil price may be, there is only so much oil that Kuwait can use. More generally, consumer tastes in a country may not correspond to the production to which that country is best suited: the Japanese may genuinely prefer Heineken to Kirin beer.

Factor endowments are, however, not the only reason why countries specialise and trade. Specialisation brings its own cost advantages as countries (and firms within countries) are able to reap the benefits of economies of scale in production. Thus, at least up to the point where diseconomies of scale set in, countries which switch resources into activities where they enjoy some initial comparative advantage can see that advantage increase as average or unit costs of production decline. So it is not only factor endowments but also the advantages of scale and experience which at various times have allowed the United Kingdom to dominate the world shipbuilding industry, the United States the world car industry and Japan the world consumer electronics industry.

INTERNATIONAL TRADE: THE PRACTICE

Trade Barriers and Protectionism

Theoretical support for free trade and exploitation of comparative advantage does not, of course, imply that in practice there will be a world free of trade barriers and protectionism. Countries may well seek to restrict imports from overseas for a variety of reasons of an economic, political or social/ethical nature. The most commonly cited reasons for protectionism include:

■ *The need to protect a country's infant industries*

A third world country seeking to reduce its dependence on primary produce by nurturing a manufacturing sector may feel a compelling need to protect its manufacturers from foreign competition while they are getting themselves established.

The problem with this argument is that protection, once provided, is notoriously difficult to withdraw. Firms become used to operating within a protective environment and can be expected to lobby long and hard against ever being exposed to the chill winds of international competition.

■ *To protect domestic industries from unfair foreign competition*

One common form of unfair competition is dumping – the practice of selling goods on export markets at less than on home markets. Such a practice may reflect nothing more than a commercial policy of price discrimination, designed to reflect the different demand characteristics of different national markets, which would be a perfectly rational practice for a profit-seeking firm to engage in.

Although two wrongs rarely make a right, it is understandable if firms facing dumping or alleged dumping by their overseas competitors react by calling for tariffs to be imposed to eliminate the price differential.

Whether or not dumping is involved, there is always a risk that a strong foreign competitor will be able to force domestic producers out of business and thereby achieve a dominant or even a monopoly position in the local market.

■ *Health/social reasons*

For health reasons you cannot normally import fresh fruit into the USA or live animals into the United Kingdom . Firearms, drugs and pornography are also typically subject to strict import controls for reasons which again have little or nothing to do with economics, but nonetheless reflect a form of protectionism.

■ *Protection of local culture or national identity*

The calls for agricultural protection widely heard within western Europe since the establishment of the Common Agricultural Policy may be said to be based on members' desires to protect local culture. The argument is given a cultural hue by countries such as France that see trade barriers as a legitimate means of helping them to preserve their rural traditions.

■ *Politics*

Political reasons for not wishing to trade with particular countries include compliance with international sanctions and a desire not to be reliant on overseas suppliers for strategically important goods such as defence equipment. Equally, countries may wish to grant preferential trading terms to a former colony/political ally. In any instance, behind all of these lines of argument there is always likely to be a domestic industry lobbying for protection for its own purely commercial motives.

■ *Protection from cheap foreign labour*

This argument has been used by labour unions in the USA, who are concerned at the replacement of US-based plants with Mexico-based ones, in the aftermath of the formation of NAFTA.

Whilst one can sympathise with those whose jobs are at risk, it needs to be remembered that the entire case for free trade is based on the premise that countries with an abundant supply of relatively cheap labour should be able to export goods with a high labour content. There might sometimes be a case for using trade sanctions to bring pressure to bear on countries or companies which were judged by international opinion to be exploiting their workers, but anyone advocating such a policy would need to be confident that the sanctions would not hurt the very workers they were designed to help. This very issue is one which was the subject of massive debate at the 1999 World Trade Organisation meeting in Seattle, where protestors were lobbying for 'fair' rates of pay for workers in the poor countries of the world, and the outlawing of the use of child labour. At this point one can see that ethical issues can become as important in international business as economic issues.

Forms of Protectionism

Protectionism takes a multiplicity of forms including:

■ tariffs – taxes or duties typically levied *ad valorem* on imports as they enter the country

■ import quotas – restrictions on the quantity of a good which may be imported, perhaps from specific countries

■ embargoes

- export subsidies

- foreign exchange controls

- other 'non-tariff barriers' such as laws, regulations and commercial practices, e.g. rules on product specifications or professional qualifications, which have the effect of favouring home producers over foreign ones.

Measures such as these can inhibit free trade, and the benefits of trade, just as surely as can more overt tariffs and quotas. For this reason, much of the thrust of trade liberalisation policy in recent years has been focused on identifying and eliminating the major legal and regulatory barriers.

GATT and the World Trade Organisation

During the first half of the twentieth century two world wars, an intervening great depression and resurgent protectionism in many countries served to severely restrict the rates of growth of both output and trade across the world. Following the end of the Second World War, however, the effects of advances in technology and its transfer across national boundaries combined with enlightened trade policies to regenerate economies. The General Agreement on Tariffs and Trade (commonly known as GATT) was established in 1947, with twenty-three founder members, although the agreement eventually extended to 100 countries. GATT's declared aim was to promote trade and reduce/eliminate tariffs.

GATT was instrumental in achieving three major rounds of reductions in tariffs and other protectionist measures before its replacement by the World Trade Organisation (WTO) in 1995. The Kennedy Round in the mid-1960s and the Tokyo Round in the mid-1970s each achieved notional tariff reductions of about a third. The Uruguay Round in 1993, which concluded seven years of difficult and acrimonious negotiations, initiated further cuts in import duties and other tariffs world-wide and created a new framework for international trade under the aegis of the WTO.

The Uruguay Round saw 125 countries agree to an average one third reduction in tariffs (36 per cent in the developed world and 24 per cent in LDCs). The negotiations also resulted in agreements to eliminate quotas on textiles and many agricultural products, thus drawing agriculture, textiles and clothing into GATT for the first time. Significantly, the Uruguay round also concluded agreements on service industries – GATS, General Agreement on Trade in Services – as well as intellectual property rights. The effect of these successive multilateral agreements on trade is estimated by Hoekman and Kostecki[3] to mean that by 1996 more than 90 per cent of world trade was covered by the framework established by GATT and followed through by the WTO.

Particular gains were expected to accrue from farm trade reform, because tariffs on manufactured goods had already been greatly reduced as a result of earlier GATT rounds. Even more gains were widely expected to come about eventually as a result of the increasing liberalisation of trade in services, together with the existence of a more disciplined international trade regime and a general growth in business confidence.

In 1996 the Ministerial Conference of the WTO further extended the range of products covered by multinational trade agreements when they announced the ITA on Information Technology products. This came into force in July 1997 with the agreement of forty-eight (including the fifteen EC member countries) countries or customs territories. The ITA agreed to the removal of all tariff barriers (but excluded non-tariff barriers) on trade in IT products by the 1st January 2000. The agreement was deemed to be very important in a world in which knowledge-based assets are becoming more valuable than traditional physical/tangible assets.

Although the gains from greater freedom of trade would not be evenly spread around the world – Europe doing best and the third world least well – the forecasters believed that in time all nations would benefit to some extent. Nonetheless, some of the poorer food importing regions might suffer in the interim from the reduction in certain food subsidies and preferential trading deals.

The WTO, and GATT as its predecessor, have set a number of important international trading rules, which serve to underpin the principle of free trade between member countries. These are shown in Table 2.1 below.

Table 2.1   *Key Trading Principles under GATT and WTO*

To establish a level playing field for trade via:
■ restrictions on the use of quotas
■ allowing of retaliation against 'unfair' trading practices
■ a requirement to grant 'most favoured nation' concessions to all member countries
■ members not allowed to treat imported goods less favourably then domestic production (except under GATS)

The whole focus of the WTO is thus one which promotes the principle of free trade, and members are deemed to support this ideal. Not surprisingly, however, the practical reality is that many member countries still seek to restrict the extent to which trade is really free, for the reasons outlined earlier in this chapter, and as a result of such restrictions members may find themselves in breach of multilateral agreements. The WTO has established a procedure for the settlement of trade disputes which it claims to be 'equitable, fast, effective and mutually acceptable' (http://www.wto.org).

The recent trade dispute between the EU and the USA over bananas suggests, however, that the settlement procedures are actually fraught with difficulties. The dispute also suggests that the world is perhaps not yet ready for 'free trade', as regional and political interests are worthy of defence. Throughout this chapter we will see that the trading environment has moved in the twentieth century from being nationally focused to being regionally based, but global free trade is not yet a reality. This is clearly illustrated in the mini case study of the 'banana war' detailed below.

The protracted 'banana war' raises fundamental questions about the future of world trade, most particularly in relation to the potential for conflict between the WTO and

The US–EU Banana War

In September 1997 the WTO issued a ruling against the EU in respect of its import rules that granted special terms of access to bananas imported from the former African and Caribbean colonies. The special access terms were originally granted under the Lome Convention agreements between the EU and African, Caribbean and Pacific nations.

The WTO ruling arose out of a complaint made by the US government following lobbying by the American banana trading company Chiquita. The complaint was that the EU arrangements breached the GATT rules on import restrictions and most-favoured nation status. The disagreement illustrates very clearly the problems that can arise out of attempts to create a free trade environment, and the potential for disputes to escalate as retaliatory protectionist policies are implemented.

The economies of several Caribbean countries such as the Windward Islands (St Lucia, Dominica and St Vincent) are heavily dependent upon the income earned from banana exports to Europe. Banana growing dominates their agricultural sector and is the main engine for economic growth and development. In each of the three islands between 30 per cent and 36 per cent of total employment is in the banana industry, and banana exports amount to 11–14% of GDP. The economic dependence of the countries on this simple product meant that the dispute raised issues about the potential conflicts between free trade and third world development, as well as generating a political row between two of the world's largest economic powers.

In November 1998, in an attempt to force a climbdown from the EU, the USA threatened to impose retaliatory tariffs on a range of goods imported from the EU, with effect from March 1999. Such retaliation is allowed within the dispute resolution procedure of the WTO, as the complainant may request the right to impose sanctions when the defendant has not complied with a WTO ruling within a reasonable period of time. The USA clearly believed that since over twelve months had elapsed since the WTO initial ruling, that the EU had failed to comply. The industries targeted for sanctions included plastics, biscuits, greetings cards and cashmere wool products. Businessmen in these industries wondered why they should be caught up, and become victims of, a dispute about bananas, a wholly unrelated product!

In January 1999 the EU changed its import rules to seek to comply with the WTO ruling, whilst at the same time retaining its commitment to the African, Caribbean and Pacific nations. The new EU rules continued to grant duty free access to a limited volume of bananas, whilst removing the individual country quotas which had been criticised by the WTO.

The response of the USA and four other countries – Ecuador, Mexico, Honduras and Guatemala – was to claim that the EU was still in breach of WTO rules, and in April that year a WTO report concluded that the EU had not complied with its 1997 ruling, and the organisation's Dispute Settlement Body established a panel to resolve the issue. The WTO report acknowledged the importance of the region's commitment to the Caribbean nations, but also ruled that the US losses resulting from the restrictions to its banana trade amounted to US$191 million per year. In September 1999 the arguments continued to rage, and the dispute was unresolved.

Sources: *Bridges Weekly Trade News Digest*, Vol.3, Nos.13–14, April 12th 1999; Caribbean Banana Exporters Association Website, http://www.cbea.org

regional economic groups. The extent to which conflicts might arise will be in part dependent upon the patterns of world trade flows, and specifically whether these flows are primarily inter or intra regional in nature. We will therefore now look at recent trade statistics to see what patterns emerge.

INTERNATIONAL TRADE: THE STATISTICS POST WORLD WAR TWO

The volume and value of world trade has increased dramatically over the half century since the establishment of GATT. For fifty years trade has been rising faster than the value of world output, thereby confirming the growing internationalisation of business. Between the 1950's and 1973, the rate of growth of international trade averaged around 8 per cent per year compared with just 6 per cent for output. From 1973 onwards, until the end of the twentieth century the annual growth rate for trade fell to approximately 4 per cent, whereas output expanded at 3 per cent per year. Much of the expansion of trade can be attributed to the reductions in restrictions which arose from GATT, with the increasing incomes and the resulting expansion in consumer demand further stimulating both imports and exports.

The decision to export or import is made not by nations but by individual producers and consumers, although the economic impact of changing levels and patterns of trade will be revealed in national economic statistics. Close study of international trade statistics is fraught with difficulties because of variations in their presentation, content and frequency of publication. They are also subject to quite substantial margins of error. Nevertheless, changes over the last fifty years indicate a number of important trends which might be expected to affect international business in the twenty-first century. In order to fully understand the implications of changing trade patterns, it is useful to begin by looking back at trade theories that identify how trade might affect the condition of a nation's economy. There are three main issues:

■ Firstly, comparative advantages change over time, and may move for or against any individual nation.

> A one-third fall in world oil prices resulted in the export revenues of OPEC nations falling by US$50 billion in 1998. This contrasted with estimated gains (over the same period) to the industrial countries of $60 billion from the cheaper oil imports.
>
> Source: *UNCTAD Trade and Development Report 1999.*

■ Secondly, individual businesses will respond at differing rates to changes in market demand, and so the gains from trade which accrue to particular nations will reflect this speed of response.

> Chile has over the last decade invested heavily in its wine industry and taken great care to also invest in well targeted marketing campaigns. As a result, the Chilean producers have gained a rapidly growing share of the expanding Western market for low priced red wine. Chile is one of the few developing countries that is combining economic growth with an improving trade performance.

■ Finally, the value added by trade in goods and services is unequal. Exporting commodities will generate lower returns than the exports of, say, consumer electronics, because the terms of trade for commodities are relatively poor. What is more, the terms of trade will change over time.

> It is estimated that throughout the 1980s the terms of trade for developing countries fell by over 5 per cent per year. The worsening terms of trade apply to manufactured goods as well as commodities, and so the export prices of developing countries' manufactures relative to those exported from the EU, fell by 2.2 per cent per year between 1979 and 1994.

These theoretical principles give rise to changes in the world distribution of production and wealth over time. The main changes that can be observed over the last fifty years include:

1 A shift in the location of world manufacturing production.

2 A rate of growth of international trade which is below that of Foreign Direct Investment (as corporations look further afield for sources of comparative advantage).

3 Increases in wealth for those nations that have benefited from favourable changes in the terms of trade.

4 A general shift towards regional, rather than global, patterns of trade.

Looking first at the issue of distribution of production, Dicken[4] suggests that manufacturing production is very heavily concentrated, but there is evidence of a shift away from the older Western industrialised economies towards the 'Newly Industrialised Countries' of the East – the so-called NIE's of Singapore, Korea, Taiwan and 'Hong Kong. The statistics in Table 2.2 reveal this trend very clearly.

Table 2.2   *Shifts in Global Manufacturing Production 1963–1994*

	% share of world manufacturing output/ value added		Average annual rate of change (%)			
	1963	1994	1960–70	1970–81	1981–87	1990–94
USA	40.3	26.9	5.3	2.9	3.9	3.2
Germany*	9.7	11.6	5.4	2.1	1.0	(–1.1)
Japan	5.5	21.0	16.6	6.5	6.7	0.03
Taiwan	0.1	1.2	N/A	N/A	N/A	N/A
S. Korea	0.1	2.7	17.6	15.6	10.6	8.2
Hong Kong	0.1	0.2	–	10.1	–	(–0.2)
Singapore	0.1	0.3	–	11.1	6.3	15.8
Thailand	–	0.8	–	–	–	13.1

* Post 1994 the statistics relate to the re-unified Germany.   Source: Adapted from Dicken (op.cit)

The table shows that over half of the wor'
produced in just three countries – the USA,
however, the US share of world output fell su'
was increasing rapidly. In 1960, Japan expor
8 per cent of its production. Twenty years
cent of output) and surpassed the US
(Cusumano[5]).

By 1995 the NIEs of Hong Kong, Sou
7th, 11th, 13th and 14th respectively
trade. The 1997 Asian crisis hit these econo...
may take some time, so their league rankings will pe..
the trade statistics reveal that there is a general shift towards ...
as a centre for global manufacturing production. The reasons for this are
more detail in Chapter 9 on Operations Management. In the meantime, we can ...
that one consequence of this shift is that other economies in the Asia-Pacific region,
such as Vietnam, are also looking at export led industrialisation as a route to economic
development.

Economists describe the pattern of economic development in Asia as following a
'flying geese' formation, as the manufacturing strength of Japan has been spread down
into the NIE's and the countries of ASEAN. ASEAN was established in 1967, to promote
mutual economic development in the member nations of Indonesia, Malaysia, Singapore, Philippines and Thailand. The 1980s and 1990s has seen these nations together
with China become major exporters of manufactured goods. For example, by 1994,
22.4 per cent of the GDP of Indonesia was generated by manufacturing industries,
compared with just 18 per cent for both the USA and UK. Between 1986 and 1993, the
percentage of the Indonesia labour force employed in manufacturing rose from just
under 17 per cent to 22 per cent. The economy would seem to be rapidly shifting away
from traditional subsistence farming with which it has been characterised for centuries.

The second major trend to be noted is the expansion of FDI* at a rate faster than
international trade growth. As the centre of production shifts across the world, so too
does the investment needed to support that production. The source countries for such
investment, and the nations and sectors where the investment is directed, will be
studied in more detail in the next section of this chapter. At this stage we are interested only in the *overall* picture of what is happening in FDI, and the story is one of
very fast growth, particularly post 1985. Between 1985 and 1990, FDI grew at 28 per
cent per year, or twice as fast as exports. 1990–1993 saw little growth due to the recession, but since then FDI has once again outstripped both export and world output
growth on an annual basis. The latest UNCTAD statistics show that total FDI rose by
almost 40 per cent to over US$40 billion in 1999, and the bulk of this investment is
focused on the Triad countries of Western Europe, Japan and North America. These
countries now account for 63 per cent of the world's FDI foreign assets.

A world in which FDI is growing faster than trade suggests that business operations
are becoming increasingly transnational. Companies are choosing to establish foreign

* UNCTAD defines FDI as 'investment involving management control of a resident entity in one economy by
  an enterprise resident in another economy. FDI involves a long-term relationship reflecting an investor's
  lasting interest in a foreign entity.

es in preference to entering overseas markets by exporting. Much of the FDI wth has arisen from cross-border mergers and acquisitions, which seem to get gger year by year. For example the acquisition of Chrysler by Daimler Benz carried a huge price tag of US$44.5 billion, and serves as an indication that companies need to invest directly in foreign bases if they are to compete in a global marketplace. As UNCTAD rightly concludes, 'FDI is becoming both a major stimulus to globalisation and, at the same time, its growth is a direct result of globalisation and economic liberalisation' (World Investment Report, 1998).

The third major trend that arises out of changes in patterns of global trade and investment is a shift in the distribution of wealth across the world. The shift is a consequence of changes in terms of trade, and in particular the long-term reductions in commodity prices. The developing countries are heavily dependent upon commodity exports and when prices fall, their economies suffer, whilst the developing nations benefit. This is clearly illustrated in the example cited earlier in this chapter in respect of oil prices. The gains to the developed world from the lower price of oil exceeded the total value of global development aid in 1998, consequently the developed world became relatively more wealthy. Over the last thirty years of the century the average trade deficits for developing countries increased by 3 per cent of GNP, and the 1999 UNCTAD Report calls for 'a long hard look at the international trading system' in which 'attention needs to be focused on market access'. Improved market access requires the removal of protectionist measures including tariff and non-tariff measures such as agricultural subsidies. Such subsidies make it difficult for developing countries to get access to the markets of the developed world. For example within the EU the subsidies granted to producers of dairy products are worth up to 100 per cent of the world market price. As a result, although the cost of dairy goods production within the EU is amongst the highest in the world, the EU producers still retain a 50 per cent share of the world market. UNCTAD's Trade and Development Report, 1999 pinpoints the consequences of this imbalance: 'income and welfare gaps have widened further' and 'asymmetries and biases in the global system against the poor and under-privileged persist unchecked'. UN Statistics on the

Table 2.3   *Changes in Per Capita Incomes 1987–95*

	Average % annual growth in Per Capita GDP 1987–1995	Per Capita GNP 1995 (US$)
Botswana	7.91	4,355
Cameroon	(0.081)	627
Hong Kong	12.58	22,898
Ghana	1.44	397
Germany (1991–95)	8.3	29,632
Japan	9.76	41,718
S. Korea	14.61	9,736
Kenya	(1.6)	330
United Kingdom	5.79	18,913
United States	4.56	26,037

Source: *United Nations Statistical Yearbook*, 42nd Issue.

changes in per capita GDP across different countries illustrates this effect very clearly, as shown in Table 2.3.

The distribution of production across the globe directly reflects the distribution of comparative advantages across nations, but it also highlights a problem for, in the view of UNCTAD, 'as the twentieth century comes to an end, the world economy is deeply divided and unstable'. The Uruguay Round would appear to have failed to generate the substantive gains that were hoped for. The Table shows the NIEs of South Korea and Hong Kong as registering the highest growth in per capita GDP. The lowest growth rates – in two cases negative growth – occurred in sub-Sahara Africa. The older developed nations are in the middle ground. The relative wealth of people in different countries cannot easily be compared using the figures for per capita GNP, due to differences in spending power, and lifestyles. Nonetheless, it is unlikely that the 90-fold difference between the richest (Germany) and poorest (Kenya) nations on the Table do not represent *real* and *dramatic* differences in living standards in the two places.

FOREIGN DIRECT INVESTMENT

As we have seen, international trade and foreign direct investment are closely inter-linked. The common factor in both instances is the international/transnational corporation (TNC), because exporting/importing or investing overseas are simply alternative ways of internationalising business. The transnational corporation is defined as comprising parent enterprises and their foreign affiliates. A parent enterprise controls assets of another entity in other country/countries usually via ownership of an equity stake. UNCTAD assume a minimum equity stake of 10 per cent as the threshold for control.

Investing in foreign affiliates requires large amounts of capital, and so FDI tends to be concentrated in the hands of the largest companies. UNCTAD estimates that there are around 60,000 TNCs across the globe, but the 100 largest concerns account for US$4 trillion of sales, equivalent to 36 per cent of total world sales by foreign affiliates. The total assets of these 100 companies are worth over US$4 trillion, they have over 6 million foreign employees, and only two of the 'Top 100' are from developing countries. The figures suggest that a vast amount of economic power lies in the hands of the TNCs and this raises questions about the extent to which they lie beyond the control of national governments.

Over the short–medium term, the corporations which make up the world's 100 largest TNCs have remained relatively stable: 85 per cent have been in the list for the last five years (UNCTAD, 1999).

The UNCTAD list of the World's largest transnational corporations has strong over-laps with the *Fortune Global 500* of non-financial corporations. The *Fortune* list ranks corporations in terms of total sales, whereas the UNCTAD list ranks by foreign assets – consequently, the overlap means that fifty-six of the firms with the largest total sales are also in the top 100 in terms of foreign assets. These huge corporations clearly have a significant economic influence upon the world, some estimates suggest that the largest 100 are responsible for between 4 and 7 per cent of World GDP.

Table 2.4   The World's Twenty Largest Non-Financial TNCs, ranked by foreign assets, 1997 (billions of dollars and number of employees)

Ranking by Foreign Assets	Corporation	Country	Industry	Assets Foreign	Assets Total	Sales Foreign	Sales Total	Employment Foreign	Employment Total
1	General Electric	United States	Electronics	97.4	304.0	24.5	90.8	111,000	276,000
2	Ford Motor Company	United States	Automotive	72.5	275.4	48.0	153.6	174,105	363,892
3	Royal Dutch/Shell Group[c]	Netherlands/United Kingdom	Petroleum expl/ref/distr	70.0	115.0	69.0	128.0	65,000	105,,000
4	General Motors	United States	Automotive	0.0	228.9	51.0	178.2	–	608,000
5	Exxon Corporation	United States	Petroleum expl/ref/distr	54.6	96.1	104.8	120.3	–	80,000
6	Toyota	Japan	Automotive	41.8	105.0	50.4	88.5	–	159,035
7	IBM	United States	Computers	39.9	81.5	48.9	78.5	134,815	269,465
8	Volkswagen Group	Germany	Automotive	–	57.0	42.7	65.0	133,906	279,892
9	Nestlé SA	Switzerland	Food	31.6	37.7	47.6	48.3	219,442	225,808
10	Daimler-Benz AG	Germany	Automotive	30.9	76.2	46.1	69.0	74,802	300,068
11	Mobil Corporation	United States	Petroleum expl/ref/distr	30.4	43.6	36.8	64.3	22,200	42,700
12	FIAT Spa	Italy	Automotive	30.0	69.1	20.2	50.6	94,877	242,322
13	Hoechst AG	Germany	Chemicals	29.0	34.0	24.3	30.0	–	137,374
14	Asea Brown Boveri (ABB)	Switzerland	Electrical equipment	–	29.8	30.4	31.3	200,574	213,057
15	Bayer AG	Germany	Chemicals	–	30.3	–	32.0	–	144,600
16	Elf Aquitaine SA	France	Petroleum expl/ref/distr	26.7	42.0	25.6	42.3	40,500	83,700
17	Nissan Motor Co. Ltd	Japan	Automotive	26.5	57.6	27.8	49.7	–	137,201
18	Unilever[d]	Netherlands/United Kingdom	Food	25.6	30.8	44.8	46.4	262,840	269,315
19	Siemens AG	Germany	Electronics	25.6	67.1	40.0	60.6	201,141	386,000
20	Roche Hildings AG	Switzerland	Pharmaceuticals	–	37.6	12.7	12.9	41,832	51,643

Source: UNCTAD *World Investment Report 1999*.

[Note: The transnationality index combines ratios of foreign: home assets, sales and employment to measure the significance of foreign operations within the whole. The higher the index, therefore, the greater the proportion of transnational involvement.]

The distribution of large TNCs and of FDI is uneven across sectors, industries and countries, and it is useful to look more closely at these distributions. A number of key points can be observed:

■ The vast majority of corporations in the top 100 TNCs have parent enterprises in the Triad nations.

■ The average (media) size of TNCs from developing countries is only $1.4 billion compared with $13.3 billion for the top 100 TNCs. The list of top fifty TNCs from developing countries is dominated by companies from Hong Kong, most of which have names that may go unrecognised in the west, such as New World Development Co. Ltd.

■ Four industries dominate the list – electronics and electrical components, petroleum, chemicals and pharmaceuticals, and the automotive business.

■ The corporations ranked most highly in terms of the transnationality figures predominantly have parent enterprises in smaller industrialised countries such as the Netherlands and Switzerland, e.g. Nestlé (Switzerland) and Unilever (Netherlands).

■ Central European TNCs are still relatively small. The region is still a newcomer to the concept of transnationality.

■ A large proportion of FDI flows are devoted to cross-border mergers and acquisitions and the UK and USA are important participants in this market.

Table 2.4 clearly demonstrates the dominance of the developed world in terms of ownership of the world's largest TNCs. The table also shows that TNCs are very large and operate in quite a limited range of business sectors.

Understanding why FDI is expanding, and the direction of inflows and outflows of investment funds – the key points raised above – requires consideration of four specific issues in relation to FDI:

■ the reasons for FDI
■ characteristics of the source nations
■ characteristics of the host nations
■ the sectoral mix and imbalance of FDI.

Reasons for FDI

The decision to invest directly in a foreign country is made at the corporate level, but the stimuli for the decision may be either internal or external to the company. FDI is just one strategic option for organisations as they seek to expand the scale of their international business, and the pros and cons of FDI from the organisation's perspective is looked at in more detail in Chapter 5 on international strategy. Nonetheless, it is difficult to understand and interpret international FDI flows without some knowledge of the reasons for FDI, and these can be summarised as follows:

Increased profit

Commercial companies are always on the look-out for opportunities to raise profits, either via cost reductions, higher sales volume or higher prices. The transfer of production abroad is a way of realising such opportunities. The theory of competitive advantage describes how nations should produce goods and services in which they have a comparative advantage. Similarly, if companies can access foreign labour/resources at a lower cost than fellow competitors, then they can gain a competitive advantage. It is no coincidence then, that a large percentage of the clothing sold in Western Europe is not produced in Europe, but in the low labour-cost nations of South East Asia and Indonesia. Even Marks and Spencer, a UK retailer which has traditionally emphasised the high UK content of its products, has been forced to succumb to market pressures and source an increasing proportion of its clothing from lower cost foreign producers. FDI is very much concerned with seeking out cost-cutting opportunities. It is also worth noting that a new trend is emerging in the type of assets sought by foreign direct investment, namely 'people skills' and 'created assets' such as technological skills, which can again be used to create competitive advantage.

New markets

When the Toyota motor company built its plant in Burnaston in Derbyshire, the plant was designed to produce cars for the whole of the Western European marketplace, not just the United Kingdom. From an operational management perspective, it does not make sense to ship cars over huge distances, and so penetration of a regional market requires the establishment of regional production facilities. Consequently, car manufacturers such as Ford, GM and Toyota will have car and engine plants strategically placed in each market bloc, to service local requirements.

Protectionism

Import restrictions may make it difficult for a company to gain a foothold in a foreign marketplace, and the only solution is to produce locally. This often goes hand in hand with mergers and acquisitions, which account for a very large proportion of international capital flows. UNCTAD describe cross border mergers and acquisitions as being the 'driving engines' behind FDI expansion in both 1998 and 1999, especially between Japan, North America and Europe – the Triad nations. In 1998 the value of majority owned cross-border mergers and acquisitions equalled US$411 billion.

Extending the product life cycle

If a company finds that a product is reaching technological maturity or the end of its life-cycle in the traditional markets, FDI may provide a means of extending the cycle by moving into new markets. The tobacco industry is a good example of this, where health concerns have led to falling demand in the industrialised world. In response, companies such as Phillip Morris have sought new markets in places such as India and West Africa, where Western cigarettes have a certain 'status' as consumption goods.

Characteristics of the Source Nations

The detailed pattern of outflows of FDI has been affected in the last two years by the Asian crisis, but a central trend remains clear, which is that the bulk of FDI flows originate from Europe, the USA and Japan. FDI outflows from the EU reached a massive US$386 billion in 1998, a rise of over 50 per cent on the 1997 figure. The United States FDI outflows for 1998 equalled US$133 billion, and those of Japan fell by 7 per cent to US$24 billion. Across the OECD countries as a whole, the value of direct investment outflows rose from US$321 billion in 1996 to over US$566 billion in 1998. What is more, the value of these flows in relation to the GDP of the source nations is rising steadily. This indicates an increasing dependence on foreign generated sources of income for these economies.

As with all statistics, the picture which emerges is dependent upon the period under analysis, but looking more closely at the statistics for the period 1996–98, outflows within the OECD are dominated by the United Kingdom and the USA. European flows to the USA more than tripled over this period. Germany and France take third and fourth place as the most active investors, closely followed by Japan. The overall story is that international investment flows are dominated by the developed nations – they were responsible for 46 per cent of world FDI in 1998 – and this picture is further reinforced when the statistics on the host countries are analysed.

Characteristics of Host Nations

The inflows of investment to the developed world amounted to 68 per cent of the world total in 1998. In recent years the scale of these inflows has reached unprecedented magnitudes as the total value of inflows to the OECD between 1994 and 1998 was greater than the total flow over the preceding twelve years of 1981–1993.

The total drawn in by OECD countries equalled US$465 billion in 1998, a rise of over 70 per cent over the previous year, and the EU is the largest recipient of the money. Inflows to the EU rose from $130 billion in 1997 to $230 billion in 1998, and the United Kingdom (US$114 billion), Germany (US$87 billion) and France (US$41 billion) were the prime recipients.

The inflow of investment to the USA was also very large in 1998, amounting to US$193 billion, compared with US$111 in 1997. A significant proportion of this was accounted for by several very large-scale mergers and acquisitions, such as Daimler Benz's acquisition of Chrysler, and other EU originated investments.

The Asian crisis has affected the attractiveness of the region to foreign direct investors. Inflows of FDI to Japan at the end of the 1990s are well below those of the EU and USA, but still remain high relative to the historic averages for the country. The purchase by Renault of a stake in Nissan is clear indication that confidence is still there, as is the fact that US firms invested $5.1 billion in 1998 compared with just $397 million in 1997. One trend which is emerging is that of countries such as Korea and Thailand proving an attractive location for European and American investors. Investment into China is also likely to be growing rapidly, but reliable statistics are difficult to obtain. There is also growing evidence that intra-regional investment in Asia is being rapidly replaced by investment from non-Asian OECD sources.

The Sectoral Mix of FDI

Perhaps not surprisingly, the extent of FDI across different economic sectors is very uneven. Furthermore, the sectors which dominate the figures vary slightly from year to year. Looking back at Table 2.4 it can be seen that a number of industries feature prominently among the world's largest TNCs: oil and gas, automotives, electronics and chemicals and pharmaceuticals. These same industries dominate the statistics on FDI. In Chapter 5 on international strategy, you will see that industries can be classified under headings of domestic, multi-domestic and transnational (global), and it is this distinction that explains why FDI is focused on specific sectors. Common sense allows us to see that cars can be sold world-wide under a common design, such as the Ford Mondeo, because local tastes do not vary so much that major design modifications are required. In contrast, some products will be very different from one part of the world to another – for example confectionery and bakery products. FDI is linked to the globalisation of business, and so the investment only tends to occur in those industries that are well suited to a global marketplace.

As a result, the global restructuring of some industries such as financial services, pharmaceuticals and telecommunications can have a very significant impact upon the size and direction of FDI flows across the world. For example, the oil and gas sector is very capital intensive and so any FDI to purchase foreign assets is likely to have a very high value. The low capital-intensive industries will conversely account for a smaller proportion of FDI. This link to capital intensiveness is clearly shown in Table 2.5 below. In the highly capital-intensive oil and gas sector the average size of deal was over three-quarters of a billion dollars. By contrast, the low capital intensity of retailing brought an average deal size of just over one third of a billion dollars.

The timing of restructuring in any particular industry can also affect the statistics from year to year. In the mid 1990s there was substantial rationalisation of the chemicals and pharmaceuticals business, whereas the late 1990s is characterised by cross-border acquisitions in the telecommunications and business services sectors (see the numbers of deals

Table 2.5   *Top Ten Industries for Mergers and Acquisitions 1998 (ranked by value)*

Industry	Deals (number)	Total Value (US$ billion)
Oil and gas	98	76.2
Automotive	144	50.9
Banking and finance	317	50.8
Telecommunications	231	50.0
Paper, printing, publishing	232	40.9
Utilities	111	39.6
Insurance	124	37.9
Business services	853	37.7
Chemicals	349	24.3
Retail	152	18.0

Source: *Financial Market Trends*, No.73, June 1999, Table 4.

in Table 2.5). Consequently, sector trends will vary across time, though the general principle that attention is focused on a relatively small number of industries remains true.

Table 2.5 identifies the top ten industries for mergers and acquisitions in 1998, and although the ranking may differ if a 1999 table were available, the same industries are likely to be featured.

We can thus conclude that international trade and FDI patterns tend to work to reinforce each other. Together they have significant influence over the distribution of income and capital, production and employment across the world, and the resulting distribution is regionally focused.

SUMMARY

There are strong theoretical reasons to support freedom of trade around the world and these provided a justification for the foundation of GATT and the WTO. Both international trade and foreign direct investment have increased dramatically over the last fifty years, resulting in changes in the geographic distribution of:

- comparative advantages
- manufacturing production
- gains from trade
- the global distribution of wealth.

Furthermore, the direction and type of trade has evolved over the years to reflect changes in technology, income levels and consumer tastes. The countries that have been able to increase their scale of involvement in international business have experienced rapid rates of economic growth, even when the changes have been relatively recent. The cases of Vietnam and Thailand are illustrations of this.

Coincidental with the rising volume of trade has been an increase in the general size of businesses, as they move into the international marketplace, and huge transnational companies now dominate certain industries. These companies engage both in international trade and in foreign direct investment, and so reinforce the links between the two. This is particularly important insofar as most investment flows are to/from the developed, as opposed to the developing nations. Consequently companies that operate internationally help in the redistribution of income in favour of the richer nations.

CONCLUSION

One of the consequences of the changing pattern of international business is the growth of regional economic blocs, which dominate the flows of goods, services and capital across national boundaries. Most importantly, these blocs have replaced the pursuit of purely national interests in the negotiation of trade agreements with that of a regional perspective. The background to such groupings and details of the various types of regional integration around the world is the subject of Chapter 3.

References

1 Heckscher, E. (1955) *Mercantalism*, 2nd edn, Allan and Unwin, London.
2 Ohlin, B. (1933) *Inter-Regional and International Trade*, Harvard University Press, Cambridge MA.
3 Hoekman, B. and Kostecki, M. (1955) *The Political Economy of the World Trading System: From GATT to WTO*, OUP, Oxford
4 Dicken, P. (1998) (p.19) *Global Shift (Transforming the World Economy)* 3rd edn, Paul Chapman Publishing, London
5 Cusumano, M. (1985) *The Japanese Automobile Industry: Tech and Management at Nissan and Toyota*, Harvard Univ. Press, Cambridge MA. (Quoted in D. Landes *The Wealth and Poverty of Nations*, Abacus (1999) p.483

Useful Web sites

www.opec.org
www.wto.org
www.unctad.org

TUTORIAL EXERCISES

1   Obtain a copy of the balance of payments for your country, and analyse the mix of imports and exports. Can you find products in which your country appears to have a comparative advantage?

2   Using the mini case study as a source of background information, enact a role-play exercise in which group members have to present their case to the WTO Dispute Settlement Body, playing the role of representatives of each of the Windward Island farmers, Chiquita, and the EU respectively. The class should then vote on the outcome of the dispute.

ESSAY QUESTIONS

1   Why might free trade areas lead to some conflict with the achievements of GATT?

2   What are the implications for the less developed nations of the current trends in trade and FDI?

Case Study: Foreign Direct Investment in China

The level of foreign direct investment in mainland China increased dramatically over the last twenty years of the twentieth century as evidenced by the following statistics:

- Between 1985 and 1990 the annual FDI inflows into China grew at an average rate of 30 per cent per year.

- Over the period 1990-97 total FDI inflows to China equalled $200 billion.

- In 1992 FDI inflows grew by 15.2 per cent followed in 1993 by a growth rate of 150 per cent.

- The value of new FDI inflows into China equalled:

    $38 billion in 1995
    $40.8 billion in 1996
    $45.3 billion in 1997.   Source: *OECD*

As a result of this very rapid rate of growth, FDI for 1997 amounted to one third of all FDI to developing countries, and led to China being ranked the world's number two host country second only to the USA.

So what makes China so appealing as an investment location? The first answer to the question can be sought in generic theories of industrial location.

Dunning argues that an MNC will only invest in a foreign location if it can obtain location specific advantages. This issue of location choice is addressed in detail in Chapter 9 but for now we can simply identify what is meant by the term location specific advantages. The main location specific factors are:

- markets
- resources – natural and created
- production costs
- political environment
- cultural and linguistic affinities.

In analysing the pattern of FDI in China, it is possible to recognise the importance of these factors in establishing the country as an attractive destination for funds. The literature on FDI suggests that there are two different types of inward investment – market oriented and export oriented. The market-oriented investors are seeking to take advantage of a large local market by having production facilities adjacent to/within that market. Export-oriented investors use the host country merely as a base from which to export goods for final sale at home or in third countries.

US and Japanese companies investing in China view the opportunity to supply the huge local market as highly appealing. An OECD study in 1998 showed that China will have the world's largest economy by 2015, and Japanese investors rank it as the world's most important market in the longer term.

It is accepted that current wealth levels in China are relatively low, but the population is

> ### Case Example
>
> Black Cat is a Hong Kong controlled fireworks manufacturer, which has invested in China to establish manufacturing plants. The plants allow Black Cat to take advantage of China's low labour costs, and given that the industry is labour intensive, this grants the company a useful cost advantage over its competitors. At the same time, China itself is a very large market, with fireworks regularly bought for community and family celebrations. In making their initial investment in China, Black Cat was possibly market oriented, but more recently their FDI policy has been extended. In 1992 the company began operating in the UK via the purchase of a German owned import business. In 1998 Black Cat bought Standard Fire-
>
> works, the main UK manufacturer, and in so doing Black Cat again initiated market-oriented FDI, but also had a wider agenda as well. The Standard Fireworks manufacturing facility in Yorkshire was closed, and the company now serves as the sourcing, distribution and marketing arm of Black Cat, providing access into the large UK and European markets. The fireworks sold into Europe are sourced from Black Cat plants in China, so that these plants are now both market *and* export oriented. The products sold in the Chinese and European markets differ, but all are produced in the low-cost environment of China.
>
> Source: *Financial Times*, November 1998

very high, and as economic growth begins to increase, there is massive medium- to long-term market potential. As the markets of the newly industrialised nations of Asia move towards maturity, investors seek alternatives, and a survey by Eximbank suggested that Japanese investors intentions re Asia were moving towards a reduced interest in Indonesia, Malaysia, the Philippines and Thailand, and in favour of China, India and Vietnam. Some countries therefore view the spectacular rise of China as an FDI host as a threat to their own ability to continue to attract FDI, but in reality both the sector and country of origin of the investments differ between China and its ASEAN* neighbours, which are technologically, educationally and industrially more advanced.

Half of the FDI in China originates from Hong Kong, which has been the largest investor since 1979. A further 25 per cent of FDI comes from Japan, Chinese Taipei and the USA. The Hong Kong and Taipei investors are predominantly small and medium sized firms, with limited resources and wealth to invest further afield than their largest neighbour. The US and Japanese investments are primarily in manufacturing facilities owned by large multinational companies. At the end of 1997, the stock of direct investment in China by Japanese and US firms was split as follows:

$13,518 million   Manufacturing
$8,234 million   Non-manufacturing

The explanation for an emphasis on manufacturing investment can be sought in the specific advantages of China as a location. A number of studies have sought to identify the key factors that attract foreign firms into China, and the findings of four important pieces of research are summarised in Table 2.6.

* ASEAN is the Association of South East Asia Nations, a group comprising Brunei, Malaysia, Thailand, Singapore, Indonesia, Philippines and Vietnam which is a Free Trade Area.

Table 2.6   *Determinants of FDI in China*

Factors motivating FDI in China	Research study
Low labour cost	Lo; Wang and Swain; Broadman and Sun; Zhang and Po Yuk
Size of market	Wang and Swain; Zhang and Po Yuk
Cost capital/High returns on investment	Wang and Swain; Zhang and Po Luk
Cultural connections	Broadman and Sun; Zhang and Po Yuk
Rate of real market growth	Broadman and Sun
Exchange rates	Broadman and Sun
Level of bilateral trade	Broadman and Sun
Cost of land	Zhang and Po Yuk
Government incentives	Zhang and Po Yuk
Stable political environment	Zhang and Po Yuk
Raw materials supplies	Zhang and Po Yuk

The Table clearly shows that four factors are cited in two or more studies, and low labour costs are found to be an important motivating influence in three out of the four pieces of research. Low labour costs, market size, and cultural affinities are all location-specific advantages as described by Dunning. The low cost of capital, which results in the potential to obtain high rates of return from an investment, is a consequence of utilising these location specific advantages. Foreign companies receive highly favourable tax treatment within China. The current tax rate for all corporations in China is 33 per cent but, after deductions, the majority of foreign companies pay around 15 per cent. The incentives granted to companies investing in special industrial development zones are even greater, as most companies will be granted two years' tax free status, plus an additional three years taxed at just 7.5 per cent. The preferential rates for foreign companies are due to be phased out following China's accession to the World Trade Organisation, in line with WTO principles. Such changes will severely hit foreign investors, and FDI may fall as a result.

One of the important subsidiary findings of the Zhang and Po Yuk study is that the dominant determining factor was labour cost, but that its importance was a function of whether the investment was export or market oriented. Three quarters of export-oriented firms cited low wage rates as the most important influence on FDI in China, compared to just one quarter of the market-oriented firms. This would suggest that companies that have well established markets outside China for labour-intensively produced goods, are seeking lower cost production opportunities. By contrast, companies which are investing in China in order to supply goods to the local market, require more than just low labour costs to induce investment. In fact, the stable political environment and government incentives were also ranked highly by such firms, suggesting that the market-oriented FDI decision is perhaps more complex and subject to a wider range of influences. Nonetheless, if the Chinese government can begin to understand what factors attract particular types of industries/companies, it can begin to adopt FDI policies which can be used to aid the nation's economic growth.

Case Study References

1 Lo, W. (1989) *New Developments in China Trade: Industrial Co-operation with the West*, The City University, Hong Kong.

2 Broadman, H. and Sun, X. (1997) 'The distribution of foreign direct investment in China, *The Word Economy*, Vol.20, No.3, pp.339–62.

3 Wang Z. and Swain, N.J. (1997) Determinants of inflow of foreign direct investment in Hungary and China: time series approach, *Journal of International Development*, Vol.9. No.5, pp.695–726.

4 Zhang, X. and Po Yuk, H. (1998) Determinants of Hong Kong manufacturing investment in China: a survey, *Marketing Intelligence and Planning*, Vol.16, No.4, pp.260–267.

CASE STUDY QUESTIONS

1 What problems might arise for export-oriented companies investing in China purely to take advantage of lower labour costs?

2 What ethical considerations might be important when considering investment in China?

3 If China is the second largest host country, does this imply there is some global shift in the distribution of industry and production? If so, what are the shifts that can be observed, and what are their implications for the future?

CHAPTER THREE

Economic Integration

LEARNING OUTCOMES

We hope that after reading this chapter you will be able to:

- Define regional integration and distinguish between four different levels of integration
- Describe the main characteristics of the EU, NAFTA, and the Asia Pacific trading blocs
- Discuss the future prospects for even larger, continent-wide regional groupings
- Critically comment upon how regional integration has affected international trade
- Explain how regional integration might be beneficial to multinational companies and stimulate their international growth

INTRODUCTION

It can be argued that economic integration around the world has been one of the most significant trends since World War Two. The creation of regional groups is intended to provide both economic stability and growth as well as increasing the level of political cooperation amongst the member nations. At the same time, the postwar growth of regional trading blocs across the world suggests that international trade is no longer focused on the national comparative advantage of individual states. Instead, the creation of such groups suggests a sense that the nation state is no longer big enough to compete in the world economy. Indeed, in seeking to explain the growth of the EU (which was the first regional economic bloc), Anderson and Goodman[1] argued that it 'has developed largely as a response to intensified competition in global markets, and as both consequence and a cause of changes in the economic role of states.'

The achievement of regional integration, via the creation of common markets and the promotion of free trade and investment flows, requires a willingness on the part of the member nations to subordinate national interests to those of the group. As we will see, it is because of limited willingness to accept such subordination, that the level of integration within most regional trading blocs remains limited. Nonetheless, these economic blocs are re-shaping the future global business relations.

THE MAIN TRADING BLOCS

Table 3.1 gives details of the largest regional economic blocs, and shows clearly that such economic integration is almost a global phenomenon – Europe, North America, South America and the Asia Pacific area all have well established trading blocs. The one exception is Africa, where the South African Development Community (SADC) with ten member states is a relatively recent, but fast growing, group. In West Africa, there is also the Economic Community of West African States (ECOWAS) which aims to form a customs union and eventually a common market, but on the whole Africa lags behind the rest of the world in its progress towards greater economic integration.

Table 3.1   *Major Regional Economic Blocs*

Group	Member countries	Type of integration/aims	Economic significance
North America Free Trade Agreement (NAFTA)	USA, Canada, Mexico	Free Trade Area	Population 281.5 million. Combined GNP greater than the EU
Asia Free Trade Association (AFTA)	Brunei, Indonesia, Malaysia, Philippines, Singapore, Thailand, Vietnam	Free Trade Area (by 2008)	Population 409.9 million
Asia Pacific Economic Cooperation Forum (APEC)	AFTA and NAFTA members plus Australia, Chile, China, Hong Kong, Korea, New Zealand, Japan, Papua New Guinea and Taiwan, Russia, Vietnam	Aim is free trade within the region by 2001 and developing economies by 2020. Bridging of the gap between developed and developing countries in the group	Population 410 million
Southern Cone Common Market (Mercosur)	Argentina, Uruguay, Paraguay, Brazil	Common Market	Population 201 million; members account for 70% of the GNP of South America
European Union (EU)	Belgium, France, Germany, Italy, Luxembourg, Netherlands, United Kingdom, Denmark, Eire, Greece, Spain, Portugal, Austria, Finland, Sweden	Economic union	Population 370 million

THE PROS AND CONS OF INTEGRATION

Not surprisingly, the reasons why most nations want to belong to a wider economic group are because it offers the opportunity for increased wealth. There is evidence to suggest that the GNP of countries that are members of major economic groups will rise faster than that of non members. This is largely a result of the fact that the removal of trade barriers stimulates a net rise in the level of trade. Other non-economic benefits that arise from regional integration are a greater level of political cooperation between member countries and a sense that it is easier to reach a consensus view with a small group. From the perspective of the nation state, there is a sense of increased power through strength in numbers, that is greater than that which could be exercised by any individual country, so that it is better to be part of a trading bloc that can argue collectively than it is to try and defend individual rights.

On the negative side, regional integration can lead to a diversion of trade which favours member countries at the expense of non-members. This would occur when a member nation chose, because of the absence of trade restrictions, to trade with a fellow member rather than externally, so that some blocs become the focus of trade for certain member countries. For example, in 1995, almost 55 per cent of the total UK imports and exports went to, or were sourced from EU countries. For France, the dependence on regional trade is even higher at 64 per cent. The same picture is true within Asia, where for the same year, more than half of Japan's trade was with Asia, Australia or Indonesia, i.e. 'local'. Direct and indirect protectionist measures can be used to establish common external trade barriers, and divert trade to member countries. For example, within NAFTA automobiles sold within the region will be free of tariffs, but only if they have at least 62.5 per cent local content. In response to such arrangements, some industries have been restructured, to rationalise production and distribution on a regional, rather than a national, basis. Holmes cites the North American car industry as an example of this type of reorganisation, but there are numerous other industries which have behaved in a similar manner. As the rate of intra-regional trade is growing faster than world trade, there is therefore some evidence that diversion of trade does take place.

There is also some concern about the possible employment consequences of greater levels of integration. Within the EU, for example, there are no restrictions on the movement of labour between countries, and there has been some concern that this has led to what has been termed a 'brain drain' in some professions (such as physicians) out of the UK. If it is possible to move freely from one state to the next, labour will be attracted to move to the state that pays the highest wages, whilst employers will be tempted to shift production to those countries with the lowest wage rates. The latter issue has led to protests by US labour unions concerned about the possible loss of jobs to Mexico as a consequence of NAFTA.

The final argument against regional integration is the possible impact upon national sovereignty. The creation of common markets and the promotion of free trade and investment flows requires a willingness on the part of the member nations to subordinate national interests to those of the group. As we will see, it is because of limited willingness to accept such subordination that the level of integration within most trading blocs remains restricted. Nonetheless, these economic blocs are reshaping the future of global business.

LEVELS OF ECONOMIC INTEGRATION

The various economic blocs, such as the European Union, NAFTA and Mercosur are all slightly different in type, and it is useful to begin an analysis of regional integration with a definition of the different types of economic groupings. In ascending order of scale of integration, the different types are categorised as:

- free trade area
- customs union
- common market
- economic union.

Within all such groups, member countries are economically inter-dependent, and the region, rather than the nation state regulates trade and serves as a focus for FDI from non-member nations.

A **free trade area** may be defined as a region within which all trade restrictions between member states are removed. In trading with non-member countries, individual states are able to retain their existing regulatory structure. In other words there is no common external tariff. The North American Free Trade Area (NAFTA), which we will discuss in more detail later, is one example of this type of arrangement.

A **customs union** takes integration a stage further because members agree a common policy for the regulation of trade with non-member countries. The European Union has, since 1968, been first and foremost a customs union, but its ambitions for economic integration have over the years moved it on into a common market and increasingly towards full economic union.

In a common market, the elimination of regulatory barriers extends beyond the trade in goods and services into the establishment of free movement of capital and labour across member states. Clearly linguistic barriers may remain, but there are no legal restrictions on workers from one member state taking up employment in another. The Caribbean Community (CARICOM), set up in 1973, is an example of this type of trading bloc.

Economic union takes economic integration to its final conclusion via the harmonisation of national economic policies, co-determined via a joint legislature. In the EMU countries, for example, a single currency is in operation – the Euro – and interest rates are common across all member nations, with the central rate set by the European Central Bank. The Treaty on European Union, which established the process for the creation of what is sometimes referred to as 'Euroland', i.e. those countries which operate under a common currency, has divided the EU into EMU and non-EMU members. The forceful debate on the pros and cons of economic union, and its effects on political sovereignty, indicate the difficulties of seeking regional economic expansion instead of national political and economic interest. Starie[2] observed that the strong political and economic ties that characterise the EU are influencing the world economic order, and it is certainly true that the 'regionalisation' of Europe has been an influential factor in the development of two other large groupings – NAFTA and APEC – and has also influenced the progress of world trade negotiations. In establishing NAFTA, US politicians were anxious to establish a group to rival what they saw as 'Fortress Europe'. In other words, it is as if the process of regional integration across the world is self perpetuating and reinforcing. Each time one group increases its power, others expand in retaliation to protect their local interests.

THE ECONOMIC SIGNIFICANCE OF THE MAJOR TRADING BLOCS

The global economic significance of the various groups shown in Table 3.1 differs widely, and this is best understood by a more detailed look at integration in the three main regions of the developed world, namely Europe, North America and Asia. These three areas, which are now viewed as the main drivers of world-wide economic prosperity, are commonly referred to as the Triad and throughout this book we will see how important the Triad is to the evolution of international business both at a corporate and at a global level.

Europe

Economic integration in Europe is dominated by the European Union (EU) which, as already indicated, is also the most integrated of all the economic blocs around the world. The EU has developed out of the Treaty of Paris in 1953, which established the European Coal and Steel Community, and the Treaty of Rome signed four years later, which created the European Economic Community. The six founding member nations had reached twelve by the time the Single European Act was passed in 1986, launching the programme for a Single European Market, and in 1992 the Treaty on European Union set the EU on the way to Economic and Monetary Union. In 1995 three more nations joined the EU, bringing the total to fifteen, and on 1st January 1999 the single currency was launched.

Estimates have been made of the benefits likely to have accrued from the 'creation' of the single market. These range from a modest 2.5 per cent of the combined gross domestic product of the member states to figures four or five times as large. They reflect not only gains from increased trade within the region, but also the belief that the single market created a generally more competitive economic environment within Europe, resulting in more efficient working practices and a superior identification and satisfaction of consumer wants.

The EU currently covers an area of 3.2 million square kilometres, and boasts a population of 370 million, and per capita GNP of just over $21,000 per annum. There is some discussion on forward expansion of membership to a number of Eastern European and Mediterranean states such as Turkey and Poland, but a few members have already expressed concerns about such proposals. Nonetheless, Turkey has adopted the external tariff arrangements, Cyprus and Malta have applied for membership and economists anticipate that Hungary, Poland, Slovakia and the Czech Republic will also apply for membership. Expansion may cause several problems however, because the economies of new entrants are not at the same stage of economic development as existing members. Consequently the EU budget may be strained by a need to support the poorer, more agriculturally dependent economies. Furthermore, the overriding influence of the founding countries of Germany and France may be undermined by an increase in the overall size of the union, and there are question marks over the political acceptability of this. Members are also debating issues such as the implications for national sovereignty of increasing economic union. There are fears that such sovereignty is being undermined, and that this is not politically desirable.

As of the start of 2001, the main concern in the group is over the prospects for the single currency, the Euro. Since its launch, it has seen its value against both Sterling and the US dollar fall substantially, despite increases in interest rates by the European Central Bank. Faith in the common currency is fundamental to the success of Economic and Monetary Union, because it was hoped that the Euro would become a major world currency for trade and investment purposes. Economists are forecasting strong rates of economic growth across the EU region over the next five years but weaker growth in North America. It is hoped that such a combination will fuel a strong recovery in the relative value of the currency perhaps to the point of dollar–Euro parity.

North America

The North America Free Trade Agreement, which links Canada, the USA and Mexico emerged in 1994 out of the Canada–USA free trade agreement. The agreement represented a continuation of growing economic ties between member countries, as Mexico and Canada were the USA's first and third most important trading partners. At the same time it represented a landmark agreement in world economic relations because it created the world's largest economic market by linking countries that were at very different stages of economic development. In the first six years of the agreement's existence Mexico's exports to its northern neighbours grew spectacularly, and now represent 90 per cent of the country's total exports. At the same time imports from Canada and USA grew almost as fast.

NAFTA is clearly dominated by the huge US economy, with the USA being the most important trading partner for both Mexico and Canada. Mexico is by far the poorest economy in the trading bloc and, as already indicated, the NAFTA agreement has given rise to complaints by US labour unions of job losses caused by companies moving production to Mexico, where labour costs are much lower. In contrast, the way in which the treaty offered access to low-cost raw materials and production facilities was seen as attractive to corporate America. In addition to raising economic issues, a number of lobby groups have also expressed concern about the environmental impact of NAFTA upon Mexico, as increasing numbers of US firms move over the border to take advantage of the weaker anti-pollution regulations.

At the summit of the Americas in 1998 a blueprint was presented for the creation of such a trading bloc covering the whole of North, Central and South America and comprising thirty-four nations. The bloc would be known as the Free Trade Area of the Americas. The difficulties of reaching such an agreement, however, are vast because it would straddle a number of existing trading blocks:

■ NAFTA in the northern part of America

■ Andean Community – a Free Trade Area comprising Venezuela, Columbia, Ecuador, Peru and Bolivia in the western side of Latin America

■ Mercosur (the Southern Common Market) which boasts Brazil, Paraguay, Uruguay as members, and Chile as an associate.

Any new Free Trade Areas would have to persuade members of existing arrangements that they would not be economically disadvantaged. There is popular support for the Free Trade Area of the Americas in Central and South America, but concern in the USA that home-produced goods would face stiff competition and so jobs would be lost. The balancing of economic and political considerations is delicate and will dictate the future development (if any) of free trade blocs in the region.

The aims of NAFTA are much less ambitious than those of the European Union. The objective is the gradual elimination of restrictions on trade and investment flows by 2010, and the possible expansion of the free trade area is now up for discussion. At the same time there are no signs that members wish to take integration any further via the agreement of common external tariffs, and no indication of a desire to pursue full economic union. Many would argue that NAFTA was a retaliation to the 'Fortress Europe' created by the single market, and this would certainly explain the limited objectives of the agreement.

Asia–Pacific

The Asia Pacific region is characterised by less structured economic blocs than those which exist in Europe and North America, which is somewhat surprising since some of the nations in the area are amongst the fastest growing economies in the world. AFTA is the only group that has formal arrangements for the elimination of trade barriers in the region, and the target date for such removal is still nearly ten years away. AFTA was formed in 1993, having developed out of ASEAN (Association of South East Asian Nations) which was established in 1967 to promote intra-regional trade and cooperation. The relative wealth and stage of economic development of AFTA members varies widely, but it is generally regarded as having been successful in increasing the level of trade within the region.

A less structured forum for the promotion of regional economic interests is APEC, which was established in 1989. The group's declared objectives are to counterbalance the power of NAFTA and the EU, and encourage the liberalisation of trade amongst group members. The target date for free trade is 2020. The major problem for APEC is the diversity of its membership, as it includes the developed nations of Australia, Japan, the USA and Canada, alongside the much poorer countries of China, Vietnam and Papua New Guinea. The geographic spread of membership is also very wide. Furthermore many members have other significant economic ties – for example Japan and the USA have ties with the OECD – and APEC nations comprise almost half of the world's trade and economic output.

This economic and geographic diversity begs the question of the relationship of APEC to the WTO, whose mission is the global promotion of trade liberalisation. It may be that they are both seeking the same ends, and if so, are both required? Perhaps the role of APEC in helping its membership to overcome the Asia economic crisis will enable it to prove it has a place as a viable force for the promotion of regional economic growth and development.

HOW ECONOMIC INTEGRATION AFFECTS WORLD TRADE

If members of regional economic groups are working together to improve their prospects, it is not surprising that a large proportion of world trade flows are actually intra-regional. Through the elimination of customs duties and trade barriers it becomes as easy to deliver car engine parts from a factory in Windsor (Ontario) across to Detroit in the USA, or from Chihuahua in Mexico to Indiana, as it would be to move the parts from one US location to another. At the same time, as companies grow bigger and more multinational in scope, the existence of trading blocs makes it possible to organise operations on a regional rather than a national basis. (This linking of structure to regional positions is well illustrated in the Ford Case Study that concludes this chapter.) As a result, regionalisation has influenced world trade flows. This is clearly illustrated in Table 3.2 below, which shows how dependent the major blocs are on intra-regional trade.

Table 3.2   *The Importance of Intra-Regional Trade Flows (1999)*

	% total imports which are intra-regional	% total exports which are intra-regional
North America	27.1	39.6
W. Europe	67.6	69.1
Asia	56.7	46.6

Source: *International Trade Statistics 2000*, WTO

The statistics show that despite their size and diversity the large regional trading blocs still engage in trade with the rest of the world. Both Asia and the EU find that over half of local requirements can be met from regional imports, but for NAFTA the level of regional self-sufficiency is much lower.

This suggests that the principle of comparative advantage still holds true, but that the advantages are measured regionally rather than nationally. For example, North America is the world's largest net importer of automotive products, whilst Asia is the world's largest net exporter. In other words, Asia retains a comparative advantage in the automotive business. By way of contrast Asia's share of clothing exports to the USA has been eroded by market share being seized by Latin American exporters, indicating that Latin America has gained a comparative advantage. It may be that this shift is a consequence of Latin American companies getting preferential trade terms because they are linked to NAFTA through regional integration arrangements.

The EU, because it has such high audiences of intra-regional trade, is the region of the world that may be best protected from economic slowdown in the USA, which is the world's largest consumer economy. Hence it may be less true than in the past that 'When America sneezes the rest of the world catches a cold'.

Detailed data from the WTO also reveal strong links between North America and Latin America, and Western and Central/Eastern Europe and the CIS. This suggests that although integration has not yet become continent-wide in scope, that trade is growing between economic blocs on the same continent.

In 1999, North American exports to Latin America accounted for 15.6 per cent of total exports. If this is added to the 39.6 per cent intra-regional trade from Table 3.2 we get a figure of 55.2 per cent for the whole of the Americas. In other words, more than half of the trade across the Americas is *within* that continent. It thus becomes easy to see the attractiveness of a Free Trade Area of the Americas, as a significant rival to the EU.

At the same time Western European countries look Eastward for markets and export 5.1 per cent of their merchandise to the Eastern States and the CIS. When combined with 69.1 per cent trade *within* Western Europe this means that just under three-quarters (74.2 per cent) of Western European exports stay within the continent.

The statistics in Table 3.2 for Asia include Japan, which receives 9 per cent of Asian exports, Australia and New Zealand (2.7 per cent) and China (3.3 per cent) as well as all the smaller Asian nations. This leads us to the general conclusion that the Asian economies are much more dependent on wider global markets for their products, with less than half of their sales being regional.

The trends in intra-regional trade over time also indicate that regionalisation works to strengthen trading ties between member countries. The rates of growth vary widely across the world, as shown by the data below, but nonetheless a clear trend is visible.

Table 3.3   *Intra-Regional Exports as % of Total Exports (excluding services)*

	1990	1999	Average Growth Rate (%) of Intra-Regional Exports 1990–99
NAFTA	42.6	54.1	10
EU	65.1	63.4	4
Mercosur	8.9	20.3	4
ASEAN	20.1	22.1	12

Source: *International Trade Statistics 2000*, WTO.

With the exception of the European Union, all regions have seen expansion of 'local' trade, so that its importance to the regional economy has increased. In fact, the fall in intra-regional exports for the EU in 1999 may well be purely because the trade figures are published in US$, even though the exports are priced in Euros. Given that the Euro fell relative to the dollar over 1999/2000, the drop may therefore simply be a consequence of currency fluctuations.

The area of fastest growth is Mercosur which covers the southern nations of Latin America. Even though the region suffered an economic recession in the late 1990s, the common market has still helped trade to grow between the member states.

THE FUTURE: REGIONAL VERSUS GLOBAL FREE TRADE

As mentioned earlier, one of the problems of regional integration is that it raises the prospect of conflict between the national sovereignty of the member states and the needs of the group. At the same time, the individual states benefit from the added bargaining power that goes with being part of a large and influential trading bloc.

From the broader global perspective, if regional integration causes a diversion of trade away from non-member countries, there may be a loss of economic welfare for the world as a whole if the result is a global failure to take maximum advantage of the laws of comparative advantage. All of this means that integration may be good for the participants, but possibly bad for the world as a whole.

Looking back to Chapter 2, you may recall that one of the problems of recent years is the growing inequality of wealth distribution across the globe, and it can be argued that regional integration is contributing to this phenomenon. Hence the developed nations are trading more and more with each other, as integration brings down the barriers, but the developing nations remains isolated from the economic benefits of such trade.

This leads to the further question of 'whose responsibility is it to promote global trade liberalisation?' It would appear to be the mantle of the WTO, but if the organisation finds itself faced with rebellion on the part of large groups such as NAFTA or the EU which may choose to engage in trade restrictions to preserve regional interests, then the WTO may be unable to act. This means that one of the most interesting questions about the future of world trade, investment and economic integration is who will win the argument – the regions or the WTO?

It would seem that there are strong links between international trade and regionalisation, and as suggested earlier, these links help influence corporate planning at a global level. It is therefore useful to conclude this chapter with a discussion on the impact of regionalisation on company strategy. This helps to set the scene for the first chapter in Section Two on internationalisation strategies of multinational companies.

REGIONAL INTEGRATION AND ITS EFFECT ON MULTINATIONAL COMPANIES

In Chapter 2 we saw that companies will often invest in a country in search of new markets, and this is a useful starting point for discussion of how multinationals are affected by the regionalisation process.

Using foreign direct investment as a way in to new markets is quite common, and particularly useful if a country has strong trade barriers which prevent multinationals from gaining market share because of import controls/barriers. For example, foreign paint companies have found it very difficult to penetrate the domestic market in Germany because non-tariff barriers have restricted access to wholesale distribution outlets. The problem with using FDI to get round such barriers is, of course, that it can tend to confine access to just one domestic market. Via GATT and the WTO, and the growth of regional trade blocs post World War Two, the scale of trade protection is falling, and this offers multinationals new opportunities. Instead of siting a plant in say, Japan, with the intention of just selling in the local market, if Japan becomes a member of an economic bloc, then the multinational now gains access to a much larger potential market – the whole surrounding economic region. The larger the bloc the greater the opportunity.

This potential to broaden the geographic scope of markets is discussed in the strategic management literature, which identifies the following three potential roles for foreign subsidiaries :

■ The supply of goods/services purely to local markets in the host country

■ The production of goods which are well established in the multinational company's product range. Using the laws of comparative advantage, companies will site subsidiaries in locations which can then export output at relatively low cost for sale in a wider regional market. This may mean that there is a widening of the geographic scope of the subsidiary, but a narrowing of the product range, as specialisation occurs.

■ Well-established subsidiaries, with high levels of expertise that can develop, produce and market new products that will significantly affect the multinational business. Such a role requires access to a much larger market area, such as an emerging trading bloc.

In other words, a company may choose to slowly upgrade the status of its foreign subsidiaries, from local supplier through to one that plays an important strategic role in the overall organisation. What is more, if multinationals are pro-active in supporting the freeing of trade restrictions in a region, then this helps to generate new market opportunities for existing businesses.

One way of looking at this is to see a region (rather than a single country) as offering broader scope for the multinational in terms of both inputs *and* markets. Within the EU, for example, Spain may be a good choice for locating a car assembly plant, because of local skill levels and the cost of basic resources, but the components could be made in any country(ies) within the EU area which has a comparative advantage. Hence the transmission systems may be made in Germany, the steering systems in the UK and so on, with the company moving all the components within the EU to the place of final assembly. Furthermore, if the region is one that is a free trade bloc, then such movement of goods will be made cheap and easy.

In this way, multinationals gain strategic benefits from operating within a free trade bloc. From a marketing perspective, there will be benefits from the faster economic growth rates that go with regionalisation, and from a supply perspective, companies can benefit from the freedom of choice on where to source components so that they can capitalise on the differing capabilities/comparative advantages of the various subsidiaries.

Of course, it is not all simple and obvious in practice. The difficulties of managing what might be described as 'many centres of different kinds' need to be resolved, and this requires that a company has a clear idea of its long term aims and objectives in the international arena. Which regions of the world will be the main producers and which will be the markets requires significant research and planning. Then choices have to be made about the role for different countries *within* the various regions. The discussion above shows that the strategic choices open to any business are influenced by the world economic background that has been described so far in this book.

SUMMARY

The post World War Two period has seen the simultaneous freeing up of world trade by GATT and the WTO, and the growth of regional economic integration. As a consequence, the citizens of the member countries have benefited from greater wealth and increased access to a broader range of consumer goods. Unfortunately, however, the benefits have not been spread evenly around the world. The developed nations within the Triad area have gained most from cooperation, whilst the developing nations of Africa have been much slower at making progress towards economic integration. Discussions on the expansion of the EU and NAFTA suggest that these blocs will increasingly dominate the world economy in years to come.

One consequence of regional integration has been the diversion of trade in favour of increasing intra-regional trade. This trend has implications for both multinational companies and global economic relations. Companies can take advantage of free trade across large regions in order to invest in a wider geographic area for both supply and marketing purposes. Consequently regional integration can indirectly assist in the international expansion of multinational companies. At the same time, because intra-regional trade is growing in importance and the blocs are becoming increasingly powerful, there is some risk of potential conflict between the WTO and the regions in the pursuit of free trade.

CONCLUSION

It would seem that the benefits of regional integration to date outweigh the costs at a global level. In the future, however, the picture may change. There may be times when greater freedom of international trade may be detrimental to regional interests, and it is difficult to see how such disputes could be resolved. Some writers suggest that the WTO may have only a limited role on the world stage by 2050 onwards – instead the regions will rule.

Unfortunately, this may lead to disputes between regions, such as we saw in Chapter 2, and also the loss of some of the economic and political gains that came from cooperation in GATT. This is the global economic scenario facing companies today as they seek to internationalise their businesses, but the economy is only one part of the external environment faced by a company seeking to develop an international strategy. Cultural attitudes and traits are another important dimension which need to be taken into account when setting strategies, and this is the subject of the next chapter.

References

1 Anderson, J. and Goodman, J. (1995) Region, States and the EU: modernist reaction or postmodernist adaptation?' *Review of International Political Economy*, 2(4) 600–31.
2 Starie, P. (1999) 'Globalisation, the State and European Integration, *Journal of European Area Studies*, Vol.7, No.1.
3 Holmes, J (1992) 'The Continental integration of the North American automobile industry; from the AutoPact to the FTA', *Environment and Planning A*, vol 24, pp 95–120

TUTORIAL EXERCISE

Collect statistical data on the average growth rate of GNP for countries in each of the EU, NAFTA and APEC, covering the period 1990–2000. Compare these with the growth rates for non-member countries in each region, as well as Africa. Discuss what this indicates about the benefits/problems of current trends in regional integration and world trading patterns.

ESSAY QUESTIONS

1 If North America is wary of Fortress Europe, why did they not seek a stronger form of integration than a Free Trade Area?

2 Is national comparative advantage now irrelevant?

Case Study: Ford Motor Company

This case looks at the current structure of the Ford Motor Company across the world, and illustrates how regionalisation can prove to be helpful to companies which are selling into a global marketplace.

Background

From its humble origins in Michigan in 1903, the Ford Motor Company has grown into the world's second largest automotive company, spanning six continents employing over 300,000 people and with world-wide sales (1999) of over US$160 billion. The company is divided into a number of different businesses, each of which are managed independently with their own profit, sales and growth targets:

FORD AUTOMOTIVE

This is the manufacturing and assembly arm of the business, producing cars, trucks and commercial vehicles world-wide. Manufacturing/assembly operations comprising 114

plants straddle more than thirty countries world-wide. The automotive brands owned by Ford are Ford, Volvo, Mercury, Lincoln, Mazda, Jaguar, Aston Martin and Land Rover. The main competitors are BMW, Toyota, VW, Nissan, Honda, Daimler-Chrysler and General Motors.

VISTEON

In June 2000 Ford converted Visteon, its spares business, into a separate company floated on the stock market, which remains a wholly owned subsidiary of Ford. The company competes in an open market for the supply of spares for Ford vehicles, and is also seeking to expand the level of non-Ford business. The main competitor in the world market is Delphi.

FORD CREDIT

This is the finance arm of the company, providing finance to both dealers and end customers. As such, its main competitors are not car producers but the big finance providers such as the major banks.

HERTZ

Hertz is the world's largest car rental company based in New Jersey, USA, but covering 143 countries world-wide. As a Ford subsidiary, it provides a ready market and showcase for Ford models around the globe. Main competitors are Avis, Budget, Alamo and Europcar.

KWIK-FIT

Ford purchased Kwik-Fit in 2000, when it was Europe's largest independent provider of maintenance and 'light repair' work on vehicles. The chain has 1,900 outlets in the UK and is seen as complementing the Ford dealer network as a provider of low cost basic maintenance services for older vehicles out of warranty. Main competitors are the fast-fit repair services offered by other main dealers, such as 'Masterfit', which is owned by Vauxhall.

The range of businesses covered by Ford is further increased if one takes into account the vast range of strategic alliances and joint ventures in which they are involved. Examples include:

COVISINT

The main automotive manufacturers in the world, namely Ford, GM, Daimler-Chrysler, Nissan and Renault, have come together to establish an Internet-based supplier exchange. The aim is to use the site to invite tenders from potential suppliers aggregating and rationalising the requirements of the different manufacturers, to create large individual contracts. It is anticipated that procurement costs will be cut by up to $2,000 per vehicle as a result.

UPS LOGISTICS

An alliance with UPS is intended to cut the delivery time from plants to dealers and on to final customers.

1999

Ford made its first purchase of a vehicle disassembly company in Florida. This marked the first stage in a plan to create a global network of vehicle recycling companies.

The range of businesses thus covers all stages in the possible life-cycle of a vehicle from purchase/manufacture of components, through assembly, sales, repair and after-sales service, to the scrap yard and disassembly. The Ford Motor Company would seem to have mastered the concept of vertical integration. The interesting question is 'how have they dealt with mastering a global market-place?'

The Global Perspective

Ford takes the view that cars/trucks/commercial vehicles are global products. In other words, they can be supplied to any market around the world with only minor modification. Ford's view was most formally expressed in their decision in 1988 to develop a new global car – the Mondeo. The company employs over 16,000 people world-wide in the area of product development, based around three main centres. Small-vehicle development work is shared equally between a UK and German centre. Large/luxury vehicle work is USA-based at Dearborn, Michigan, alongside the Truck Vehicle Centre at the same location.

The Mondeo brought together designers and engineers from around the world to create a car which acknowledged the convergence of tastes and motoring needs across all continents. The vehicle, which sold in Europe, Taiwan and the Middle East as the Mondeo, and North America as the Ford Contour and Mercury Mystique, offered what Ford themselves describe as 'a prototype for a new approach to product development – a global "platform strategy" that uses many components to produce vehicles that are widely differentiated to meet the varying needs of different regions'.

This global product was the first tangible outcome of the company's Ford 2000 project which had been launched in 1995. Ford 2000 consolidated North American and European operations under a global management team, with the aim of creating a unified global operation by 2000, and the Mondeo provided the first product designed for this environment.

How do Regional Economics Groups help Ford?

Ford recognises the need to be a global competitor in the automotive business, and in particular the importance of gaining a strong foothold in the emerging markets, where sales growth is likely to be greatest. The problem, however, is that historically many developing nations have placed tariff barriers or other import restrictions on vehicle imports, which has made it difficult for Ford and other overseas producers to gain market share. For example, Korean tariff barriers mean that imported vehicles represent less than 1 per cent of the local market.

Ford is responding to import barriers in a number of ways:

- by supporting WTO initiatives to open up markets to free trade

- via investment in manufacturing facilities in the developing nations, so that vehicles can be sold as locally produced rather than imported

- through active support and promotion of various regional initiatives to promote free trade and economic cooperation. In supporting the talks on a Free Trade of the Americas, the company is recognising the growth potential of the Latin American markets, and the opportunities for export that this would afford its existing plants in North America. This complements Ford's existing support for NAFTA.

Similarly, by expressing support for the APEC goals of free trade, and encouraging APEC to designate automotive production as a sector worthy of priority consideration, it creates more opportunities for Ford's US plants (the USA is an APEC member) to take advantage of the area's fast growing consumer markets. It can be argued that commercial interests also lie behind Ford's desire to see China admitted to membership of the Word Trade Organisation. The company already has joint ventures and minority stakes in component and manufacturing plants in China. WTO membership for China would enable the output of these plants to be freely exported across the Asia–Pacific region.

In other words, the growth of free trade around the world and more localised regional economic blocs is potentially beneficial to Ford. Nonetheless, it leaves them with the problem of how to combine the apparently divergent forces of globalisation and regionalisation in the day to day management of their businesses.

Fitting Regional Organisations into the Global Structure

With markets, component and assembly plants distributed around the world, it is not surprising that Ford is a major exporter as it moves components, assembly kits and finished goods between its sites. The main producers and buyers of these exports (in terms of location) are as follows:

Exporting Nation(s)	No. Units
USA and Canada	140,152
Europe	63,162
Asia/South America	16,064
TOTAL	**219,378**

Importing Nation(s)	No. Units
Mexico	60,912
Puerto Rico/Brazil/Argentina	33,700
Middle East/North Africa	31,335
Western Europe	24,201
Australia	9,246
Rest of the World	59,984
TOTAL	**219,378**

Source: media.ford.com

The Table shows that there are regional linkages between exporters and importers. The Latin American markets can be served by either the North American or South American producers; Western Europe buys cars from its own region, and Asia can sell on its output to the Middle East and Australia. North African countries may buy products from either Europe or Asia. In other worlds, regionalisation of both production and markets is possible within the Ford Motor Company. This regionalisation is seen more clearly when one looks at the structure of Ford operations in Europe, North America and Asia respectively, and how these relate to Ford Global.

The regional divisions of Ford operate as separate Strategic Business Units responsible for meeting specified profit, sales and growth targets. This means that the performance of each region is seen as vital to the overall results of Ford Motor Company, and so regional operations are supported by global 'centres of excellence'. The global structure, as illustrated below, therefore works by replicating 'miniature' Ford Motor Companies in each geographic region, which provide a comprehensive range of services to each locality, with the support of central company services for core facilities.

GLOBAL STRUCTURE OF FORD AUTOMOTIVE REGIONAL GROUPINGS

NORTH AMERICA (including Mexico)
Accounts for more than half of world-wide employment, and 65 per cent of vehicle sales

Canada
production plants + dealerships

USA
37 manufacturing plants + research development + sales marketing + Ford Credit

Mexico
Production plants + dealerships

EUROPE
47 manufacturing locations in UK, Spain, Germany, Belgium and Portugal
+ Research and Development (UK and Germany) + dealer networks + Ford Credit

ASIA
Manufacturing/assembly plants in Malaysia, Philippines, Thailand and Vietnam
+ sales marketing + leasing company + B-Quik servicing company

---

SUPPORTED BY GLOBAL CENTRES OF EXCELLENCE

1   **DESIGN**
    e.g. Large vehicle centre, Dearborn, Michigan

2   **PROCUREMENT**
    Through Covisint

3   **CORE COMPONENT MANUFACTURING**
    e.g. Dagenham. The engine plant is Ford's sole global source of diesel engines

4   **MARKETING**
    Via dealership network and provision of Ford Credit Facilities

5   **REPAIRS/SERVICING**
    Dealer network plus Kwik-Fit

It can be seen that regionalisation has helped Ford in the organisation of its global markets. Automotive production is a high volume business and it would be expensive to establish separate manufacturing, parts, marketing and after-sales services on a country by country basis.

In a world in which there are large free trade areas, however, it becomes economically viable to establish regionally focused facilities, which supply markets in several different countries simultaneously. Structured in this way, the Ford Motor Company can maintain a presence which crosses all of the continents but provides overall support in the core functional areas of research and development, purchasing and key component provision. This way of balancing global and local needs is vital to success in international business, and Ford's ranking in the world automotive industry suggests that it has found a successful formula.

CASE STUDY QUESTIONS

1 Find out the detail of the scale and type of Ford operations in your home country, and discuss how it fits into the broader regional picture.

2 Why is it important to centralise research and development facilities in Ford?

3 Conduct a survey of classmates and see how many can correctly name more than 3 brands owned by Ford. Explain your results in terms of whether they support or oppose the ownership of separate brands under a common organisation.

CHAPTER FOUR

The Role of Culture in International Business

LEARNING OUTCOMES

This chapter will enable you to:

- Understand and explain the term 'culture'

- Critically comment upon a variety of alternative classifications of national cultural characteristics

- Explain why culture might influence management practice in each of the key business functions

- Discuss the role of culture in relation to marketing, human resource management, operations management and finance in a multinational company

INTRODUCTION

'The vodka is OK but the meat is underdone' is an oft quoted Russian mis-translation of the English proverb 'the spirit is willing but the flesh is weak', which symbolises the problems of cross-cultural relations. When transporting ideas, products or symbols from one culture to another direct translation does not work, because sensitivity and adaptation is required to send/collect the message. In the case quoted here, the words 'spirit' and 'flesh' have been misinterpreted by being translated literally, with the result that the central message of the proverb is lost.

The need to avoid cultural misunderstandings is vital to successful international business expansion, but it must be recognised that culture can affect many aspects of corporate activity. The topic is considered sufficiently important to have generated its own distinctive field of study – comparative management – which looks specifically at how management styles vary across national cultures. The overall impact of culture on international business, however, goes right through an international company because it affects the core functions of HRM, marketing and finance as well as corporate strategies, organisational structures and general codes of business conduct and ethics.

It is the aim of this chapter to demonstrate that cultural understanding is a vital ingredient for global success in business and that culture influences the fundamental practice of management in a multinational organisation. The starting point is a definition of culture, which is then followed by consideration of the work of key writers in analysing national cultural characteristics under a variety of headings. Recognising that patterns of behaviour and social values vary between countries implies that management styles are also likely to differ from nation to nation. There is a mass of literature on the topic of comparative management and you may find it valuable to look at books on a country of your choice, but comparing managers in, say, Italy with those in Japan is not the function of this chapter. Instead, and in keeping with the functionally based structure of this book, we look at how cultural differences can impact on the different functional elements in a multinational corporation – in other words, how does culture affect marketing, finance, operations and human resource management?

WHAT IS CULTURE?

Although we may all believe that we have an intuitive understanding of the term culture, expressing that understanding in the form of a definition is more complex. Kroeber and Kluckhohn[1] found over 160 definitions of culture, and a selection of alternatives is shown below:

'shared patterns of behaviour' (Mead[2])

'collective mental programming' (Hofstede[3])

'a set of base assumptions – shared solutions to universal problems … handed down from one generation to the next' (Schein[4])

'the essential core of culture consists of traditional (i.e. historically derived and selected) ideas and especially their attached values' (Krober and Kluckhohn[1])

These definitions have certain common features, which recur in the social sciences literature on culture: a recognition that culture affects beliefs, values and behaviour and that culture is shared and passes through the generations. It may be useful to briefly outline some examples of cultural differences under each of the subheadings of values, beliefs and behaviour.

BELIEFS

People's beliefs are most obviously expressed in religion, but the importance of religion and the specific beliefs vary across countries. For example, in Middle Eastern countries, Islam is a very important influence within societies, but in Western societies which are predominantly Christian, the social significance of religion is declining rapidly.

VALUES

The relative value attached to the individual versus the group varies across national cultures, and affects the process of social interaction. For example, Middle Eastern and

Japanese societies place a strong emphasis on the collective view, and this is reflected in the responsibility of children in a family, to care for parents and help provide for younger siblings once they reach adulthood. By way of contrast, in the USA and UK it is expected that young people will leave home and live independently of their family in their late teens or early twenties. In these cultures, the individual perspective takes precedence over the collective view.

BEHAVIOUR

Beliefs and values influence behaviour, even in small ways such as daily habits and timetables. The Dutch may be contrasted with the Spanish in this regard. Dutch people are well known for their adherence to schedules, and it is their habit to eat at home as a family between 6pm and 8pm. By way of contrast, the Spanish relaxed view of time means that they will frequently go out (as a family) to eat at the much later hour of 10 or 11pm, and adherence to the daily schedule is less predictable and significant.

In comparing cultures, care must be taken on a number of counts, including:

■ Recognition that cultures are not monolithic. Within any culture there are numerous subcultures that may be explained by social divisions, e.g. working class culture, or the caste system in India, place of residence, e.g. the Basque people, French Canadians or Chinese Malays, or demography, such as 'youth culture'. What is more, the cultural heritage, and interpretation of it is highly individual, and so it cannot be assumed that two different people from the same country will behave in similar ways or have common beliefs. The cosmopolitan nature of major cities such as New York and London is witness to such a mixture of peoples.

■ The separation of cultural issues from economic and political is complex, as all three factors interact to influence views and beliefs.

■ Defining the degree of difference between cultures is not straightforward because recognition of differences is a subjective issue.

■ As the level of international trade and travel increases, cultures become increasingly intermingled and this cultural diffusion may dilute the significance of national cultures. Many children of immigrants to the UK, for example, are more familiar with British cultural traditions than those of their parents, and this can cause family strife.

ALTERNATIVE CLASSIFICATIONS OF NATIONAL CULTURAL CHARACTERISTICS

A number of researchers have devised frameworks for the analysis of national cultures, and we can now look at these in some detail, beginning with the work of the Dutch writer Hofstede.

Hofstede

Hofstede, an engineer turned psychologist, based his classification upon evidence from questionnaires completed by employees at all levels of the multinational company for which he worked. The American multinational had operations in more than fifty countries, and so Hofstede's database was culturally very broad. The research was undertaken in the late 1960s and early 1970s, and so it is perhaps useful to interpret the findings with some caution, as attitudes may have evolved over the intervening forty years, but it provides a useful starting point for consideration of national cultural characteristics.

Hofstede developed four dimensions which can be used as a basis for comparison of national cultures. These dimensions are as follows.

Individualism versus collectivism

This distinguishes societies in which the individual and their close associates are the focus of attention and commitment, from those characterised by arrangements through which personal commitment to a broader group of extended family and community is common. Members of an individualist society enjoy the challenge of hard work but demand alongside this the right to a private life. The opportunity to lead is desirable, in contrast to the opportunity to belong which features in collectivist cultures. Consequently the collectivist societies emphasise the right of everybody to share access to good training and remuneration. These differences of approach are illustrated in some detail in examples included in Chapter 10 on human resource management.

Perhaps not surprisingly, Hofstede found that the level of individualism was closely linked to wealth, so that the poorer countries of Latin America and Africa were more collectivist, whilst the wealthy nations of North America and Western Europe were highly individualist in character. The Scandinavian nations, however, were found to be a little more collectivist than their level of wealth would lead one to expect. The Eastern cultures also emphasise the importance of the group rather than the individual, with China, South Korea, Taiwan, Malaysia and Singapore all classified as collectivist. Japan, surprisingly, lies midway between the Western and Eastern cultures in the spectrum, as do the Arab countries.

Power distance

Power distance measures the degree of tolerance for differences in power in given national cultures. In the cultures which score highly on power distance, managers tend to have greater power over their subordinates, and exercise of this power is accepted. Hofstede based the national scores for power distance on answers to questions relating to the frequency with which subordinates were afraid to disagree with their superiors, and the level of preference for a directive as opposed to consultative style of management.

A high score for power distance thus indicates a culture in which the management style is tending towards the paternalistic and there is minimal participation by lower levels of staff in the decision making process. The findings suggest that the poorer nations are characterised by high power distance combined with collectivism, in contrast to the richer Western countries which are individualist and low on power distance. France is an important exception to the pattern however, because it is distinguished by its highly individualist society which also scores highly on power distance. The Scandinavian nations also differ from the norm insofar as they are distinctively low on power distance, which fits with their more collectivist stance.

Uncertainty avoidance

This third dimension measures the extent to which people are nervous of the future and what may/may not happen. Cultures which score highly on uncertainty avoidance have a preference for trying to predict the future, and a general dislike of uncertainty and ambiguity in managerial and social situations.

In some societies life is taken 'as it comes' whilst in others there is need to control events. Control is implemented through orderly methods of working and careful planning, although the level of adherence to procedures and rules will vary across countries. Greece and Portugal head the list of nations which Hofstede found disliked uncertainty the most, and they are closely followed by other Latin European nations and the Latin American states. Singapore was the nation most willing to tolerate uncertainty, but Denmark, Sweden and Norway also gained low scores on uncertainty avoidance. Amongst other Western European nations, the Germans dislike uncertainty more than the disorderly British, who have a fairly easy going style of management. If you think about what these attitudes might imply in relation to how meetings are organised and decisions taken, it is easy to see that there may be considerable differences of style when several cultures try to work together.

Masculinity v femininity

The words are used here in a deliberately stereotypical way, with masculine being used to describe a society which promotes the 'macho' norms and values of ability and earning power. Feminine cultures place a high value on interpersonal relationships, caring and the overall quality of life.

Masculinity can be linked to assertiveness in attitudes to work, where the pursuit of success, high earnings and personal recognition are dominant characteristics. In contrast, feminine societies place greater emphasise on the qualitative dimensions of work, such as good working conditions, personable colleagues and a generally pleasant environment.

In Hofstede's research, Japan was found to be the most masculine country and Sweden the most feminine. Other Scandinavian nations are similarly feminine in orientation, and this ties in with their collectivist attitudes and low scores on power distance. In contrast, anyone who has watched television clips from Japanese game shows where contestants are given often gruelling physical challenges which would not be tolerated by, for example, the British, can identify with the idea of Japanese cultural masculinity. The masculine assertiveness can be linked to the fact that the Japanese also have a strong dislike of uncertainty, but it does not fit so well with the Asian approach of respect for elders and authority. Consequently some writers* consider that Japanese culture is a unique mix probably 'unmatched by any other society.'

In Western Europe, the Latin nations of Portugal, Spain and France tend towards the feminine, whereas the more northern Anglo Saxon countries of Great Britain, Germany and Austria score relatively high on the masculinity scale. The USA and Canada also demonstrate more masculine characteristics.

In 1988 Hofstede and Bond[5] identified a fifth dimension of culture, namely Confucian Dynamism. The concept is important because the economic success of the 'Tiger Economies' of Hong Kong, Singapore, Taiwan and South Korea has been attributed to Confucian values. The cultural values associated with the religious philosopher Confucius are thrift, hard work, relationships ordered by status and a long-term planning horizon. The case study at the end of this chapter clearly illustrates how these values can permeate society's attitudes towards the most basic ideas.

Confucian Dynamism is associated with the peoples of South East Asia, particularly Thailand, Hong Kong, People's Republic of China, Korea and Japan. There is evidence, however, that although Hoftede's description of psychological traits is generally true at this macro level, it is nonetheless the case that the strength of the cultural bias will vary across nations and across individuals. In other words, Confucian Dynamism can exist anywhere in the world, but is likely to stronger in communities which have a large proportion of South East Asian members.

Confucian Dynamism links directly to Hofstede's other four cultural dimensions insofar as evidence of strong empathy with Confucian principles is associated with low levels of individualism, mid-range masculinity, and high levels of power distance. There seems to be no observed correlation with levels of uncertainty avoidance.

Clearly it is difficult to create cultural groupings based on just five specific characteristics, but Hofstede's work is important is setting in motion a train of research on national culture, and when the findings are combined with those of other researchers, a number of patterns begin to emerge.

Hall and Hall

Supplementing the work of Hofstede is that of Hall and Hall, who suggest that national cultural differences can be classified in terms of attitudes to time and use of language. Hall[6] distinguishes between countries which he terms *monochronic*, where time is regarded as a precious commodity, and *polychronic* nations, where time is seen as less significant, because it can be 'expanded' to accommodate the necessary activities. In general, the north-western European nations and the USA can be regarded as monochronic, and Southern Europeans, African and Arabic nations as polychronic.

As an example of differing attitudes to time, I will recount one of my experiences as a member of a multicultural research team looking into corporate strategy in Europe post 1992. The team leader was French, and we worked to a specified time schedule each day. Over the course of the first few days it began to emerge that the afternoon meetings regularly started late, and so one day the UK and German research

* See for example Chapter 7 of *Management Worldwide* by Hickson and Pugh (Penguin Business)

teams decided to return to the meeting room later than the scheduled start time, in anticipation of a delay. The justification for arriving late was simply that time was precious and should not be wasted waiting for the meeting to start: the time could more usefully be filled working in our own rooms. The late starts were inevitably the result of lunch-time socialising and discussion on the part of the French, Spanish and Italian researchers who held a polychronic view of time. They were of the opinion that if the meeting started late it did not matter – it could finish late if necessary. Varying attitudes on such a simple issue can cause huge problems in establishing working guidelines, and fundamentally affect business performance.

In respect of language, the distinction made by Hall and Hall is between high and low context cultures. In the high context culture, great significance is attached to the relative status of people, and the long-term evolution of a relationship. Trust is emphasised and relied upon more than legal formalities in a business relationship, because peripheral information is deemed to be important to decision making. The countries of the Middle East and Japan are examples of high context cultures, where protracted negotiations are held as a precursor to the settlement of any contract. The negotiating period is seen as a vital part of understanding the other party to a contract, and the assessment of trustworthiness.

Trompenaars

Another writer who has sought to establish a classification system for national cultures is Trompenaars[7].

In his book *Riding the Waves of Culture*, Trompenaars identifies three criteria which can be used to differentiate cultures. These are:

- Relationships with people

- Attitude to time

- Attitude to the environment.

In contrasting cultural approaches to relationship with other people, Trompenaars utilises the five dimensions for analysis of relationships which were first developed by Parsons[8] in the early 1950s, and in fact there is also substantial overlap with the some of the cultural characteristics described by Hofstede, as described earlier. The five dimensions that characterise relations with other people are:

- *Universal v particular.* The universalist cultures see relationships as essentially rule based, so that there is a clear definition of correct or incorrect behaviour, and there is always a consistency of approach. Adaptation is seen as risky and the exercise of discretion not permissible. America is generally seen as an example of a 'universalist' national culture. The particular culture is more sensitive to changing circumstances, recognising that this can affect the way in which people interact, and also that personal obligation is important. The result is a fluidity in relation-ships where behaviour is flexed to meet local needs and informal networks are vital to mutual understanding. The legalistic aspect of a relationship is thus less important than the informal, and Japan would be considered to be an example of a 'particular' type of culture.

- *Individualism v communitarianism.* This is the same as Hofstede's individualism versus collectivism. The key issue is the focus of responsibility, and the significance attached to individual as opposed to the concensus view. The differing perspectives can be characterised by their use of either 'I' or 'we' in discussion. In the business context, decision making will often be slower in communitarian cultures, because of the unwillingness to delegate responsibility to a single individual.

- *Neutral v emotional.* The difference here relates to the willingness to express emotion, including the use of humour. Neutral cultures cannot be viewed as 'cold', but merely as ones in which it is deemed inappropriate to publicly reveal one's personal thoughts and feelings. Emotional cultures are those in which touch, gesture and vehement expression of opinion is the norm. Trompenaars found that cultures varied within continental boundaries, but Japan, Hong Kong, China, the UK and USA could all be classed as 'neutral' cultures, whereas Spain, Russia, Italy and some Arabian countries such as Saudi Arabia and Oman were highly emotional.

- *Specific v diffuse.* In many respects this is related to the distinction between universal and particular cultures. Specific-oriented cultures are those which clearly distinguish between personal and business agendas; work is concerned with the achievement of a clear set of objectives which means that working relationships are structured and purposeful. In a diffuse culture, there is more intertwining of the personal and business dimensions of a relationship. Understanding the other person's position, and taking time to develop that understanding is important to a business relationship. There is some overlap between the specific and neutral cultures, and also those which can be seen to be both emotional and diffuse. Hence, the UK and USA are (in varying degrees) both specific and neutral, whilst the Arab nations and Southern Europeans are emotive and diffuse.

- *Achievement v ascriptive.* These dimensions are used to describe the factors which engender respect within a culture, and grant status to individuals. Some peoples will celebrate personal achievements, whilst others (ascriptive cultures) attach more value to educational or personal background. In the latter case, the use of titles and respect for superiors is of great importance, and there is often a tendency towards a male dominated hierarchy. Achievement-based cultures grant promotion according to proficiency and respect is based upon how well a person does their job. The USA is clearly a culture within which success is achieved rather than ascribed, and Trompenaars found that 87 per cent of Americans disagree with the idea that status depends mainly on family background. The UK, Ireland, Norway and Sweden were also found to be 'achievement' cultures. In contrast, French culture might be described as ascriptive, because great significance is attached to background and education: the managerial elite of France are recruited from the *Grandes Ecoles*, and as Hofstede observed, the French scored highly on power distance, indicating that status is important to them.

In classifying cultural attitudes to time, there is some overlap between the work of Trompenaars and that of Hall and Hall. The key issue is that of how we manage time, and whether we view it as sequential or synchronic, because if we are future oriented then we will use our time differently to if we are past oriented. Trompenaars neatly distinguishes between the two views of time by describing how a butcher might serve his customers. The sequential view, where jobs are done in a specific order and one at a time, would lead a butcher to serve customers in turn according to their place in the queue, even if two people required the same thing. The sequential view would lead the butcher to, for example, say 'I am cutting rump steaks, does anyone else want some?' so that the same job meets the needs of several customers simultaneously, regardless of their place in the queue (sequence). Whether cultures are long-term or short-term in their orientation is also significant in influencing the way in which we do business, with Americans thinking short-term in contrast to long-term Japanese planning horizons. Indeed even the importance we attach to planning differs between synchronic and sequential cultures, because the latter are more concerned with achieving the final goals than planning how they will be achieved. Consequently, the sequential cultures can have more problem in dealing with unexpected events than the synchronic, who just adapt to the new situation. Italy and Spain are examples of 'synchronic' cultures, and the USA, UK and Sweden examples of 'sequential' cultures.

The final cultural characteristic identified by Trompenaars was that of our attitude to the environment, and in particular whether we see it as a factor to be controlled or something that influences and controls us. Put into a business context, the differing viewpoints can affect our willingness to listen to, for example, customers, and adapt products to their needs. In some societies, such as the USA and Northern Europe, it would be seen as a sign of weakness to allow oneself to be influenced by outside events, and businessmen have to be taught to 'listen to the market'. In other cultures, particularly those of Asia and Japan, this recognition of the significance of environmental influences is intrinsic.

Lewis

The most recent author to seek to classify national cultural characteristics is Lewis[9], in his book *When Cultures Collide*, which was published in 1996. Lewis suggests that national cultures can be described under one of three headings, which mark out the factors that dominate the thinking and behaviour of the culture. The three alternatives are:

■ *Linear active.* These cultures place great emphasis on planning, scheduling and ensuring that everything is well organised and only one thing is done at a time. In many ways this definition matches the monochronic culture of Hall and Hall, and the sequential culture of Trompenaars. Lewis cites the Swiss and Germans as examples of people who display these characteristics.

- ■ *Multi-active.* Like Trompenaars' synchronic culture, multi-active cultures do lots of things at once, prioritising appointments on the basis of interest or importance rather than time. Italians, Latin Americans and Arabic cultures all fall into this category.

- ■ *Reactives.* Unlike the others, these cultures see courtesy and respect as having priority over time related matters. Listening, and understanding the views of partners is vital to business success. Lewis suggests that the Chinese, Japanese and Finns can be described as reactives. This term is equivalent to the 'diffuse' characterisitc described by Trompenaars.

It is difficult to reconcile and acknowledge the completeness of Lewis' categorisation of cultures, because it is limited in its scope. The linear and multi-active categories describe attitudes to time, whereas the reactive categorisation is a description of how relationships are managed, which is a very different issue. Nonetheless, it is useful to include his analysis because it completes the picture of major studies of cultural characteristics. We can now ask what all of this means for international business.

IMPLICATIONS FOR MANAGEMENT

Regardless of the specific nature of the variations, if one accepts the view that national cultural characteristics influence people's behaviour and beliefs, then it is reasonable to expect that this will also mean that management styles are not common throughout the world. The various definitions of what constitutes management are not different in black and white terms, because of course there is some cross-cultural common understanding of the purpose of business and the nature of the management task. Nonetheless, there are differences of emphasis, priority, and understanding which may also create a variety of styles and practice. In fact, the differences can be narrowed down by the creation of clusters of countries which demonstrate similar characteristics, and reference to such clusters can be helpful to the businessperson who when dealing with a country for the first time can simply look at the salient features of the culture of the relevant group, with which he may find he is in fact familiar. Figure 4.1 illustrates one such group classification of national cultures.

The figure is based on work which synthesised the findings of several research studies on national cultures, such as those of Hofstede, Hall and Hall, Trompenaars and Lewis. It demonstrates that there is a level of cultural affinity between groups of nations, and so a general understanding of management practice is made easier if one realises that it is only necessary to grasp the key characteristics of the seven groups. This is not, of course, to say that the Russians are exactly like the Latvians, but merely that they are more alike than the Russians and the Americans.

One of the dangers of creating groupings of countries is that it assumes that it is possible to make generalised statements about either the groups themselves or their constituent countries. This is not advisable. The detail of how the people of one nation or group of nations behave in certain situations can only be discovered by personal experience, and discussion with colleagues who have worked in a particular place for a

Figure 4.1 *A Pie Chart of Cultural Groups*

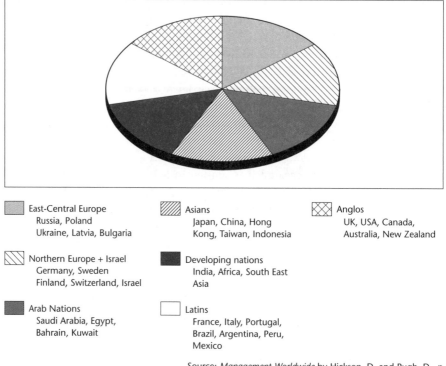

◻ East-Central Europe Russia, Poland Ukraine, Latvia, Bulgaria	◻ Asians Japan, China, Hong Kong, Taiwan, Indonesia	◻ Anglos UK, USA, Canada, Australia, New Zealand
◻ Northern Europe + Israel Germany, Sweden Finland, Switzerland, Israel	◻ Developing nations India, Africa, South East Asia	
◻ Arab Nations Saudi Arabia, Egypt, Bahrain, Kuwait	◻ Latins France, Italy, Portugal, Brazil, Argentina, Peru, Mexico	

Source: *Management Worldwide* by Hickson, D. and Pugh, D., p.44

long time. Nonetheless, understanding national and group characteristics at a very general level can be extremely useful in international business, because, as we have seen above, management styles tend to mirror individual cultures and most importantly each of the major business functions will be affected by cultural differences.

When devising an international strategy, a company needs to consider what it is going to sell where, and the acceptability or otherwise of given products/services is likely to be dependent upon the level of cultural similarity between the domestic and target markets. At the same time, staff will need to be employed in a variety of capacities in the overseas locations, and so human resource managers will need to be sensitive to any cultural needs that might be specific to individual countries. Similarly, if a company decides to establish foreign production facilities, culture may affect the ways in which production can be organised, and the content and format of any financial reports produced to report company performance. It is useful to look in some detail at how each of the marketing, human resource management, operations management and finance functions might be subject to cultural influences, and we can begin with the one which is perhaps easiest to understand: marketing.

The Impact of Culture on International Marketing

There can be no doubt that the cultural diversity of the world's many nations offers both challenges and opportunities for international marketing. On any foreign holiday or business trip you will encounter things that you may regard as 'strange' –

perhaps a different product not sold at home, an unfamiliar advertisement for a well known brand, or different opening hours for shops/restaurants. All of these are aspects of marketing which are adapted to local requirements and practice, and so pose potential difficulties for marketing managers.

One of the major issues for international marketing managers, which is discussed in detail in Chapter 8, is the extent to which it is possible for an international company to sell identical goods/services across the world. Maintaining a standard product design helps to keep costs down, but it also fails to recognise that customer tastes/needs may vary from one country to another, and so there is much debate about the feasibility of such a strategy.

The categorisation of national cultural characteristics, and the creation of cultural groupings can be very helpful to managers seeking to find new overseas markets for their goods. Most importantly, the country groups can be used to identify the places that are culturally closest to the existing markets; in other words, culture can be used as a way of segmenting the market. For example, a Kiev-based food processing company may be looking for new markets for its highly acclaimed tinned borscht. Borscht is the national soup of the Ukraine, and the name is derived from the old Slav word for beet, so the soup is basically a vegetable soup with beetroot as the main ingredient. In Figure 4.1 above, the Ukraine belongs to the Eastern European cluster of countries which includes Russia, Poland and Bulgaria, and so the company's marketing manager may take the view that it will be easier to find customers for the soup in any of these countries rather than in other places which fall within a different cultural grouping such as the Latin nations. Indeed, although borscht originally comes from the Ukraine, it is a food commonly found across most of Eastern Europe, and so it is likely that the Kiev company could successfully export to other countries in the region.

One of the features that links countries in the same groupings tends to be the roots of the language. This is most obvious in the Anglo-Saxon group, but it is also true of the other clusters as well. Avoiding linguistic mistakes can be fundamental to ensuring success in a new marketplace. In his book *Mother Tongue*, Bill Bryson[10] offers the following advice: 'If you are thinking of launching a new product yourself I can tell you that among the names that you cannot use are Sic, Pschitt, Plopp, and Super Piss. The first two are the names of soft drinks in France, the third is a chocolate bar in Taiwan and the fourth is a Finnish de-icer.' From the Anglo Saxon perspective, none of these products would be attractive to an English-speaking customer, except perhaps for their novelty value, and such bizarre examples go to illustrate how language can be vital to market success. The next time you go abroad, look out for such strangely named products yourself – you will find that they may have a local market but not an international one – for example the Aeroplane brand of tinned mango slices from India, or the Soberano brandy sold in Spain.

In practice, culture might affect all of the following aspects of marketing:

- Product
- Price
- Promotion
- Place.

The example of borscht illustrates how some products may appeal in some cultures rather than others, and so the actual product *per se* may be linked to culture, particularly in respect of food items. A less obvious example is that of washing powder, the composition of which reflects different climatic and cultural histories. In the USA, washing powders are made to function at low temperatures – usually 30°C or below. In the UK, perhaps because of our cooler climate, washing is done at much higher temperatures, and so washing machines all work on a mix of hot and cold fill and powders are not intended for use at temperatures below 40°C. You might think this a pointless piece of information, but it is very important if you are a company such as Unilever, marketing washing powder across the world. If you try and sell a powder that is ineffective at the normal local washing temperature, you will not find many customers. Consequently, the way in which products are linked into culture may actually be quite subtle and require extensive local research in order to ensure marketing success.

Price is a cultural issue because it needs to be matched to the level of economic development in a country. In rural Africa, for example, chewing gum is sold not in packets of five sticks, but as individual sticks, in order to make it affordable to the local population. This is a packaging issue as well as a pricing one, and the custom and practice on packaging may vary from culture to culture. For example, in Belgium and France it is common practice for supermarkets to charge a small deposit on wine bottles, which the customer then returns to the shop for recycling by the vineyards. In contrast, in the UK no such deposits are charged and the responsibility for recycling of glass rests with local authorities not private companies. In fact, a large number of bottles simply end up in rubbish bins, and are never taken to recycling depots at all.

Promotion refers to the methods used by companies to encourage people to purchase their goods – it may involve general advertising on billboards/televisions, house to house leafleting campaigns or branding. In practice, the most effective form of promotion will be culturally influenced. In the less developed world, for example, billboards and radio advertising are likely to be more effective media, which reflect the lower levels of exposure of the population to the mass media. In contrast, in rich countries such as the USA, the use of the Internet as a prime choice for advertisements is now commonplace.

The final way in which culture affects international marketing is in relation to place – where products are sold. As the internationalisation of business increases, place may become less important – you may have noticed yourself that walking down a shopping street in Frankfurt, you see many of the same shops that you might see in London, Paris or New York – and so the retailing has itself become international. Nonetheless, some items, especially food products, tend to be purchased in different places according to national culture. Chocolate products are one example of this, as in the UK most chocolate purchases are made at small confectionery/newsagent outlets; this perhaps reflects the fact that this market consumes a large amount of chocolate in the form of individual bars such as Kit Kat, Snickers and Mars. By way of contrast, in continental Europe most chocolate is sold through supermarkets, where large blocks of chocolate are bought as part of the weekly shop, and purchased for family rather than individual consumption. The marketing manager of the Swiss company Nestlé, therefore needs to be aware of such differences if they are to be successful in establishing a strong market for their products in the UK, and it is clear from their market share that they do have this knowledge and use it very effectively.

Human Resource Management

The HRM manager in a company is responsible for establishing policies in respect of recruitment and training, working hours/methods, and remuneration systems for staff. In a company that operates across international boundaries it is likely that the staff will be of mixed nationalities and so this creates the possibility for cultural misunderstandings.

In recruitment, some cultures will operate a very formalised recruitment process, based on the specification of particular qualifications for each job and interviews and tests to assess the relative ability of applicants. In other cultures, the method of recruitment may be more informal, based on employer networks, educational background or personal recommendation. Familial societies such as those of Africa, Asia and Arabia view it as a personal duty to use one's position to help other family members obtain work, although such an approach would be deemed wholly inappropriate and unfair in the West. In Chapter 5 you will see that attitudes to training also differ between cultures, with some countries such as Japan and Germany placing a strong emphasis on in-house training and accumulated experience as the criteria for advancement, in contrast to the USA and UK where it is common for staff to attend formal training courses that are run outside the business.

Hofstede's concept of power distance is also highly relevant to HRM management because it relates to an individual's attitudes to hierarchy and the way in which this might be translated into various ranges of pay levels between the highest and lowest individuals in a company. In France, which Hofstede scored highly for power distance, the gap between the highest and lowest paid employees is much greater than in the more collectivist and low power distance countries of Scandinavia. Differences in attitudes to the very fundamental issue of pay mean that in managing staff from a variety of different cultures care needs to be taken to accommodate different viewpoints and perhaps particular attention given to the pay differential between expatriates and local staff.

Working methods, and the relative importance of the individual versus that of the work team will usually reflect the level of collectivism within a society. The individualist Anglo-Saxon societies tend to place more emphasis on the need for personal assertiveness as a route to success and so team working is less likely to be accepted (or will at least be questioned), and the preference will be for remuneration systems based on personal effort, such as performance-related pay for managers. This in turn implies that the methods of working and the associated payment systems cannot be transported wholesale by a company to its overseas subsidiaries without careful thought – they may not work in a different cultural context.

Operations Management

The relevance of culture to operations management is quite subtle and indirect, insofar as one needs to think about how a country's economic conditions may impact on local culture. Operations management is concerned with solving the problems of how, when and where a product or service is to be made and delivered and the problem solving process is supported by good information systems. In reality, the production methods used in manufacturing will be selected on the basis of the factors of production that are available to the company in the form of labour and capital. The richer and more developed societies are likely to have access to more sophisticated production technologies than those which are poorer and with a population that is less well educated. Consequently, an operations manager in a multinational company which is setting up a foreign production facility will be conscious of the possible difficulties of introducing complex technologies into simple, labour-dominated societies. In such situations, it may be both cheaper and easier for multinational companies to adapt production methods to suit local resources rather than adopt a common global approach.

In addition to the technology of production itself, there is also the question of how sophisticated is the information system that supports it. Advanced computer-based systems can supply real-time data on such things as stock levels to remote sites across the world, in contrast to older manual systems which may be permanently several days or even weeks out of date. Clearly the use of computer systems requires the employment of staff with a high level of educational ability, which may not always be available, and so once again culture becomes a factor in operations management.

Finance

The finance function within a business is concerned with ensuring that sufficient funds are available to pursue the company's objectives, that they are used efficiently, and that the company's financial performance is monitored and reported regularly to both internal management and external parties such as banks, the government and shareholders. The elements of the finance function that are affected by culture are sources of finance, and external financial reporting practice.

The sources that may be used by companies to expand their business tend to vary from country to country, as they reflect the political economy of the nation as well as its state of economic development. In Chapter 6 you will see that in some countries the usual form of business finance is bank borrowing, with the loans often underwritten by the state – Japan and Germany are examples of such countries. In contrast, businesses in the USA and the UK are much more reliant of raising money via the sale of equity shares in the stock market. In order to expand across national boundaries, companies may choose to raise the necessary funds in either the home or host nation, or possibly a third country. If markets are highly localised or small then the number of options is reduced, and in this way national custom and practice may affect the finance decision. For example, when McDonald's opened their first restaurant in Moscow, it was set up as a joint venture with the Moscow City Council, and although all of the funding came from the Canadian franchisor and the US headquarters, the terms of the deal required payments to be made to the City council in return for the right to operate in the city. The agreement reflected the Russian political system in which the state and business are closely intertwined, and so the financial arrangements were partially determined by culture.

In a similar way, there is no universal approach to the external reporting of financial results via annual reports. For example, there is the so called 'continental' approach of nations such as Germany, France and Italy, which is heavily influenced by tax regulations. The information contained in the reports is primarily designed to enable tax authorities to compute liability. In contrast, the approach of the Anglo-Saxon group of nations, which includes Australia, the USA and the UK assumes that the investor (shareholder) is the primary user, and so information is provided which allows shareholders to assess the performance of their investments.

Such differences are of importance to multinational companies, because if they establish overseas subsidiaries then those companies will be required to comply with the local reporting rules. What is more, back at the parent company base, the financial information from all of the subsidiaries will need to be combined in order to produce what are called the consolidated accounts. For companies operating in lots of different countries each with their own system this could prove a massive headache, and so it is common practice for multinational companies to establish a common reporting system based upon the home nation's rules, that is then used by all foreign subsidiaries in the preparation of their accounts. Local staff in each foreign location are then employed to 'rewrite' the report in terms of the local rules. All of this complexity adds to costs, and many large companies are therefore exerting pressure for the introduction of common international accounting standards. In the meantime, culture affects accounting systems.

SUMMARY

The aim of this chapter has been to demonstrate that cross-cultural understanding is a vital ingredient of success in international business, and that culture affects the core functions of business, namely marketing, human resource management, operations management and finance. You have seen that culture is strongly linked to national boundaries, and influences people's attitudes to one another and authority as well as their willingness to take risks, plan for the future and accept/reject uncertainty. Writers such as Hofstede and Hall have used a variety of different factors to classify national cultural characteristics, and further work by Hickson and Pugh[11] has sought to group nations together to create culturally similar clusters of countries.

Understanding the cultural characteristics of different countries is useful to multinational companies because they can use the information when managing their business. In marketing, the product, price, place and promotional methods that may be used are all culturally sensitive. In HRM, recruitment, training, remuneration and work systems are similarly subject to variation across cultural boundaries. For the operations manager, economic development may influence the availability of alternative production systems, and identical products may need to be made in different ways in different parts of the world. Finally, even the financial management of business is subject to cultural influence. The sources of funds for business expansion vary from place to place, as too does the style and content of financial reports, and companies incur high costs in complying with varying reporting regimes around the world.

CONCLUSION

All of this leads us to the inevitable conclusion that culture is a factor that cannot be ignored in international business. There will be times when it plays a dominant role in business decisions perhaps, for example, in relation to the selection of new markets. In other instances, the effects may be more subdued, for example in respect of training programmes for new recruits. In the view of David Hickson 'it is not easy, some would say futile, to try to disentangle what is due to a society's culture with any precision and clarity.' The international company need not ask the question *why* is something different, it simply needs to recognise and acknowledge the difference if it is to progress on the global stage. The succeeding chapters of this book suggest ways in which such progress can be made.

This marks the end of the first section of the book, where attention has been focused on the broad external environment of international business. Companies need to understand and adapt to that environment and so we begin Section Two with a study of how companies plan their overall international strategy, taking into account the current economic, political and cultural framework that has been outlined.

References

1 Kroeber, A. and Kluckhohn C. (1952) *Culture: A critical review of concepts and definitions*, Harvard University Press, Cambridge, Mass.
2 Mead, M. (1953) *Coming of age in Samoa*, Modern Library, New York
3 Hofstede, G. (1980) *Culture's Consequences*, Sage, Beverly Hills, California
4 Schein, E.H. (1985) *Organisational culture and leadership*, Jossey-Bass, San Francisco
5 Hofstede, G. and Bond, M.H. (1988) *The Confucius Connection: From Cultural Roots to Economic Growth*, Organizational Dynamics, 16, 4.
6 Hall, E.T. and Hall, M.R. (1990) *Understanding Cultural differences*, Intercultural Press, Yarmouth, ME
7 Trompenaars, F. (1993) *Riding the wave of culture*, Economist Books, London
8 Parsons, T. (1951) *The Social System*, Free Press, New York
9 Lewis, R. (1996) *When cultures collide*, Nicholas Brealey Publishing, *London*
10 Bryson, B. (1990) *Mother Tongue – The English Language*, Penguin, London
11 Hickson, D. and Pugh, D.S. (1995) *Management Worldwide*, London, Penguin

Further Reading

Barsoux, J.L. (1993) *Funny Business*, Cassell, London

Barsoux, J.L. and Schneider, S. (1997) *Managing across cultures*, Prentice Hall, Hemel Hempstead

Bartlett, C.A. and Ghoshal, S. (1989) *Managing Across Borders*, Hutchinson Business Books, London

Calori, R. and Lawrence, P. (1991) *The Business of Europe*, Sage, London

Calori, R. and De Woot, P. (1994) *A European Management Model – beyond diversity*, Prentice Hall, Hemel Hempstead

Clark, R. (1979) *The Japanese Company*, Yale University Press, New Haven, Conn.

Hickson, D.J. (ed.) (1993) *Management in Western Europe*, de Gruyter, Berlin

Holden, N. and Burgess, M. (1994) *Japanese–LCU Companies*, McGraw–Hill, London

Horovitz, H. (1980) *Top Management Control in Europe*, Macmillan, London

Randlesome, C. (ed.) (1990) *Business Cultures in Europe*, Butterworth Heinemann, Oxford

Weinshall, T.D. (1977) *Culture and Management*, Penguin, Harmondsworth, Middlesex

---

TUTORIAL EXERCISE

Each student should describe three examples of situations that they have encountered in their foreign travels which illustrate the differences between the culture of a foreign country and their own culture. Foreign students should find this very easy, as they can relate the problems they faced in coming to study in a different country.

The list of examples based on holiday experiences can then be used as a basis for discussion on what the experiences might imply for methods of conducting business in each selected country, e.g. length of the working day, methods of working, styles of decision making etc.

ESSAY QUESTIONS

1 Do you agree with the idea that the globalisation of business has led to a dilution of national cultures?

2 In selling goods abroad, cultural considerations are much less important than a strong brand image, as illustrated by big names such as Reebok and Nike. Discuss the arguments for and against this statement.

3 What does the evidence about national cultural characteristics suggest about the optimal strategy for international business success – should a company be regionally focused or can it 'risk' going global?

Case Study: The Impact of Culture on Advertising in China

In 1998 the US-based food and drinks company Procter and Gamble was ranked top of the world's multinational companies in terms of its advertising spend – a massive US$5,754 million – and Unilever, an equally well known household products company was ranked third, spending almost $3,500 million in one year. One market that is targeted by both of these companies is that of China, which attracts huge foreign interest because of its sheer size and the fact that local demand for basic goods is growing very rapidly. The Chinese population is clearly divided between rural and urban, and the city dwellers are in the highest income brackets which are targeted by foreign companies. The largest ten cities in China hold just 4 per cent of the population, but nonetheless account for over 22 per cent of the country's earned income. The average income per head in these cities is US$610 per year, but with just ten cities holding a population of 45.5 million, it is not surprising that they offer the best potential markets for consumer goods.

The rapid growth of markets is creating a hugely competitive environment in which to sell, almost regardless of brand, and so foreign companies face a huge challenge in terms of getting their products noticed. Statistics from the *International Journal of Advertising* indicate that between 1987 and 1997 China was the fastest growing advertising market in the world, registering growth of over 1,000 per cent. The estimated total expenditure on advertising in China for 1999 is RMB185.6 billion. In addition to competition from fellow advertisers, foreign companies also face marketing difficulties because of the way in which advertising in China is subject to local cultural influences. The three largest advertising agencies – Saatchi and Saatchi, McCann

Erickson and J.Walter Thompson are all of foreign origin, but in advising clients and designing advertisements for the Chinese media they must recognise and be sensitive to local cultural needs.

In any nation the media is used to disseminate political as well as social and commercial messages, but the balance between the three tends to reflect the political situation, so that centralised economies, or totalitarian states may emphasise the political, whereas decentralised democracies will incorporate more widespread commercial use of the media. Chinese thinking and behaviour reflects the principles of Confucianism, which provide a strong contrast with Western cultures based on individualism. At the same time the economy has been centrally planned and based on socialist principles since the days of Mao Tse-Tung in the 1950s, and it has only recently begun to engage in economic reform and become more commercial in its orientation. The Chinese government has reacted to the fast growth of advertising and the media via a 'spiritual civilisation' programme which promotes national cultural traditions and 'socialism with Chinese characteristics'.

Within the cities, television is the most popular advertising media, and by 1996 it accounted for almost one quarter of the nation's advertising spend. Shanghai Unilever Toothpaste Co. Ltd spent RMB16 million, and Procter and Gamble spent RMB9.3 million on television advertising in that one year. The Chinese television industry is now very fragmented with just one national channel operating alongside a much greater number of provincial, city, cable and foreign satellite channels. Such fragmentation poses big problems for advertisers who must decide whether to focus on city or provincial channels, and also compete in a marketplace perhaps reaching saturation. Advertising breaks last for an average of ten minutes, with some breaks of thirty minutes being recorded, during which over 100 commercials are shown! In the key cities of Shanghai and Beijing consumers may be faced with 600–800 television advertisements per week, compared with a UK average of 300, and such saturation makes it difficult to attract the attention of potential consumers.

In order to protect Confucian principles, legislation to control the content and style of commercial advertising was passed in October 1994. The law requires that commercials must be clearly distinguishable from 'real' programmes and uphold Chinese social and cultural beliefs by maintaining the following principles:

■ People cannot laugh at the misfortunes of others

■ Elders must be respected

■ Children must comply with their parents' wishes

■ The dignity and interest of the state should be upheld.

The desire of the state to be involved in controlling the commercial activity of advertising is a reflection of the strength of feeling that core value needs to be protected. The introduction of private ownership and entrepreneurship into a previously centrally planned economy is viewed as a possible threat to traditional morality, and the principles laid down in the laws on advertising are derived directly from Confucius. Confucianism requires that a number of key relationships within society must be upheld, namely those between father and son, ruler and subject, husband and wife, child and parent and elder and younger friend or brother. The idea of respect for elders is fundamental and so it is

embedded in the legislation. Such regulation upholds the spiritual civilisation programme and is enforced by censorship by the managers of the individual television stations, who have the right of acceptance or veto over any particular advertisement. One problem for advertisers is that there is some ambiguity over what is/is not acceptable under the law, and so whilst some stations may be willing to show an individual advertisement, others may not. There is some evidence that 'guanxi' can be very important to acceptability, because guanxi describes the bonding or relationships by which people interact and feel mutually obligated. Where business relationships are strong, the bonding will create obligations which may help advertisers to gain acceptance of their commercials. Building business relationships is therefore very important to successful advertising in China.

The final factor which foreign companies need to be conscious of when designing advertisements aimed at the Chinese market is the nature and price of the product. What is a basic household item in the West may be deemed a luxury in China; for example products such as instant coffee are used as gifts by the richer city dwellers because they are very expensive relative to local equivalents. In such circumstances it can be difficult even for strong brands to overcome consumer resistance to purchase. Another example of how products are viewed differently in China is the case of toilet cleaners, because most Chinese households use the washing up water to clean their lavatories. Consequently, S.C.Johnson faced a big challenge in trying to launch their 'Toilet Duck' cleaner into the Chinese market. They needed to be sensitive to the idea that people might ask 'do we need toilet cleaner, let alone one that attacks germs under the rim?' In other words, something that is taken for granted as being a necessity in the West, may be seen as of little value in a different cultural context. The difficulties of marketing basic household goods are aggravated by the fact that under the Chinese remuneration system many workers obtain basic household and food products free from work, and so it is difficult to sell items which compete directly with free alternatives.

In conclusion then, foreign advertisers in China need to place their products into a cultural context which reflects Confucian principles, income levels and remuneration systems and lifestyles, all of which help to define attitudes and behaviour. This is no easy task.

Sources: www.shanghai-ed.com; International Journal of Advertising

CASE STUDY QUESTIONS

1 Identify three ways in which Chinese culture directly affects the design of advertisements in China.

2 Is guanxi a purely Chinese phenomenon or does it have equivalents in other cultures?

3 What do you think might be the current attitude of the average Chinese city dweller to the ten minute advertising breaks on provincial television stations? Explain your answer and comment on whether you believe this attitude might change over time.

4 What does the fragmentation of the television industry imply for a foreign company thinking about moving into the Chinese marketplace in terms of how to begin a marketing campaign?

The Internal Company Environment

CHAPTER FIVE

International Strategy

LEARNING OUTCOMES

When you have completed this chapter you should be able to:

- Understand the distinction between corporate, business and functional strategies and the interrelationships between them
- Describe and explain the factors that may lead a company to seek to internationalise its operations
- Explain and critically discuss the staged theory of internationalisation
- Explain and critically discuss the contingency theory of internationalisation
- Understand and comment upon the relationship between organisational structure and strategy
- Comment upon the global versus local debate in terms of its implications for company strategy and the structure of international organisations
- Demonstrate that successful internationalisation is dependent upon a solid strategic foundation at functional, business and corporate levels

INTRODUCTION

We now move away from the global and environmental perspectives of the preceding part of this book, into a corporate view of the world. Why do companies choose to move into the international marketplace? How do they progress from a domestically focused operation to a fully fledged multinational organisation? What problems do companies face in developing an international strategy? What are the critical factors determining the success of an international strategy? These are the type of questions addressed in this chapter, and followed through in chapters 6–10 in relation to functional strategies.

> 'The end product of strategic decisions is deceptively simple; combination of products and markets is selected for the firm.'
>
> Drucker

Behind the 'deceptively simple' process of selecting a product and market combination lie all sorts of problems, and the problems are increased when a company is seeking to determine an international rather than just a domestic strategy: the number of alternative combinations is increased dramatically. So how do companies begin to decide which products to sell overseas, and which markets to target? As commercial organisations the driving force will be the need to increase profits and the market value of the company, and so care must be taken to avoid expensive mistakes. The selected strategy must match corporate capabilities but at the same time grant some form of competitive advantage, thereby increasing the value of the company.

One way of minimising the risk of making a strategic mistake is construct a detailed matrix of alternative product and market combinations, and to formally assess each alternative. The criteria for assessment will reflect management's attitude to risk, their priorities, and their understanding of current market and competitive conditions. The final selection that is made at Board level represents the strategy for the organisation as a whole, but this will have implications for subdivisions of the organisation – both businesses and functions. Analysing product and market combinations in this manner in order to develop a position of competitive advantage is otherwise known as strategic planning, and it is a continual process. Over time, the market and product options may change and a company will need to review its strategy in the light of these changes. Consequently, strategic planning can be portrayed as a looped process, within which new opportunities/changed circumstances (inside and outside the firm) will lead to a revision of current plans. This process is portrayed in Figure 5.1.

The process starts with an analysis of the external environment – the political, economic, social and technological factors which currently influence the company's operations. The analysis will include some forecast of future trends, so that a strategy can be developed which fits the changing environment.

The second stage requires that the company reviews its own position within that external environment, by looking closely at its internal strengths and weaknesses, and its ability to either exploit new opportunities or respond to perceived threats. Focusing on the things that it can do well in the current environment, the third stage is one in which general corporate objectives and a mission statement are defined. These define the company's overall perception of its market position.

Specification of a strategy requires that the company defines precisely how it will achieve the declared aims, and this is stage four of the planning process. Corporate strategy must then be broken down into business and functional strategies if the objectives are to be achieved, and these plans must then be further divided into operational, i.e. year by year plans. Operational planning allows a company to subdivide its objectives into yearly/quarterly targets, which can be used for performance measurement and progress reviews. The outcome of performance reviews allows managers to see whether they are on target to achieve the declared objectives, and where targets are missed, the strategic plan needs to be revised. The causes of failure to achieve targets may be internal or external to the business, and so any new plan needs to review the internal and external environments. The cycle therefore recommences, but it is continually ensuring that the company is in a position of

Figure 5.1   *Stages in the Strategic Planning Process*

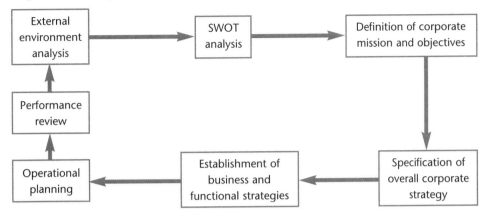

having achieved, as Drucker suggests, 'a combination of products and markets...
selected for the firm.'

The strategic planning process shows that strategies need to be developed at a
number of different levels within a company. It is therefore helpful to begin consideration of international strategy with a clarification of the different levels of strategy
within any organisation.

LEVELS OF STRATEGY

It is the responsibility of senior management to ensure strategic consistency across
different sections of a company. Consequently, it is helpful to understand the distinction between corporate, business and functional strategies.

■ Corporate strategy asks the question: what should be our portfolio of businesses?

■ Business strategy asks the question: how do we compete?

■ Functional strategy asks the question: how does this function, e.g. marketing,
   need to be organised so that business and corporate strategies are fulfilled?

The link between corporate, business and functional strategies can be understood by
consideration of Porter's[1] value chain. The value chain portrays the full collections of
activities which companies perform, subdivided into primary and secondary functions. The primary functions are those which are required to create the physical
product/service and distribute it to the marketplace. The support functions, such as
Human Resource Management, Finance, and Research and Development serve to facilitate the primary activities. A diagram illustrating the composition of the value chain
is shown in Figure 5.2.

Looking at the value chain from the perspective of international strategy, the aim
is maximisation of total world-wide profits from the chosen product and market mix.
A company may be made up of several different businesses, and each business

Figure 5.2   *Porter's Value Chain*

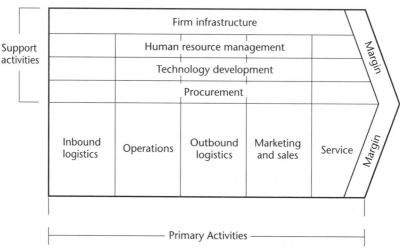

segment will have its own specific value chain, although support activities will often be shared by a several businesses.

For example, the international auctioneers and valuers Phillips has a world-wide network of salerooms which covers fifteen different countries. Each country's activities could be classified as a 'business' in its own right, and a value chain constructed accordingly. The organisation of functions may vary between, say, the UK operations of Phillips and the European operations, and these variations will affect the relative profitability of each business. This means that Phillips needs to establish strategies which allow it to plan and make decisions at functional, business and corporate levels which are complementary in nature. Let us suppose that Phillips' corporate strategy is to raise its share of global auction receipts by 12 per cent over the next five years. The flow chart below shows how this might be done.

Figure 5.3   *Interlinking Strategies*

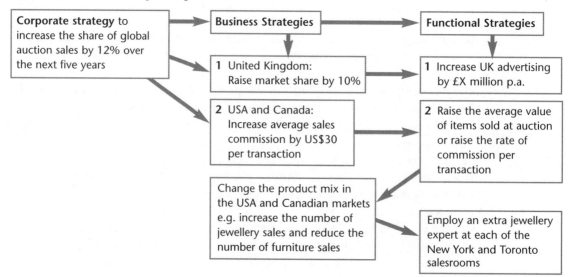

The chart clearly shows that decisions on corporate strategy have implications for the individual businesses, and these in turn have an effect at the functional level. Choosing to increase global market share requires decisions on which specific 'businesses'/countries will be the focus of attention for growth. At the same time, the decision on how to boost market share differs between the two businesses, and so the implications for the management of the marketing and HRM functions differ in each case.

Effective strategic planning, which links the various different levels of an organisation, helps to ensure that companies maintain profits and competitive advantage over the long term. Dudley[2] demonstrates the case for planning when he says 'the squandering of corporate strengths and competitive advantages through inaction or inappropriate adventures occurs when strategic elements in business management are lacking.' In other words, strategic planning is vital to corporate success.

One way of understanding what is meant by strategy is to see it as a route plan for taking a company forward from its current market position and profit level, to a new and stronger position in the future. In other words, if a company knows where it is now in relation to the competition AND where it wants to be in the future, then the strategy is designed to bridge the gap between the present and future positions of the company.

In the example of Phillips Auctioneers we saw how an international strategy must be specified at the three different levels of function, business and corporate strategies. The example also raises questions about the precise nature of differences between national and international strategies, and so this is the issue which we address next.

IS INTERNATIONAL STRATEGY ANY DIFFERENT?

Yes and no

Yes, because it involves analysis of a more complex environment. No, because ultimately it still has the same aim – identification of a competitive advantage. Let us look at each of these issues in a little more detail.

The product/market choice at an international level is made more complex because of the greater level of information required to make informed decisions. The different geographic regions of the world exhibit political, cultural, legal and economic differences all of which have both strategic and operational implications. As we saw in

---

Mini Case Study

New marketing strategies may be required

The way in which chocolates and confectionery are purchased differs between nations. In the UK, the main market is in items referred to as count-lines, which are sold via local newsagents and confectioners. The count-line is individual chocolate bars such as Mars, Snickers etc., and such shops carry a wide range of choice in these lines. In continental Europe, confectionery is sold primarily through the major food outlets such as supermarkets, or specifically as chocolate gifts sold via specialist retailers, e.g. Godiva in Belgium. This means that it may be difficult to penetrate the market in mainland Europe with a new count-line, as the distribution outlets are not the same.

Figure 5.1, strategy needs to be fine tuned to match the external environment, and so differences in environmental characteristics across different countries will require strategic refinements that would not be necessary in a domestic market.

The example demonstrates the need to be aware of differences in methods of operating between countries. Good background research is required by companies to ensure that they understand the new market they are entering. The example also shows that a UK chocolate manufacturer would need to devise a different strategy for the European market, either in terms of its products – moving away from count-lines – or markets – finding new distributors.

Other areas of difference between international and domestic operations which may have strategic implications include:

Cost structure of operations: For example, wage rates in Germany are higher than in the UK, which means that the cost structure of overheads:direct costs will not be the same for the German and UK plants of BMW/Rover, even though they may be producing the same motor vehicles. These differences mean that BMW's corporate strategy will need to specify the model types and volume of cars to be produced in each plant, and selling prices for vehicles may vary between the two countries to accommodate for the higher UK costs.

Competitive strategies: Local forms of competition may vary. For example, it is suggested that penetration of Japanese markets is very difficult because of the difficulty of accessing distribution outlets for consumer goods: control of competition takes the form of control of access to customers. The same is true for certain types of products in Germany, such as household paint. In the USA, in contrast, market share for consumer goods is tied to access to funds for extensive advertising. These differences mean that the way in which a company seizes competitive advantage may vary internationally.

Organisational structure and control systems: The type of organisational structure and control system in any country or region will be linked to the management style of that culture. Consequently, a company may need to be more flexible in specifying performance measures for international operations than it would be in the domestic environment. For more detail on these differences refer to Chapters 4 and 10.

The factors identified above indicate real differences between international and domestic strategy setting. At the extreme, the result can be that a business needs to have an overall international strategy, combined with substrategies for each geographic area of operation. These substrategies can then take account of operational differences between countries.

There are, nonetheless, some similarities of approach in strategic planning in domestic and international settings.

Mini Case Study

The Toyota company has expanded from a relatively small base into a truly global company by means of exploitation of cost advantages. This initial advantage has now been converted to a new competitive advantage gleaned from scale of operations and technical expertise. This strategy has made the company a huge success as a major player in the mid-range car market.

The Toyota story illustrates that there are only so many ways of gaining market share and competitive advantage. In the language of Porter, a company can seek to gain an advantage from lower costs or from product differentiation, and this strategic choice applies in both the domestic and international environments.

The simultaneous exploitation of both cost and niche product advantages is difficult, especially on the international playing field. Porter cites the example of Laker Airways failing because they began by seeking to attack a niche market, at a particularly low price which was dependent on volume sales for profit. The aim was to exploit a cost advantage in a very specific market, but when Laker sought to compete in the broader airline market it failed. The combination was doomed. It is interesting to note that the new breed of low cost airlines, such as Easyjet, 'Go' and RyanAir are all tightly focused on winning market share via low pricing combined with flexible and easy booking procedures. Maybe they have learned from Laker's mistake.

In practical terms then, businesses must make a choice: to compete on the basis of price via the exploitation of cost advantages from economies of scale, or to specialise, either in geographic or product terms, and gain a niche market advantage by differentiation. Depending on the type of product involved, high volume producers may be able to move into global markets with minimal adaptation of strategy. Niche products may require substantially more strategic adjustment. In other words, the extent of difference between national and international strategies is very dependent upon the type of product/service. This issue of the distinction between global and non-global markets is discussed more fully later in this chapter when we look at the link between structure and strategy, and again in great detail in Chapter 8 on international marketing.

GOING INTERNATIONAL – WHY BOTHER?

So far we have reached a point at which it is possible to conclude:

■ strategy is concerned with competitive advantage

■ functional and general strategies need to be fully integrated

■ formulation of an international strategy can present additional challenges to management

■ the extent of variation in strategies across national boundaries is dependent upon the type of product/service.

In a competitive world it is hard enough to survive on the domestic front, and maintain acceptable levels of profitability, so what is the point of increasing the burden on management by internationalising operations?

The answer lies in the need to challenge the competition in order to ensure the long-term survival of the business. Failure to take up the challenge of internationalisation can sound the death knell for a company. As Henry Ford observed, the true cost of change lies in what happens if you don't make the new product or try the new process, not what happens if you do. Ultimately, selling or producing overseas is simply a variation on an existing strategy, pursued because existing markets or sources of supply are inadequate or too expensive to maintain. You will recall that at the beginning of this chapter Drucker was quoted as saying that a product and market combination is the end result of strategy. Hence, if existing product or market portfolios are inadequate, new strategies must be devised. The 'new' component may be becoming international.

The factors that drive firms to internationalise are explained in internationalisation theory, but before looking at the theory in some detail, it is worth noting that external environmental and social factors play a very important role in creating optimal or suboptimal conditions for international business expansion. In Chapter 1 the current political, economic and technological environment was shown to be creating conditions that favoured the globalisation of business. International trade agreements, and the growth of regional trading blocs encourage internationalisation at least on a regional scale, not least because they raise the level of international competition in any given market. Political stability serves to further encourage trade, and technological developments which have reduced transportation time and vastly increased the global telecommunications network all work to favour the internationalisation of business.

Of course the decision as to whether or not to internationalise is ultimately made at the level of the individual business, as managers weigh up the strategic benefits versus the additional cost of increased complexity. Furthermore, there is no single route mapped out which allows a firm to progress from being a purely domestically focused company into one which is multinational in orientation. Internationalisation theory seeks to explain the variety of routes followed by companies as they become international, and so the core elements of the theory are the next topic of discussion.

THE PROCESS OF INTERNATIONALISATION

Welch and Luostarinen[3] define internationalisation as:

> 'the outward movement in an individual firm's or larger grouping's international operations.'

The speed at which companies move outwards and expand their geographic coverage, and the way in which the geographic mix is selected will involve strategic choices, and a large number of academic papers have been written on the topic of how and why internationalisation occurs. The result is that there exist a number of alternative theories, and it is helpful to look at the respective merits and limitations of each, before drawing some overall conclusions about the process of internationalisation.

Theories of internationalisation address two specific issues:

- Why do companies internationalise?

- How do companies internationalise?

Staged Theory

Writing in 1975, Johanson and Wiedersheim-Paul[4] sought to offer an explanation of how firms moved from comparatively small domestic operations into fully fledged multinational corporations, based upon their research on four Swedish companies – Facit, Volvo, Sandvik and Atlas Copco. They concluded that 'the firm first develops in the domestic market, and that internationalisation is a consequence of a series of incremental decisions.' What emerged out of this research was the famous paper by Johansen and Vahlne[5] published two years later, which formulated the staged theory of internationalisation. In essence, the theory argues that companies move into the international arena via a gradual and incremental process of increasing international involvement.

As Table 5.1 below demonstrates, there are a number of proponents of staged theory, but there is a lack of agreement on either the definition of the various stages, or the absolute number of stages involved. The only agreement is in respect of the description of internationalisation as an orderly and progressive sequence in which management attitudes and the orientation of the company changes as different stages are reached.

Table 5.1   *Stages in the Internationalisation of a Company*

Author(s)	Stages
Johanson and Wiedersheim-Paul[4] (1975)	Indirect exporting (agents)
	Direct exporting
	Local sales office
	Local manufacturing
Ansoff[6] (1982)	Direct export
	International company
	Multinational company
Rothchild[7] (1983)	Domestic
	Quasi-domestic
	Multinational
Root[8] (1987)	Indirect/ad hoc exporting
	Active exporting and/or licensing
	Active exporting, licensing and ownership of foreign equity stake
	Multinational marketing and production
Ellis and Williams[9] (1995)	National market
	International market entry
	International–regional
	World-wide

It may be argued that whether it takes just three stages (as per Ansoff[6] or Rothschild[7]) to move from being a domestic to a multinational company, or four stages (as per Johanson and Wiedersheim-Paul[4], Root[8] and Ellis and Williams[9] does not matter. Nor do the names given to the different stages What is at issue is *how* the process occurs. In this sense, Table 5.1 paints a picture of a theory that is still under development, and the literature on the subject (Welch and Luostarinen[3] and Leonidou[10] for example) criticises internationalisation research for its failure to address the dynamics of the international growth of the firm. That is to say, the theory does not explain what causes a firm to progress from one stage to the next, it merely describes the fact that they *do* progress. A further problem is the acknowledgement by a number of writers, including Root[8], Welch and Luostarinen[3], and Ellis and Williams[9], that the sequence of stages is not necessarily followed in precise order, and companies will often retract back a stage if their international experience is bad. One example of such behaviour is illustrated in the following extract from The *Financial Times* of February 1996:

> 'Sega Enterprises, one of Japan's largest games groups, yesterday announced the closure of its European sales subsidiary and its replacement with a smaller operation … The group is moving its European headquarters to smaller premises in London and reducing its workforce in Europe from 300 to 125.'

The company also closed its sales offices in Austria, Belgium and the Netherlands, in a response to a decline in European games sales. In other words, having progressed up the scale of internationalisation by establishing a number of European offices, Sega chose to move back a step, and disentangle itself from such extensive European involvement, because of marketing problems. A more recent example of withdrawal from international operations is the decision by the UK retailer Marks and Spencer to close all of its stores in Europe and re-focus on the domestic market.

Understanding how internationalisation can follow an orderly process is perhaps most easily understood by reference to an example, such as that in the case study below.

Mini Case Study

Electrolux

Electrolux is one of the world's largest electrical appliance manufacturers. A Swedish-based company, it owns businesses in more than fifty countries, and overseas sales account for more than 90 per cent of total sales. The Group operates in three main business areas: consumer durables (primarily white goods such as refrigerators and washing machines), outdoor products (gardening equipment, chainsaws etc.) and professional appliances (food service and laundry equipment). Total sales world-wide amounted to 119,550 million Krona in 1999, and operating income for the same period equalled 7,204 million krona.

The mix of products sold in different regions of the world varies, but the USA is the largest single market for the group. The markets served cover most of the globe, and include Europe, Asia, Oceania, Latin America and Africa as well as North America.

In 1994 Electrolux celebrated its first 75 years of operation, and an analysis of the company's history is a useful way of understanding the company strategy. Throughout its history, Electrolux has adopted a policy of growth through acquisition and they see this as a way 'to obtain market positions and sales volumes in our key areas that create a framework for long-term competitive strength.'

The search for growth by acquisition began in 1962, after Electrolux had begun to experience declining profits due to its limited product range and lack of research and development facilities. That year, the company bought ElektroHelios, and expanded its product range to include cookers, freezers and a new type of washing machine. Despite poor economic conditions in the domestic market, by 1965 group sales exceeded one billion Krona for the first time. Throughout the 1960s Electrolux continued to acquire companies in related industries, but maintained a concentration on the Northern Scandinavian markets where its brand name was well recognised.

In 1974, the company chose to expand its acquisitions horizons beyond Europe. National Union Electric/Eureka, from the United States, and the world's largest manufacturer of vacuum cleaners, was bought. The European horizons moved wider in 1976, when Arthur Martin, a French white goods company was acquired.

Up until the mid-1970s it seemed that company strategy had concentrated on expanding in core areas of business in which it was well experienced. If small, fringe businesses accompanied the purchases, they were taken on board, but they were not the focus of great attention. This policy served to reduce the risks of the acquisitions, and reduce the level of restructuring required.

In the latter half of the 1970s, the company began to diversify a little. When in 1978 it bought Husqvarna, a Swedish household appliances company, the business included a chainsaw production operation. The purchase tied in with Flymo, a small lawnmower business which had been bought nine years previously, but was a relatively insignificant part of Electrolux's operations. Together, Flymo and Husqvarna formed the core of what is today Electrolux's outdoor products business, and offered the opportunity for the company to broaden its product base.

Key acquisitions since 1979 show how Electrolux has grown further as a Group.

1979	Tappan, a US household appliances manufacturer
1980	Granges, a Swedish metal and mining company with a large share of the European aluminium market
1984	Zanussi. Electrolux took a 49 per cent stake in the Italian white goods company. In 1986 this was converted to a majority holding.
1986	White Consolidated, the US's third largest white goods company
1986	Poulan Weed Eater, a US garden products company
1988	American Yards Products, a US garden equipment supplier
1991	Lehel, the main refrigerator manufacturer in Hungary
1992	A joint venture with AEG Germany, for product development in the washing machine, tumble-drier and dishwasher markets. Electrolux took a 10 per cent stake, which has been increased to 20 per cent by 1994
1996	Purchase of Refripar, the second largest white goods manufacturer in Brazil, which was later renamed Electrolux do Brasil

The company's strategy appears to be one of maintaining a position of leadership in major geographical markets by means of acquisition rather than organic growth. Simultaneously, Electrolux is seeking out long-term synergies on a global level in such areas as product development, purchasing and production of components, and marketing. Most significantly, the progress of the company over the last forty years seems to fit the staged theory of internationalisation very well. The initial business was concentrated in Northern Scandinavia, and throughout the 1970s and 1980s attention was focused on consolidating strength and market share in the European and US markets. Sales to other regions of the world have been met by supply from existing bases, until the 1996 move into Brazil, which marks the final phase of the progress towards being a truly transnational company.

The idea that international involvement increases via a number of stages may be effective as an illustration of the internationalisation of Electrolux, but the theory may be questioned by reference to the way in which some Korean, Japanese and Chinese companies have entered the global marketplace in recent years. As already suggested, Toyota has expanded into a global company via the exploitation of cost advantages created by large volume production in the mid-range car market. Toyota did not progress from a domestic producer, to an exporter serving just one or two foreign markets and then on to regions and the global market – instead it leapt from domestic into regional, effectively omitting the second stage of the internationalisation process. The progress direct into regional markets was essential to the strategy of exploitation of the scale economies which are so fundamental to car production. Similarly, the growth of Internet-based commerce, whereby companies can immediately enter a global marketplace, without ever limiting the scope to just a domestic environment, raises questions about the future validity of the staged theory. In very many cases, the staged theory of internationalisation offers a useful and valid explanation of company behaviour, but care must be taken to recognise that the theory is not one that can be universally applied.

In critically reviewing the staged approach to internationalisation, a number of questions remain unanswered:

- What are the factors that trigger a company/business to progress from one stage to the next?

- What determines the speed of progress towards a transnational organisation?

- Why do companies sometimes retract from international involvement only to re-enter (perhaps in a different country) some years later?

Some of the answers to these questions lie in a different theory of internationalisation – contingency theory.

Contingency Theory

As already suggested, the staged theory of internationalisation may be criticised for its failure to address the fundamental question of *how* companies progress from one stage of international involvement to another. Contingency theory argues that the internationalisation process is driven by a company's response to a mix of internal and external factors. Responses to the different factors are determined by management attitudes to risk, their vision for the future of the business and their knowledge of different markets, and it is recognised that these evolve over time as a business moves through the different phases of internationalisation. Leonidou[10] likens the process to the learning curve, whereby given stimuli encourage firms to progress to the next stage, but having progressed, corporate attitudes, perceptions and abilities change accordingly.

For example, a company which is still domestic in its orientation may view a sales enquiry from overseas as an opportunity, but one to be rejected because it would make the business more complex. By contrast, a company which is already well established internationally, may see the chance to sell into a new national market as an exciting opportunity, which will diversify risks still further. The difference in attitudes between the two companies will be a consequence of *changes* in management styles as internationalisation has progressed.

Contingency theory also suggests that management may be regarded as being either proactive or reactive in their approach to internationalisation. The more forward looking and aggressive the management style, the more likely it is that internationalisation will stem from a positive choice, rather than a reaction to an external event such as an overseas sales enquiry. Reactionary managers are likely to be more cautious and their businesses expand more slowly.

Important proponents of contingency theory include Leonidou[10], Reid[11] and Turnbull[12] amongst others. These writers refute the idea that exporting is necessarily the first stage of an international business, and suggest instead that the internationalisation process is a response to market circumstances, corporate resources and managerial attitudes.

REASONS FOR INTERNATIONALISATION

All companies are different, and so the precise reasons for internationalising will vary across organisations to reflect their individual circumstances. Nonetheless, a number of common themes emerge, which highlight a mix of factors seen as influencing the decision to sell or produce internationally. These are summarised in Table 5.2 below, and explained in the succeeding discussion.

Table 5.2   *Factors Influencing the Internationalisation of a Company*

Internal Stimuli	Proactive	Reactive	External Stimuli	Proactive	Reactive
Excess capacity	No	Yes	Market opportunities	Yes	Yes
Search for economies of scale	Yes	No	World economic trends	No	Yes
			Trade liberalisation	No	Yes
Unique product	Yes	No	Social change	No	Yes
Senior management characteristics/personality	Yes	Yes	Government incentives	Yes	Yes
			Competitive environment	No	Yes
Poor overall financial performance	No	Yes	Technological change	Yes	Yes
Organisational learning	No	Yes	Receipt of unsolicited order from overseas	No	Yes
Exploitation of core competencies	Yes	No			

It is acknowledged that the factors shown in Table 5.2 do not necessarily work separately and discretely. Leonidou, for example, argues that internal and external factors will interact to determine the dynamics of internationalisation for any individual firm. Before considering any such interactions, however, it is useful to look at each of the factors in turn.

Internal Factors

Research by Calof and Beamish[13] found that managers cited changes in a firm's internal environment as the most important cause of progression towards internationalisation, and a change in company strategy was the most common reason for the changed environment. For example, managers saw that product/market diversification was an important stimulus, along with a desire to grow, and a change in company resources. In fact Table 5.2 clearly shows that the majority of internal factors are associated with a proactive approach to internationalisation.

Excess capacity

Regardless of its cause, excess capacity means that a business could increase profits by increasing production volumes. Consequently, when excess capacity coincides with a domestic market which is saturated, a company may be pushed into looking abroad for new markets. Companies from the oil-producing countries of Kuwait and Iran are examples of this. The domestic markets are too small to absorb all of the petroleum which is processed in these states, and so selling to foreign customers is the only way to utilise the spare capacity.

One common cause of spare capacity is that a product is reaching the end of its life-cycle, and the potential for future sales growth in the domestic/original market is limited. For example, the US tobacco company Philip Morris has suffered from declining sales in the North American and European markets, as Western consumers have acknowledged the bad effects of cigarette smoking on health. In response, the company has sought to replace lost income and expand sales of their Marlboro cigarette brand by attacking markets in the less developed countries such as India, where smoking Western brand cigarettes is a form of status symbol.

Product life-cycles can be extended by innovation through research and development. Access to the technical know-how may, however, require a firm to purchase a foreign operation with the research expertise. Similarly, innovative marketing or distribution channels can be used to extend life-cycles or expand markets. A joint venture between Nestlé and Coca Cola to market Nestlé hot drinks via Coca Cola vending outlets is one such example of innovative marketing.

Economies of scale

The search for economies of scale is often cited as a reason for internationalisation, and this factor may be particularly important when the market for a product is price sensitive. Companies may need to actively seek out ways of both producing and marketing their products in high volumes in order to take advantage of cost reductions associated with increased scale.

Dicken[14] estimates that pre 1970, in the period of mass production, vehicle manufacturers in the automobile industry needed to produce 2 million units per year in order to gain maximum scale economies. Historically, this provided a massive stimulus for companies in the industry to internationalise. With the onset of lean production systems, the optimal size for an assembly plant has fallen to one quarter of a million units per year, and so the opportunities to exploit economies of scale is diminished. As a result, the reasons why car manufacturers continue to expand internationally have changed over time – the reasons are now linked to market rather than production issues.

A more recent example of an industry where scale economies have encouraged internationalisation is the mobile phone market. The telecommunications industry is one in which companies need to make large infrastructure and network investments in order to function, but once the investment has been made the key to success is increasing customer volumes. The takeover of the German company Mannesmann by the UK operator Vodafone in 2000 is an example of how this search for greater scale economies through a larger customer base can spur further internationalisation in an industry that is already far from domestic in its orientation.

Interestingly, Leonidou found that although scale economies was the most quoted reason given for firms becoming international, it was given just fifteenth place out of nineteen by managers who were asked to rank motivating factors in order of significance.

Unique product

Where a company makes a product that has unique qualities, it may be able to exploit those unique qualities to find customers in markets around the world, and so there is strong reason to internationalise. Clearly, such an opportunity to exploit foreign markets is also linked to the additional profit that they might generate, but the initial stimulus comes from the uniqueness of the product.

The automobile industry provides an example of how this might arise, in the case of the McLaren F1 sports car. There are few who would argue that this is the ultimate road car, with a top speed of 231mph and a price tag of over £600,000. Exclusivity was maintained by the fact that sales were restricted to 100 vehicles over the period 1993–97. The F1 is essentially a Formula 1 road car sold to the public, but in the company's home nation, the UK, few members of the public could afford the high price tag, even if they wanted such a vehicle. The price was set high both for prestige, but also to recover the massive research and development costs that had gone into the vehicle, but the unique nature of the product meant that it was easy to market it globally, in order to achieve the necessary sales.

Another example of a company where internationalisation has been driven by the unique product characteristics is a small concern called Impact Development group based in the UK Lake District. The group began running group team building exercises for managers at an adventure centre in the Lake District National Park twenty years ago, and it now runs similar courses in over thirty different countries, including Japan, Italy and Thailand.

Senior management characteristics/personality

Table 5.2 shows that management personality can affect internationalisation via both proactive and reactive behaviour. In fact many writers would argue that the attitude of senior management is the most important factor in the growth of a business, likening it to the idea that it is the jockey that wins the race not the horse. A whole variety of both internal and external stimuli might be in place to encourage internationalisation, but what really matters is how managers respond to those stimuli. Moving into either international markets or international production requires managers to agree to commit resources, and individual attitudes to risk may affect their willingness to make such a commitment.

One example of a company where management attitudes have positively spurred international growth is Val do Sol Ceramicas, a Portuguese producer of terracotta ware. Over the course of eleven years, the business has expanded from a small workshop outside Lisbon, to an organisation employing over 200 people across three production plants. The company took advantage of the growing demand amongst retailers in the 1990s for rustic-style products, and it now exports over 95 per cent of its production. The United States and Europe are the main markets, but despite the Asian economic crisis, Val do Sol Ceramicas began exporting to Japan, and the managing director takes the view that 'opportunities can open up in the midst of economic crises for small companies like ours.' As further proof of this positive attitude, three years ago the company spent US$500,000 on establishing its first overseas production plant in Brazil, in a joint venture with a local concern. This is despite the fact that many observers would view Brazil as a highly risky location. Of course it may yet be the case that Val do Sol Ceramicas suffer a financial crisis as a result of their risk-taking approach, but they remain an example of how management attitudes are a strong influence on business decisions.

Poor overall financial performance

Falling profits and falling sales can act as a strong incentive to look for new markets, but when companies internationalise for this reason they are reacting to events rather than behaving proactively: if profits did not fall, they would not look abroad for new custom. The importance of such events as a trigger for the development of a new strategy are of particular significance in the market-based economies of the USA and Europe, where shareholder pressure can lower stock prices and put pressure on management to create more shareholder value.

It is often difficult to distinguish between the influence of poor financial performance and that of excess capacity, which was discussed earlier. Weak financial results always have a cause, either in relatively poor sales and/or relatively high costs, and both of these may lead to surplus capacity.

In the UK, the retailer Laura Ashley found itself facing the problem of falling market share in the late 1980s. One element in the reorganisation programme for the company, aimed at returning them to high levels of profitability, was a cost cutting exercise which involved the transfer of sewing work on the ladies clothing goods from Mid-Wales to the Pacific Basin. The result was a large percentage fall in the cost of getting each item of clothing into the shops. Even in the high-class retailers, customers remain a little price sensitive, and the lower costs allowed Laura Ashley clothing prices to become competitive once again.

In similar vein, but ten years later, the behaviour of the UK retailer Marks and Spencer can be used to illustrate how both falling sales and relatively high costs can act as an incentive to internationalise. Marks and Spencer, in common with many other general retailers, began to lose sales in the late 1990s, and one of its responses was to change its long-held policy of using domestic UK suppliers for the bulk of its clothing products. Like Laura Ashley before them, Marks and Spencer found that it could reduce costs and so maintain/reduce selling prices by ordering from textile manufacturers in the Far East. Marks and Spencer was already international in its sales base, with stores across Europe and ownership of Brookes Brothers in the USA, but in production terms its outlook had been primarily domestic, and the need to revive profits served as an incentive to internationalise still further.

Organisational learning

The term organisational learning refers to the way in which management attitudes to international involvement develop in response to their accumulated experience; consequently it serves a potentially reactive stimulus to internationalisation. Positive experiences – the discovery that it is possible to sell abroad – encourage firms to try harder and become involved. The converse can also be true.

A small English fashion design business, 3F, obtained export orders to the value of just £46,000 when they went on a Department of Trade and Industry-funded trip to Japan in 1997. The next year the Asian crisis began to take hold, and orders and payments from the region began to drop. Learning from the experience, 3F has chosen to move into the Australian market, where the colours used in designs are similar, and use their Sydney office to re-launch in Japan when the economy picks up again. The organisation learned that there was an overseas market for their products, and used that knowledge to expand their international involvement.

Core competencies

Many companies begin their international involvement by selling or producing the product that is most popular in the domestic market. This strategy will often succeed, if the product is fundamentally well designed and has relatively universal appeal, but often it is more helpful to think in terms of core company skills, rather than products, when thinking about entering a foreign market. Ellis and Williams' story of Honda's first moves into motor cycle production in California illustrates this idea well.

In the 1960s Honda set up a North American plant to produce large motorbikes for the Western US markets, with the aim of competing with Harley-Davidson and other similar manufacturers. The bikes did not sell well. The production plant covered a large area, and in order to move staff quickly around the plant, Honda provided them with small-engined motorbikes, and company employees were frequently seen using the same vehicles to shop in the city areas adjoining the plant. The motorbikes were completely different to the large luxury products traditionally sold in the USA. Local sports goods dealers (not motor dealers!) started to ask Honda about obtaining supplies of the bikes, and at that point Honda management realised that their core competence lay in motorbike production, regardless of size, and that maybe they should try to penetrate the US motorbike market via the sale of small, differentiated models rather than competing for the same large bike market as everyone else. Honda now has a very large share of the US motor cycle market.*

The example illustrates the way that becoming international can be aided by thinking in quite broad terms about company skills. Thinking in such a way, however, requires a proactive management style, where management are willing to take a risk to seize a potential opportunity.

External Factors

External influences on company behaviour may operate at a number of different levels. At a macro level, world economic trends, international trade policies and the growth of new markets will provide potential business opportunities. At a national/industry level, changes on the competitive environment, government policies and social and technological changes are relevant. At a corporate level, there may be pressure from shareholders, or the threat of a take-over or merger to focus management minds on the need to look for new strategies. Regardless, however, of the level at which the stimulus operates, it will only be effective if management respond.

Macro-level influences: market opportunities, world economic trends and trade liberalisation

As already suggested, the world economic environment is one which is evolving in a manner that encourages the internationalisation of business. The elimination of trade barriers in the large regional trading blocs, the growth of GATT and rapid economic growth in new areas of the world are examples of such positive influences. Freer trade may also increase the level of competition faced by a firm in the domestic market, and cause it to react by looking for ways to enter competitors' markets. As companies increase their level of international involvement, they are able to geographically diversify their risk.

Certain product types may be particularly susceptible to economic conditions. For example, Jaguar or other luxury cars will see a downturn in demand when a market is in recession. To compensate for this, when the world economic environment is favourable to increased international trade and investment, companies can seek foreign markets as a means of creating a portfolio effect. When the economy in one market is in recession, it can be expected in a multinational company that one of the other economies is still showing high levels of demand.

The early 1990s' recession in the United States and Europe had a severe impact on the results of Jaguar, but the company's decision to market aggressively in Japan helped to stabilise the company results. It must also be noted that the need to seek out such a portfolio is reduced in the case of large, diversified organisations. The portfolio effect is already being experienced internally in the organisation by means of the wide product range.

* *Source:* based on Ellis and Williams *International Business Strategy*, illustration 1.2, p.13.

In conclusion then, the macro-level effects are important in facilitating the international diversification of business, which in turn serves to reduce the level of business risk.

National/industry level influences

The competitive environment and the size of the remaining national market may both act to push a company into the international arena. Increased competition in the domestic market was a factor which helped to push the UK bank Abbey National plc. into the international market. The bank faced competition in its core mortgage business from a range of new providers, and so Abbey decided to look for new opportunities overseas, in Malta, Gibraltar and Spain. The first two locations had the advantage of large English-speaking populations, to whom the brand name may also be familiar. Spain offered opportunities for selling peseta-denominated mortgages to the large numbers of English people buying second homes or retiring there.

In some instances, companies are approached by a foreign competitor or supplier asking whether they are interested in buying the business. Although this might at first sight sound unlikely, Calof and Beamish[13] found that managers were able to cite a total of thirty-five instances in which this served as a trigger to increased international involvement.

A number of governments offer significant help and incentives to companies that are selling overseas, and the existence of these incentives can help to encourage internationalisation. The example of the design company 3F, cited earlier is one such case. The company went to Japan on a government-sponsored trade mission, whereby businessmen/women are given access to low cost travel and accommodation and meetings with potential suppliers/customers are arranged through the commercial attachés at the embassy. It is also quite common for displays/exhibitions to be mounted to help sell the products. Small companies may not know where to begin to find customers in a foreign location, but travelling on a mission such as this, with the arrangement/meetings set up for them and translation services on hand, helps to build up confidence. Many new export orders arise out of such trade missions.

Government policies may also serve as a positive encouragement to companies to invest overseas. Many nations now operate entrepôt ports and export zones, within which imported goods are then processed for re-export free of trade controls. Additionally, nation states will 'compete' in the incentives that they are prepared to offer to large multinational concerns looking for greenfield sites. When Toyota announced that it was looking for its first European manufacturing site, it found itself in a position of being able to compare the cash value of offers of tax benefits, versus preferential purchase prices on land versus employment cost subsidies in a number of different countries. The very large global companies are wooed by governments seeking inward investment flows.

Social change at both national and international level can also create international opportunities. As people travel more widely, consumer tastes change. Some would argue that tastes are becoming more global, as everybody eats pizzas and curries these days, and brand names such as Nike or Adidas are universally recognised. If consumers are becoming more open to new ideas and products, then it makes it much easier for a company to succeed internationally.

Technological changes may affect production techniques, product design and marketing at industry, national or local levels. The most obvious recent innovation is the growth of Internet-based retailing, which allows companies to sell to anyone in the world who connects in to their web site. Even so, not all firms that operate interactive web sites will sell to non-nationals, because of the complexities of dealing with different requirements for export packaging, labelling, completion of customs declarations etc. The proactive managers see new technologies such as the Internet as opportunities, but others see them as a threat. Once again, it is the internal management response that counts most.

Corporate level influences

Sometimes the factors that push a company into the international arena are a response to external factors peculiar to the individual firm. For example, a very successful company may find that it has a very high share of the domestic market but wishes to continue to grow. Under such circumstances, looking abroad for new markets is the only realistic way of sustaining sales growth.

Hozelock, a UK manufacturer of garden hoses, sprayers and pond equipment cites precisely this reason for its decision to target the European market as its route to expansion. Hozelock has a 70 per cent share of the garden watering equipment market in the UK, and a 40 per cent share of the UK market across its full range of garden products. In contrast, its European market share is just 2 per cent. Hence the view that expansion of sales in Europe is the route to further profit growth.

In other cases, a company may have recently merged or been taken over, and the new management has a much more proactive approach to internationalisation than the previous management. It may be something as simple as a new marketing manager who has linguistic skills, or experience of export marketing. Demergers, or the sale of foreign-owned subsidiaries can work in the opposite direction and reduce international involvement. The recent decision by BMW to sell the Rover company is an example of this.

Another spur to action, as mentioned earlier, can be shareholder reaction to poor financial results. The reaction is peculiar to the individual company, but is externally generated, and managers often respond by developing an international dimension to their strategy.

INTERNATIONALISATION THEORY – SOME CONCLUSIONS

So far we have seen that internationalisation theory describes the process by which companies progress to becoming multinational organisations as one that follows a sequence of stages. The stages may be leapfrogged by companies, and sometimes they may move back from international involvement, but the idea of a steady increase in internationalisation is broadly accepted in the literature.

Contingency theories seek to explain what pushes a company into further international involvement. The triggers may be internal or external to the business, but a variety of factors interact to create conditions that encourage internationalisation.

Calof and Beamish[13] found that managers explained their progression from one stage of internationalisation to another in terms of internal, external, attitude and performance based stimuli. They further found that internal factors were the most important in explaining changes in a company's positioning on the international stage. The interaction of the different influences is, however, very difficult to explain and it is thus safe to conclude that there is currently no existing theory that serves to adequately and fully explain both how and why companies choose to internationalise. Indeed it may be that no theory can ever emerge, because every firm is different, and so generalisations are inappropriate.

CORPORATE STRUCTURE AND INTERNATIONALISATION

The link between strategy and structure was first highlighted by Chandler[15] almost forty years ago. His argument was that structures are the framework that facilitates the implementation of strategy and so as strategies evolve, so too must organisational structures.

The term organisational structure refers to the vertical and horizontal framework that defines the vertical and horizontal lines of communication within an organisation. Organisations may be multi-layered, with a large number of vertical levels. Alternatively, they may be relatively flat structures, which have long horizontal lines of communication, but few layers between the top and bottom.

Effective communication is essential to co-ordinate the work of a company which may contain a variety of functional, products, and geographic components and it is fair to assume that companies will try and establish the structure that best facilitates this co-ordination process. In their book *In Search of Excellence*, Peters and Waterman[16] noted that 'excellent' companies recognised that the choice of structure was dependent upon a variety of key variables including corporate culture, leadership styles, and existing operating and control systems as well as strategy. This view of how structures are determined is merely an extension of Chandler's approach, and can be regarded as a contingency approach to structural determination. There are alternative theories of corporate structure but these are beyond the scope of this book, and so we will from this point forward adopt a contingency view of corporate structure.

In defining a framework for communication, decision-making and control, the optimal approach will differ between companies. Where sales are dominated by one particular geographic region, but there are exports to several other countries, the optimal structure is likely to be very different to that of a very large global organisation, with large sales volumes and production facilities in all continents of the world. In the light of this, a number of alternative structures for internationally active companies can be identified, and a company's progression from one type of structure to another can be likened to the staged theory of internationalisation. The progression through different structures is most easily understood if it is split into two distinct phases. In Phase 1, the company is limited in its scale of international involvement, so that international operations tend to be grouped together, crossing both product and geographic boundaries. In Phase 2, the international component of operations becomes fully integrated with the rest of the company's operations, and the overall

Figure 5.4   *Stages in the Evolution of Corporate Structures for International Companies*

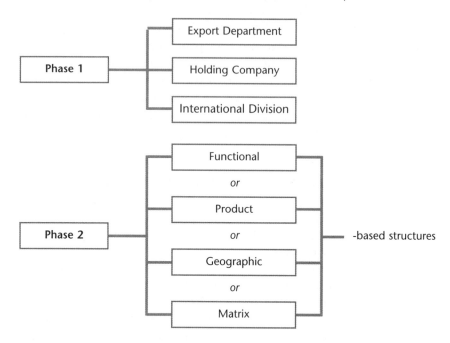

configuration of the structure is rebuilt around either functional, product, geographic or matrix lines. These stages are illustrated in Figure 5.4.

In line with the staged theory of internationalisation, it is likely, though not absolutely certain, that Phase 1 will precede Phase 2. The only instances when this would not happen is when a company does not start from a domestic base, but immediately operates in a broad international market.

Phase 1

For the company that is focused on the domestic market, the receipt of occasional overseas orders may prompt the establishment of an export department. This is separate from the mainstream business, and simply arranges the supply of goods for foreign customers as and when required. By definition, the export department implies a relatively limited level of international involvement, and certainly no investment in foreign-held production or marketing facilities.

Once sales to a particular foreign market reach a critical level, the company may decide that it is worthwhile investing directly in the country/region, and establish an overseas subsidiary. The subsidiary may be just a sales office, or it might extend to a small production unit and sales operation combined. As the company continues to grow, and foreign sales take on more significance, it is likely that additional overseas subsidiaries will be established, so that a holding company structure begins to emerge, with the original home company acting as the parent to a number of different foreign subsidiaries.

The final stage of Phase 1 is reached when the scale of international operation is such that it warrants the establishment of a separate international division, such that the domestic and international elements of the company's operations are the responsibility of different senior level management. The advantage of separating out an international division lies in the fact that it recognises that different, specialist skills are required to deal with foreign markets, for example, the management of foreign exchange risk, or product modification to meet specific design requirements. The international division allows all such skills to be centralised, and also ensures that the international interests of the company are taken into account more explicitly in strategic planning and resource allocation.

By this stage in its international development, a company is likely to already have quite extensive levels of foreign direct investment. The problem that may next be encountered, and which triggers the progression to Phase 2 of the cycle, is the need to integrate the domestic and international elements of the business. One might ask 'why integrate something that has just been split up?' The answer lies in the conflicts that can begin to arise in allocation of the limited resources between the international and domestic divisions. For example, if a company is nearing the limits of its production capacity for a number of different products, some of which are sold only at home, and others of which are only sold in specific foreign markets, then a choice may need to be made as to how to allocate investment funds on increasing production. Should the investment be oriented in favour of the domestic or the foreign products, and which products in particular? The choice will be determined by company strategies in relation to its product and market mix, and also the financial benefits of the different alternatives. Nonetheless, the need to make a choice highlights the fact that in terms of resources, the company can be regarded as a single unit, and so it would make some sense to also structure it that way. It is for this reason that many companies find that the period during which they operate with an international divisional structure is relatively short lived.

Phase 2

Integrated international structures are usually centred around one specific factor that is deemed central to international success, namely the functions, products or geographic regions. The question of what is critical to success is very much dependent upon the industry in question, and the product/service type, as explained below.

Functional structures are characterised by the existence of functional divisions, in which functional managers are responsible for the supervision of their function across all products and all geographic areas. Such a structure can be illustrated as in Figure 5.5.

Figure 5.5   *Functional Structures*

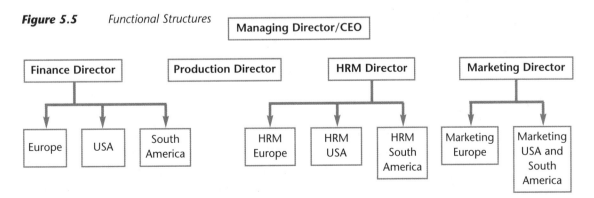

Functional structures are particularly useful where there are minimal differences between products across the different countries of operation. A diversity of products would require the functional manager to understand all of the differences and relate them to changing functional requirements, which would be difficult. Similarity of products means that the methods used to manage production, for example, in Brazil will be basically the same as those used to manage production in France. A company such as Wendy's, the hamburger chain, can therefore apply a functional structure to its organisation, because the basic burger product is largely unchanged across geographic boundaries. In contrast, a company such as FKI plc., which deals in materials handling, industrial hardware and engineering has such a diverse range of products and services that the functional structure would be inappropriate.

For the company seeking to manage international production and sales of a diverse product range, perhaps characterised by very fundamental differences from country to country, a product or geographically based structure is more appropriate. For example, the Japanese electronics company Sony produces and markets a very wide range of audio-visual, personal hi-fi, home entertainment and personal computer products, from CD players and hi-fi systems, to notebook computers and games consoles such as the Playstation. In addition to its wide product range, the company also has to manage sales which are spread widely across the globe – in 1997 US sales accounted for 31 per cent of the world total, Europe 23 per cent, Japan 27 per cent and the rest of the world 19 per cent. In order to co-ordinate and cope with this diversity, the company is organised around product divisions. This structure recognises that the geographic distribution of sales will vary between products, so that the personal CD player might have been replaced by the mini-disc player in the US market, but in Latin America sales are still growing. The product-based structure also ensures that divisional managers are experts in their product group, and understand the life cycle of that product such that they can effectively co-ordinate marketing and promotional campaigns on an international scale. This allows for market segmentation, because a particular class of products may have only one regional market.

The disadvantage of a product-based structure is that it requires duplication of provision of core functions; the support functions of finance, HRM and IT services are required by all product divisions, and so these services may be replicated several times within the organisation. Equally, the structure does not encourage the exchange of useful local information between divisional managers. There may, for example, be some quirks in the rules in advertising in France which would be relevant to all product managers, but the lines of communication laid down in the product structure do not encourage the sharing of regional knowledge, despite the fact that one division could well benefit from the experiences of another. Daniels and Radebaugh[17] cite the example of Westinghouse as an illustration of this point, because at one stage one national subsidiary was paying high interest rates on local borrowing at the same time that another subsidiary in the same country was sitting on surplus cash. The example of Akzo Nobel, the international chemicals company described below, provides an illustration of a product-based structure.

The use of geographic divisions is the other main alternative that is open to international companies. This approach is favoured where it is believed that the company's dealing with, or operations in, different parts of the world are more significant than product differences. The geographically structured company gives divisional managers full responsibility for all of the functions and all of the products within a defined region. This has the advantage that it allows managers to become expert at under-standing the needs and idiosyncrasies of their particular area, but has the disadvan-tage that functional roles will be duplicated across regions. There is also a potential problem for product managers, who may be harassed by the divisional heads to make sure that products are 'fine-tuned' for their particular region. Such refinements cost money, and the product manager will have a problem in determining which areas to prioritise, particularly as he/she will be operating at a lower level in the managerial hierarchy than the divisional managers. A diagrammatic representation of the geographic type of structure would look something like this:

Figure 5.6   *Geographic Structure*

Mini Case Study

Akzo Nobel is a Dutch-based international company that operates in a number of product areas, and recently underwent a structural re-organisation. The company has over 350 sites in more than fifty countries, and in strategic terms views itself as globally active in specific product areas, particularly in respect of chemicals.

The product groups supplied by Akzo Nobel are chemicals, pharmaceuticals, coat-ings and fibres and the corporate structure is now essentially product based.

World-wide, there are two key sites per product, and selection of location has been primarily market driven. The market proximity is viewed as being essential to fast responsive-ness to customer needs. At the same time, the company recognises that where the markets are global, technological advances are vital to maintaining market share, and so a structure is required that allows operating units access to centrally co-ordinated technical skills and research.

Independent business units have been established, which operate autonomously but are structurally attached to a particular product group. This allows the company to view each product group as a strategic busi-ness unit, the performance of which can be clearly identified and compared. Within the product groupings, the smaller independent business units can also be monitored in terms of profit performance.

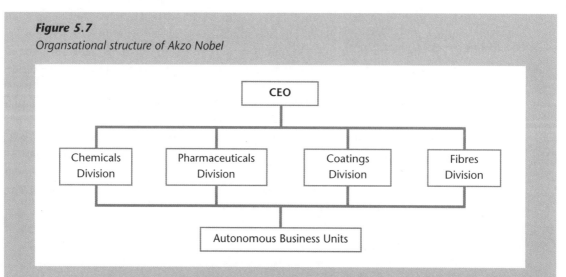

Figure 5.7
Organsational structure of Akzo Nobel

The organisational structure of Akzo Nobel can be graphically portrayed as above.

The structure is one which provides very direct lines of control, and also facilitates regular performance review of key product areas. Prior to the restructuring, the company was organised on a geographic basis with, for example, a European director responsible for all the various products in that region. This could be viewed as limiting the vision of the management, and also their understanding of the particular market needs for individual products. The change has been seen as bringing the business closer to the marketplace.

It is easy to see that a company may find it difficult to identify the most appropriate structure, and furthermore the ideal format may change as the company evolves. There is no such thing as an ideal organisational set-up; the best approach depends on the individual position of each company at a particular point in time.

Many companies operate a similar organisational structure based around strategic business units. Within individual companies the precise terminology may vary, but the basic structure is the same. GEC was the originator of the strategic business unit concept, but other users now include 3M and Gillette, as well as Akzo Nobel and many more.

The Akzo Nobel example illustrates the core of the problem with each of the structural forms that make up Phase 2. Each form has different advantages and disadvantages, but they share a common problem in that they all give priority to one particular dimension. This prioritising may be unsuitable for some companies that feel perhaps that equal weighting should be given to product and geographic/functional issues. The organisational form which seeks to address this dilemma is the matrix, in which organisational responsibilities for individual national subsidiaries rest with more than one manager. For example the UK director, whilst being answerable for all that happens within his area, must report to a Head of Europe, perhaps the product managers for each product group sold in the UK, and also the functional managers. Such a structure is commonly portrayed as a cube, with functional, product and geographic responsibilities represented by the three dimensions of the cube.

Needless to say, perhaps, the main problem with the matrix structure is the difficulty of balancing off the different dimensions. In practical terms, for the day to day

Figure 5.8 *Matrix structures*

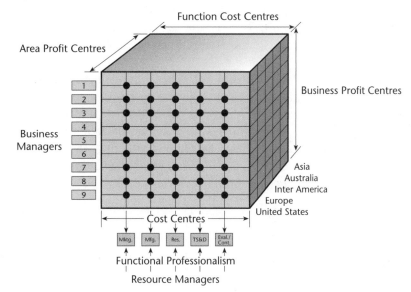

Source: Janger, A.R., *Matrix Organizations of Complex Business*, the Conference Board, New York, 1979, p.31

running of an organisation some issue will take priority. The matrix allows for the possibility that what is the priority will change over time, but it does not contain a mechanism for determining what is the most important issue at any particular point in time.

One theory of structural design which recognises the problems encountered as companies develop and grow, is that of Bartlett and Ghoshal[18], and their approach is a consequence of the local:global debate within international strategy. It is therefore useful to begin by considering the main aspects of that debate.

THE GLOBAL VERSUS NATIONAL DEBATE

The global–national debate may be regarded either as a strategic or as a marketing issue: either way, it forces companies to make fundamental planning decisions. In this chapter, we look at the strategic issues only, with the marketing perspective being considered in Chapter 8.

There are two alternative ways of operating in international markets, which represent alternative strategic approaches: the multi-domestic or the global. The focus is on the level at which the company finds itself competing.

■ A multi-domestic strategy is one in which the company views individual countries or geographic regions as the competitive base. Retailers might compete within the North American marketplace, but would view Europe as a different market. It is unlikely that many retailers would accept that it is possible to view the whole world as a single market. As we will see, there are some exceptions to this rule, but this is the general position.

■ A global strategy means that a product can be sold world-wide with minimal adaptations, and there are large scale economies to be gained in manufacturing and marketing. Competition is in a global marketplace, and examples of products which fit this category are cars and commercial aircraft.

The main issue in the global versus multi-domestic debate is therefore the extent to which facilities can be integrated as opposed to remaining responsive to the needs of individual markets. A secondary issue is what happens in the middle. Do firms which are multi-domestic progress to becoming global organisations, or is there a third category of companies between the two extremes, which is itself a stable state, and not purely transitory? These are issues which are currently the subject of research.

The ability of a business to transfer competitive advantage between countries, whilst remaining locally responsive, creates a strategic tension. The company will be affected in a number of different ways, according to the choices it makes, and writers tend to focus on particular aspects of the debate. Porter views the conflict as being expressed in terms of a tension between co-ordination and configuration. This can be illustrated as in Figure 5.9 below.

Figure 5.9   *Co-Ordination Versus Configuration Chart*

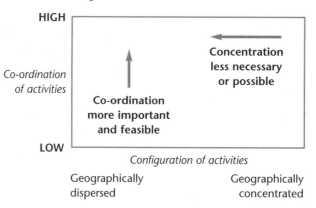

(Source: Porter, 1986)

Porter argues that the multi-domestic firm manages its international operations as a portfolio, with the activity in each location having a significant level of autonomy. In effect, the international strategy can be collapsed down into a collection of domestic strategies. This also implies that a geographic-based structure is adopted, perhaps based on countries clustered into regional groups.

In contrast, the global firm seeks to take advantage of the linkages between countries, and is sensitive to the geographical configuration of each element in the value chain. Close attention is therefore given to the comparative advantage available in the different locations, whilst at the same time concentrating on maximising the integration of world-wide activities. This does not mean that the country perspective is completely ignored, but getting the local–global balance right is not easy.

Prahalad and Doz[19], look at the dilemma specifically in terms of an organisational framework. They see individual managers in international companies as being required to balance off economic and political imperatives. The economic imperatives, in the form of global competition, force companies to transcend national boundaries and seek global strategies. The political imperative, imposed by the requirements of host governments, pushes companies towards local responsiveness which acknowledges the diversity of national markets. Prahalad and Doz suggest that there is no single organisational structure that can be put in place to resolve the dilemma. Instead, decision tools are used to allow managers to assess the global–local trade-off in respect of individual decisions. They argue that the international company should be organisationally capable of 'shifting the locus and logic of decision from a national concern to a global view, and vice versa, from decision to decision.'

To adopt such a system requires new management skills, and implies a structure not dissimilar to the matrix arrangement. Bartlett and Ghoshal concentrate on the organisational issues facing cross-border operations in emphasising the importance of a company's organisational and administrative heritage. The way in which international operations are managed will be influenced by the organisational structure which has evolved over time, but they also suggest that environmental influences are important.

Bartlett and Ghoshal identify three types of organisational structure, and each can be associated with a different cultural history. The three models are:

- Decentralised Federation
- Co-ordinated Federation
- Global organisation.

The decentralised federation is characterised by its local responsiveness, with assets and responsibilities being managed independently by the foreign units. The structure is seen as typically European in origin.

A co-ordinated federation operates through a system of greater control over the foreign subsidiaries than in the decentralised model. The subsidiaries are more dependent on the parent both for expertise and control. The geographic origins of this structure are seen to be American.

The global organisation is one which fits the Japanese management model. There is centralisation of both assets and decision making, with tight control of subsidiary activity. The Bartlett and Ghoshal approach offers an alternative to the Chakravarthy and Perlmutter view of international organisation which used the classifications of ethnocentric, polycentric and geocentric to differentiate styles of control.

From an organisational point of view, the two extremes of decentralised versus global organisations each present their own problems. In the decentralised company, the emphasis is on flexibility, with individual subsidiaries able to adapt to particular market needs. This will have implications in terms of costs, production management and possibly corporate image.

The global concern faces the difficulty of managing the integration of its worldwide operations. Utilising the individual strengths of each particular subsidiary, whilst avoiding the risk of internal fragmentation is not easy. Care must also be taken not to lose markets because of an unwillingness to be locally responsive.

Observation of the way in which many companies have changed their organisational structure several times in recent decades, suggests that there is no easy solution to these problems. Companies inherit an organisational structure from their past, which may not meet their new operating requirements. When the structure is changed they are on a huge learning curve, and new problems will arise.

To summarise, it is possible to note some important aspects of the debate on international organisational structure:

- The structure is dependent on the individual product and market type.
- Company organisation will be a consequence of its cultural and individual history.
- Organisational structures are continually evolving.

SUMMARY

This chapter has sought to investigate the ways in which companies devise an international strategy and organisational structure, and the associated problems. A trend has emerged, which suggests that strategies are evolving over time, as the scale of companies changes, and world markets alter. The historic view that a company could dabble in exports and progress to direct investment when it was ready no longer holds strictly true. Technological changes have pushed down labour costs and automation has meant that it has become much easier for companies to site themselves anywhere in the world. Simultaneously, vast improvements in information technology have made control of world-wide operations much easier. At the same time, communications technology opens up the eyes of the customer, so creating global consumer goods markets.

In line with these changes companies have been forced to rethink their markets and the organisational structures that will allow them to tap those markets. The consequence is that international business now requires companies to choose between pursuing a global strategy, or looking to niche markets which are locally responsive. This is the strategic dilemma of the twenty-first century.

CONCLUSION

The dilemma of how to develop an international strategy is made easier if companies recognise that choices are restricted by the type of products/services in question, the company history, size and strategic capability, and the willingness to respond to changes in the external environment. The other very important factor that constrains what companies can do, and when, is their access to funds for overseas expansion. This is the topic of the next chapter.

References

1 Porter, M.E. (ed.) (1986) *Competition in global industries*, Harvard Business School Press, Cambridge, Mass.
2 Dudley, J.W. (1990) *1992 Strategies For the Single Market*, Kogan Page
3 Welch, L.S. and Luostarinen, R., 'Internationalisation: Evolution of a concept', *Journal of General Management*, 14(2) Winter, pp.34–55
4 Johansen, J. and Wiedersheim-Paul, F. (1975) 'The Internationalisation process of the firm: four Swedish case studies', *Journal of Management Studies*, October, pp.305–22
5 Johansen, J. and Vahlne, J. (1977) 'The internationalisation process of the firm: a model of knowledge development and increasing foreign market commitments', *Journal of International Business Studies*, Spring–Summer, pp.23–32
6 Ansoff, H.I. (1982) *Strategic dimensions of internationalisation*, European Institute for Advanced Studies in Management, Brussels, mimeo, October
7 Rothchild, D. (1983) 'Surprise and the competitive advantage', *Journal of Business Strategy*, 4(3), pp.10–18
8 Root, F.R. (1987) *Entry strategies for international markets*, Lexington Books, D.C. Heath and Company, Lexington, Mass.
9 Ellis, J. and Williams, D. (1995) *International Business Strategy*, Pitman Publishing, London
10 Leonidou, L.C. (1995) 'Export stimulation research: Review, Evaluation and Integration', *International Business Review*, 4(2), pp.133–156
11 Reid, S. (1984) 'Market expansion and firm internationalisation' in *International Marketing Management* ed. Kraynak, E., Praeger, New York, pp.197–206
12 Turnbull, P.W. (1987) 'A challenge to the stages theory of the internationalisation process', in *Managing export entry and expansion*, ed. Rosson, C.T., Read, S.J., Greenwood Publishing group Inc., Westport
13 Calof, J.L. and Beamish, P.W. (1995) 'Adapting to foreign markets: explaining internationalisation', *International Business Review*, 4(2), pp.115–131
14 Dicken, P. (1998) *Global Shift* 3rd Edition, Paul Chapman Publishing, London
15 Chandler, A.D. (1962) *Strategy and structure: Chapters in the history of the industrial enterprise*, MIT Press, Cambridge, Mass.
16 Peters, T. and Waterman, R. (1982) *In search of excellence*, Harper and Row, New York.
17 Daniels, J.D. and Radebaugh, L.H. (1998) *International Business* 8th edition, Addison Wesley, Reading, Mass.
18 Bartlett, C. and Ghoshal, S. (1990) *Managing Across Borders: the transnational solution*, Hutchinson Business Books, London
19 Prahalad, C. and Doz, Y. (1987) *The multinational Mission*, Free Press, New York
20 Chakravarthy, B.S. and Perlmutter H. (1985) *Strategic Planning for a global Business*, Columbia Journal of World Business pp.5–6

Further Reading

The following books are strategic management texts which offer some useful insights into the problems of managing a global business.

Bartlett, C., Doz, Y. and Hedlund G (eds) (1990) *Managing the Global Firm*, Routledge
Forsgren, M. and Johansen, J. (1992) *Managing Networks in International Business*, Gordon and Breach, Philadelphia
McKiernan, P. (1992) *Strategies of Growth, Recovery, Maturity and Internationalisation*, Routledge
Wortzel, H.V. and Wortzel, L.H. (eds) (1990) *Global Strategic Management: The Essentials*, 2nd Edn., Wiley, New York

If you prefer to read something shorter than a book, then there are a number of journals that regularly contain articles on issues of international strategy. Some of the more popular ones are:

Journal of International Business Studies
Strategic Management Journal
Harvard Business Review
Columbia Journal of World Business
Long Range Planning

TUTORIAL EXERCISE

Look on the IKEA website (www.Ikea.com) and see what changes, if any, there have been in the company's pattern of international sales and sourcing of products. What new markets have they entered since 1998? What problems might these changes create for the global management and control of the business?

ESSAY QUESTIONS

1 Is strategy concerned only with products and markets?

2 List the functional areas in which an international company needs to formulate a specific strategy. Would your list be any different if drawn up for a domestic company?

3 Why does it not make sense to argue that the sequential theory of internationalisation is correct, particularly as it tends to mirror the development of structures in an international company?

4 'The matrix structure sounds good in principle but is unworkable in practice.' Is this true?

Case study: IKEA

The international furniture retailer IKEA was founded in Sweden in 1943, and by the end of 1998 it had built up a network of over 140 stores in 28 countries of the world. The IKEA group is a private group of companies owned by a charitable foundation in the Netherlands, and is made up of the companies responsible for product development, trading and wholesaling. IKEA stores are operated on a franchise system, which is co-ordinated and managed from the Netherlands, and the granting of franchises is linked directly to the overall corporate expansion plan.

Reflecting its Swedish roots, product development and purchasing is still the responsibility of IKEA Sweden but the group's international headquarters is based in Humlebaek, Denmark. Headquarters staff are responsible for decisions relating to new target markets, store openings and re-furbishment of existing stores.

Sales and marketing in individual countries are the responsibility of individual country managers once a region has more than two stores. The core product range is common to all stores world-wide, but as the total range encompasses approximately 12,000 items, both stores and countries vary in the specific stock they carry. The average full-range store carries 10,600 lines. Country managers are given some discretion in their selecting of products to augment the core range to suit particular local tastes/needs.

IKEA's declared objective is to 'offer a wide range of home furnishing items of good design and function at prices so low that the majority of people can afford to buy them'. Low prices and high sales volumes are achieved by keeping styles simple, materials colourful and emphasising practicality. Products are sourced (see figure 5.10) from 2,400 suppliers in 65 different countries supplying to 14 distribution centres; costs are kept low via the use of flat-pack packaging, designed for customer self-assembly. Evidence of the attractiveness of this style of furniture retailing is the fact that *Fortune* cited the traffic chaos caused when an IKEA store opened in New Jersey, USA, in 1995. 26,000 shoppers turned up on the opening day and the result was a nine mile tail-back on the New Jersey turnpike. It is estimated that in the US market, IKEA prices are 20–40 per cent below those of most other furnishing retailers.

In common with many Scandinavian companies, IKEA seeks to be environmentally 'friendly' in relation to its sourcing of materials, product design and marketing. Examples of this policy include:

- the company banned the use of HFCs and CFCs in its products some years ago

- the IKEA catalogue is printed on chlorine free paper, and contains 10–15 per cent recycled paper waste

- the use of formaldehyde is forbidden in paint and varnishes, as it can cause allergic reactions

- the teak used in outdoor furniture is from sustainably managed plantations in Java, Indonesia

- tropical (rainforest) wood is only used for furniture production when it can be obtained from sustainably managed forests.

Table 5.3 below shows selected key dates in the international growth of the IKEA group.

Table 5.3 *Historical Development of IKEA*

Year	Event
1950	Furniture is introduced to the product range.
1953	First furniture showroom opens in Sweden.
1956	Self-assembly, flat-pack furniture is introduced by IKEA.
1963	Oslo, Norway, first foreign store opens.
1973	Switzerland – opening of first non-Scandinavian store.
1975	Australian store opens.
1976	First Canadian store opens.
1978	First Singapore store opens.
1983	IKEA opens in Saudi Arabia.
1985	USA store opens.
1990	IKEA moves into Eastern Europe with stores in Hungary and Poland.
1998	First store opens in mainland China.

The global distribution of sales is shown in the pie chart below. The company is currently opening approximately one new store per month, expanding its presence in existing markets. For example, new stores are planned for Bremen (Germany) and Moscow and Khimki in Russia in the first three months of 2000.

The IKEA group employed the equivalent of 30,500 full time 'co-workers' in 1998. The term co-workers is used because of the organisational structure of the business. This represents an average annual employment growth rate of 11 per cent since 1994. Over the same period, sales have increased by 13.5 per cent per year, but long-term sales growth is more clearly shown in the bar chart below.

Figure 5.10

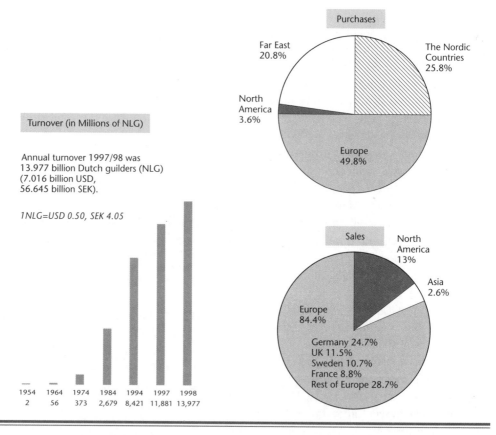

Turnover (in Millions of NLG)

Annual turnover 1997/98 was 13.977 billion Dutch guilders (NLG) (7.016 billion USD, 56.645 billion SEK).

1NLG=USD 0.50, SEK 4.05

1954	1964	1974	1984	1994	1997	1998
2	56	373	2,679	8,421	11,881	13,977

Purchases

Far East 20.8%
The Nordic Countries 25.8%
North America 3.6%
Europe 49.8%

Sales

North America 13%
Asia 2.6%
Europe 84.4%
Germany 24.7%
UK 11.5%
Sweden 10.7%
France 8.8%
Rest of Europe 28.7%

CASE STUDY QUESTIONS

1 In what respects is the international structure of IKEA well suited to corporate skills and the market requirements of furniture retailing?

2 Does the current world trading environment help or hinder IKEA's future growth as a multinational?

3 Why is the global distribution of supplies different from that of sales? Does the pattern displayed by IKEA match up with theories about the changing global economic map?

4 Why is a company the size of IKEA concerned about environmental issues?

CHAPTER SIX

The International Financial Markets: Sources of Finance for International Trade and Investment

LEARNING OUTCOMES

When you have completed this chapter you should be able to:

■ Briefly discuss the role of the finance function in an international business

■ Outline and comment upon recent developments in the international financial markets, and explain how the markets are becoming more integrated

■ Describe the main sources of export finance and their respective advantages and disadvantages

■ Detail the financial markets that serve the short-term funding needs for international firms

■ Describe the operations of the international capital markets, and the types of finance available within them

■ Explain the reasons behind the continued absence of a Euroequity or world-wide equity market

■ Explain the underlying features of regulations governing the taxation of foreign earnings, and the significance of overseas taxes to financial planning

INTRODUCTION

In Chapter 2 we saw how both the volume and the value of international trade and investment flows have increased dramatically in recent years, in line with the rapid globalisation of business. In Chapter 3 the importance of regional integration, and its effects on multinational companies was discussed. The focus of that earlier stage in the book was the changing patterns of trade and investment flows in terms of their impact upon the world economy. Our concern now is in viewing the same issue from a micro, rather than macro perspective – that of the corporation – because it is multinational corporations that are the initiators of many of the trade and investment flows.

The chapter will begin with a brief discussion of the role of the finance function in a business before moving on to focus on how companies can obtain the funding needed to expand their international operations. This involves a brief look at recent developments in the international financial markets, followed by a detailed discussion of the alternative sources of finance for trade and international investment.

THE ROLE OF THE FINANCE FUNCTION

In the last chapter on international strategy you saw in Figure 5.1 that the overall company strategy needs to be broken down into separate functional strategies, one of which is finance. In fact there is a two-way link between corporate strategy and finance strategy because the potential to follow *any* strategy is restricted by a company's access to finance. This means that the Board of Directors need financial information when producing their overall corporate plan, but at the same time, what emerges as the overall plan will have more detailed implications for the finance function. In other words finance both influences and is influenced by corporate strategy.

Within any organisation the finance function has a mix of roles which have both an external and internal focus. These roles may be summarised as follows:

- *Management accounting* – to help management to ensure that they have adequate financial resources to achieve the desired strategic objectives, and to make good business decisions. This requires the construction of budgets that forecast the resources required, and performance measurements to monitor the costs and revenues resulting from any strategic decisions.

- *Financial accounting* – involves continual monitoring and maintenance of records of the cash and other assets of the business, as well as any debts/liabilities that need to be paid.

- *Treasury management* – is the term used to describe the management of financial resources in a business. If managers make a decision that requires that additional funds need to be raised, then the Treasury Department will take responsibility for identifying and advising managers on alternative sources of funds and their relative costs, and then going into the financial markets to raise the required cash. Additionally, in an international business, there are likely to be requirements to make payments and collect income in currencies other than the domestic currency of the home nation. Treasury staff will take responsibility for management of the risks that may arise from transactions in foreign currencies, to help minimise the financial risks to the organisation.

In this book we focus on the treasury management elements of the finance function. Management accounting is a discipline in its own right, and there is some argument that management accounting principles are universal, so it does not warrant detailed discussion in an international business text. Financial accounting is a highly specialised field, and the rules and regulations on accounting vary across the world and are the subject of a number of major textbooks. You simply need to be aware that companies in different countries may have to follow different rules in preparing their annual financial statements, but the detail of those rules is beyond the scope of this book.

So why is treasury management so important to international business? The answer can be split into two parts. Firstly, when a company chooses to internationalise, this places heavy pressures on its financial resources, and unless overseas involvement occurs on a very small scale, then the need arises to make new investments which require financing. The sources of finance for international operations are rather more diverse than those used by companies for domestic purposes, and so it is useful to look at them in some detail. This is the subject of this chapter. The second reason for focusing on treasury management is that raising money (or spending it) overseas creates new financial risks, and these need to be managed. Foreign exchange risk management is the subject of Chapter 7.

We therefore begin with an introduction to the financial markets.

FINANCIAL MARKETS: THE BASICS

The financial markets are institutions that deal in accepting deposits or raising finance over short, medium and long timeframes. In other words they act as intermediaries to bring together parties who have surplus cash with parties that need cash. Examples include the Eurocurrency market which provides short-term capital, the Eurocredit market for medium term finance, and the national stock exchanges, where long-term equity funds can be raised via the issue of shares.

If a company begins to export its products, the time before payments are received may rise, leading to an increase in the short-term funding needs of businesses. This means additional working capital has to be raised. At the same time, if a decision is made to invest directly in the establishment of foreign production/distribution facilities, foreign currency funds may need to be raised to pay for the investment. The new financing requirements associated with engaging in international business therefore cover the full spectrum of short, medium and long-term funds. At the same time, the sources of funding for international operations extend beyond those sources traditionally available to domestic businesses and understanding these markets is an important aspect of international business.

DEVELOPMENTS IN THE INTERNATIONAL FINANCIAL MARKETS

In the process of sourcing, manufacturing and selling goods and services across the globe, companies need to raise finance. Consequently, in parallel with the internationalisation of business there has been an internationalisation of the financial markets. Indeed it is interesting to note that the world's three main financial centres, New York, London and Tokyo, are also the commercial hubs of the Triad which dominates world trade and investment. The evolution of global business and the international financial markets are inextricably linked. Reed's[1] listing of the twenty-five cities which control the world's financial transactions shows only five of the cities (Rio de Janeiro, Sao Paulo, Mexico, Sydney and Melbourne) lying outside the Triad zone.

The growth of the international financial markets over the last quarter century has been characterised by a number of significant triggers of change, including:

- deregulation of the financial markets
- changes in the trading systems used for securities
- eastern Europe and the expansion of the European Union
- introduction of the Euro and the single currency
- cross-border alliances and mergers in the financial services sector.

By looking at each of these issues in turn, we can begin to understand the current structure of the world financial markets.

Deregulation of the Financial Markets

Dicken[2] suggests that the 'internationalisation of financial services and the deregulation of national financial services markets are virtually two sides of the same coin.' It is certainly true to say that the financial markets cannot *yet* be described as borderless because of the existence of national regulations and supervision, but post 1980 deregulation has been growing apace. In the major economies of the USA, UK, France, Germany and Japan the barriers to competition and foreign involvement in financial services are being dismantled. The deregulation within the national states has further been encouraged by parallel dismantling of regulations at the level of the major trading blocs such as the EU and NAFTA. For example, the EU introduced the Investment Services Directive in March 1997 which served to reinforce the existence of a single market for securities transactions, and was a follow up to legislation to ensure a single market in insurance services. In the NAFTA bloc, there is an agreement to remove all barriers to an open market in financial services by 2007, and within the World Trade Organisation an agreement was signed in 1995 to remove barriers to open international competition in such services. Furthermore, the establishment of Economic and Monetary Union (EMU) in January 1999 created further incentives for additional dismantling of the barriers between domestic financial markets within Europe.

For the individual company seeking to raise finance for investment in, say, a foreign production facility, this deregulation is good news because it offers the company access to a larger array of finance sources than would be available within the domestic market. Furthermore, the additional competition in this larger marketplace has served to drive down the cost of finance.

TRADING SYSTEMS IN THE FINANCIAL MARKETS

New technology has changed the way in which securities are traded around the world, and increased the opportunities for investors in, for example, the United Kingdom, to buy stocks quoted in the USA. Technology has cut the cost of accessing information as well as speeded up the rate at which information can be passed around the world, but in relation to the buying and selling of shares it has also altered the method of trading.

In recent years there has been substantial growth in the level of disintermediation in the securities markets, i.e. the elimination of the dealer as an intermediary in the trading process. Traditionally, a buyer or seller would need to go to a dealer to obtain a price for the shares, and the price paid would include a commission to the dealer. Today, what are called Proprietary Trading Systems (PTS), such as Instinet and Posit in the USA, are used to link buyers and sellers directly, thereby eliminating dealers (and their charges) from the transaction. Research by Steil suggests that fund managers in Europe expect almost 70 per cent of equity trades to be handled in this way by the year 2000. If this forecast is accurate then it implies lower costs for investors, which might be expected to lead to an increase in the size of cross-border portfolio investment flows. This additional investment activity would work to the benefit of multinational companies via larger markets to provide the capital needed for international expansion.

Eastern Europe and the Expansion of the European Union

The collapse of the Berlin Wall in 1989 and the subsequent introduction of free market trading into countries of the former Eastern Bloc has resulted in a substantial increase in the flow of funds both into and out of Eastern Europe. Simultaneously, the new private enterprises in Eastern European economies now have access to new capital markets where funds can be raised via the sale of bonds and equity shares.

Equity trading began in Moscow in the mid 1990s and by the end of 1996 the market value of the stocks traded totalled US$55 billion, or 19.5 per cent of GDP. The Zagreb stock exchange, created in 1991, marked the opening of the Croatian capital market. Most of the securities traded in the market have arisen out of the privatisation of state concerns, and a number of foreign companies have used the market to acquire significant stakes in local firms. For example, Tuborg Carlsberg has purchased large holdings in Croatian breweries, and Ericsson purchased a 49 per cent interest in the electrical equipment company Nikola Tesla.

At present the East European stock markets, including Moscow and Warsaw, are small and lack liquidity, perhaps because they are dominated by local firms. There is, however, clear evidence that the existence of these exchanges may have two potentially important implications for international business:

■ foreign companies can use the stock markets to purchase large stakes in local companies, thereby gaining access to relatively low-cost productive capacity, as well as the opportunity to sell into new markets

■ the new capital markets provide local companies with a means of raising new capital with which to expand their businesses. As the former communist economies gain expertise in private enterprise, these companies will increase the level of competition in certain industries, and this will in turn affect both consumers and companies in the West.

In the newly expanded EU, and amongst countries where membership has been applied for, it is also noticeable that the size of the national stock markets has increased in recent years. Table 6.1 below shows the rapid increase in the number of companies with stock market quotations in Finland and Sweden (which joined the EU in 1995), and the large emerging market of Turkey, which has applied for EU membership.

Table 6.1   *Number of Companies with Shares Listed*

Country	1990	1994	1998	Foreign companies listed 1998
Finland (Helsinki)	77	65	131	2
Sweden (Stockholm)	132	228	276	18
Turkey (Istanbul)	110	176	278	1

Source: *FIBV*

The Table also shows that these markets although very small, are, like their counterparts in Eastern Europe, dominated by local companies. In reality, however, many of these will be part-owned by foreign concerns.

This leads us to the conclusion that both the collapse of communism in Eastern Europe and the expansion of the EU have both served to generate new capital markets which make it easier for companies to expand internationally, particularly via foreign acquisitions or mergers. The 1999 World Investment Report published by UNCTAD estimates that the value of world-wide foreign direct investment could exceed US$800 billion in 1999 because of the boom in cross-border mergers and acquisitions, and most of these investment flows are between the USA and Europe.

Introduction of the Euro

The combined impact of deregulation, disintermediation and the growth of national stock markets within the EU all indicate that capital markets within Europe are becoming more integrated. The introduction of the Euro single currency can only serve to enhance this integration.

The most important effect of the single currency is that it eliminates currency risk between the eleven member states. Export contracts can now be invoiced in Euros, and the rate of exchange between the Euro and the domestic currency of any of the member countries is fixed. Within the financial markets, companies can now borrow in Euros, or issue bonds and shares priced in Euros. If shares are quoted on more than one exchange, there will be price transparency, and consequently increased competition which may well lead to the closure of some exchanges and consolidation into a single market. The net effect of all of this will be to reduce the cost and eliminate the currency risk of raising cross-border finance for intra-EMU projects. At the same time, if companies express confidence in the Euro by raising finance in this way, it is likely that the new currency will become the world's second most important reserve currency, after the US dollar.

World capital markets are now dominated by institutional rather than individual investors, and the single currency will affect these institutions. Historically, national regulations have restricted the level of foreign currency denominated investment which can be undertaken by institutional investors such as pension funds, unit trusts and insurance companies. The single currency now means that such restrictions are meaningless within the EMU zone, and this could result in large scale intra-EMU investment as fund managers diversify their portfolios and move out of domestic markets.

The attraction of raising finance in Euros rather than a national currency is highlighted later in this chapter, in the statistics on debt and equity markets in Europe. At this stage it is sufficient to propose that the single currency is expected to increase the attractiveness of investing in Europe, and make it cheaper and easier for multinational companies to raise finance for the such investments.

Cross-Border Alliances in Financial Services

The final piece in the jigsaw, which completes the picture of integrating financial markets, is the number of cross-border alliances between financial institutions over the last decade. A Bank of England paper[4] identified 247 cross-border alliances amongst financial institutions within the European Community over the period 1987-93, but even this large number is acknowledged as not being comprehensive. The Bank of England data suggest that French institutions were most active in initiating alliances, as they accounted for 74 out of the total of 247. Prime targets for the French were UK (18) and Spanish (19) institutions. France also appeared to be a popular target country because of its large potential market for retail loans, mortgages, and private banking services.

The most common form of alliance is one in which a large foreign institution buys a stake in a smaller concern. In wholesale banking, outright acquisition has been favoured, such as in the Deutsche Bank purchase of Morgan Grenfell. There are also instances of joint venture companies and cooperation agreements which involve cross shareholdings. The arrangement between Banco Santander and Royal Bank of Scotland is one example of this.

This opening up of markets to foreign participants is not confined to intra-European activity. In recent years the personal credit market in the UK has been targeted by American credit card companies looking for new markets. The effect has been much increased competition, wider consumer choice, and lower interest charges on many credit cards.

Viewed from the perspective of the multinational company, international alliances in financial services can be seen to be beneficial because they result in:

- lower transaction costs
- faster processing of cross-border transactions
- easier access to foreign banking facilities for overseas operations.

In conclusion then, developments in the international financial markets over the last quarter century have led to more integrated markets in which financial institutions operate on an international scale that mirrors that of their main customers, the MNCs. The financial system thus supports and encourages the internationalisation of business.

We can now look in detail at how companies use the different financial markets to develop their international trade and investment.

Sources of Finance for International Trade and Investment

In looking at sources of finance for overseas operations it is useful to divide the topic into three main sections.

■ Export finance: for companies in the early stages of international involvement, this is the area which is of most interest.

■ Short term and medium term finance, raised in the international markets, e.g. the Eurocurrency and Eurocredit markets.

■ Long term sources of finance, and the international bond and equity markets.

When raising corporate finance, it is vital that a Treasurer pays close attention to the relative cost of alternative sources. Differing taxation regimes may significantly affect the cost of raising funds in different parts of the world. In the light of this, the chapter takes a brief look at strategic tax planning, whilst noting that tax rules will influence general location choices as well as financing choices for international companies.

EXPORTING: THE IMPORTANCE OF TERMS OF PAYMENT AND SETTLEMENT IN DETERMINING FINANCE REQUIREMENTS

There are very few international companies that do not export at least some of their output. The cash difficulties that may result from extended delays in obtaining payment for exports has led to the development of special types of export finance, which supplement the short-term financing options available to all companies.

In comparing the relative merits of the various sources of export finance it is vital to consider the terms under which the export contract operates. Needless to say, contract terms will be dependent on the relative size of the two parties, and the extent to which the exporter is prepared to accept risk.

The risks encountered by an exporter take three forms: political, physical and commercial:

Political risk

The political risk relates to the threat of government intervention to control exchange rates or access to foreign exchange. The controls may also extend to import tariffs or quotas, and licensing. Many governments restrict the funds available for imports, or operate tiered restrictions. In the latter case, it is easy to obtain the foreign currency to pay for industrial components, for example, but perhaps impossible to access the funds for consumer goods imports.

In such an environment, the exporting company needs a basis for assessing the risk that payment may be subject to severe delay. The trade departments of most governments offer an information service to exporters, which provides guidance on the level of political risk. Similar services are provided by most large commercial banks.

Physical risk

The physical risk is related to the fact that transit distances are greater in export markets. Goods in transit face the risk of damage, deterioration, theft or fire.

Commercial risk

Commercial risk is used to describe the possibility that payment may be short, paid late, or never received at all. Credit risk appraisals on commercial companies are widely available, both from government and private sources, such as Dun and Bradstreet. These may be supplemented by bank and trade references to help build a complete picture.

All of the above risks require insurance cover, and this may be available either via governments or the private sector. The role played by governments varies from nation to nation. In the EU, all governments with the exception of the UK provide export insurance services to cover all types of risk. In the UK, cover for all short-term export contracts, i.e. with payment terms of six months or less, is now only available through private firms. Government cover is still available for longer term contracts. Standard terms generally offer 90 per cent cover for commercial risk, and 95 per cent cover for political risk, but the cost of cover escalates when firms wish to insure only a part of their export business.

Payment Terms

Once a company has satisfied itself that the risk levels are tolerable, it can begin to negotiate contract terms. Payment terms are critical here, in limiting risk as well as reducing the amount of additional funding that may be required. At one extreme, the exporter may demand payment up front, and at the opposite extreme he will be prepared to trade on open account. Open account trading is similar to sales within the domestic market. Title is passed on delivery of the goods, subject to payment being received. The purchaser is granted credit, with the usual payment period being between 90 and 180 days.

The general rule is that open account terms should only be offered to highly creditworthy customers. In other cases, alternative terms need to be considered. The alternatives may be any of:

■ payment upon shipment
■ bank collection
■ discounted bills of exchange
■ letter of credit.

Payment upon shipment requires the foreign buyer to pay whilst goods are in transit, and he does not acquire title until the payment has been received and cleared.

Bank collection works by a bank being responsible for collection of payment before issuing of the transfer of title.

A Bill of Exchange is a form of promissory note, and if drawn against a creditworthy party the bill may be sold on, or discounted, in the financial markets. The bill is drawn up by the exporter, and its signature (acceptance) by the importer implies a willingness to accept the liability to pay. The bill may be a sight draft, whereby the importer must pay for the goods immediately on presentation of the bill. Time drafts allow a specified credit period to elapse between the time of presentation and payment. An accepted Bill of Exchange can be sold by the exporter. The buyer is effectively purchasing an entitlement to a sum of money due to be paid at a specified future date, and so pays below the face value, i.e. discounts the bill.

Letters of credit, which are linked to bills of exchange, are very widely used in international trade. Letters of credit work by obliging the importer's bank to accept a bill of exchange and the bill may be in any currency agreed by both importer and exporter.

The onus is on the bank to make payment when the bill is presented and so the bank specifies terms for the exporter, which are required to be met before payment will be made. Most commonly, there is a requirement for the exporter to provide documentary proof of shipment, origin of the goods, and clearance by the importer. Incomplete documentation will mean payment will not be made.

The fact that the system works by passing the responsibility for payment from the importer to a bank serves to reduce the credit risk. There may be a problem, however, if a foreign bank is willing to make the payment but exchange regulations prevent the foreign currency being available. To avoid this difficulty, it is possible to organise a 'confirmed' letter of credit. In this case the exporter's bank confirms its willingness to pay the exporter once the importer's bank is satisfied that the terms of the letter of credit have been fulfilled. The fact that payment is now coming from a domestic bank means that exchange controls no longer affect the likelihood of payment. One problem here is that, not surprisingly, it is often difficult to find banks that will confirm letters of credit in countries where access to foreign exchange is restricted.

Even greater security can be obtained via a confirmed irrevocable letter of credit. Irrevocable letters of credit require agreement by all parties if the terms are to be altered.

Settlement

Regardless of the contract terms, the longer an exporter waits to receive payment, the greater the short-term finance he requires. Comparing payment on shipment with a 180 day bill of exchange could mean a total time difference of eight months if shipment takes two months to complete. If payment is then made by cheque, further delaying effective receipt of the cash, the total financial cost could be very high.

Comparing the cost of alternative contract terms

Example

Suppose that a UK-based company estimates that one third of its £9 million turnover comes from export sales. We can compare the impact of choosing different contract and payment terms by making a number of assumptions.

Let us assume:

1 The company works on a gross profit margin of 20 per cent. This would mean that for the £3 million of exports, costs of £2.4 million would be incurred

2 Suppliers and other creditors are paid after 90 days

3 Short-term credit is raised via an overdraft facility, which costs the company 8 per cent per annum.

4 *Option 1:*
   Accept payment against shipment, with payment by cheque which will take seven days to clear.

   Option 2:
   Take payment by banker's draft against a confirmed letter of credit which is expected to be paid ninety days after delivery. Shipment takes twenty-one days.

Solution

Comparing the costs of the two alternative payment systems:

Option 1

Costs to be funded £2.4 million

Credit taken 90 days

Credit granted 7 days

Net funding period: 83 days, i.e. payment is received 83 days before the company needs to pay its own creditors.

Value of saving = £2.4 million x 83/365 x 0.08
                = £43,660

In other words, by collecting payment before shipment, and negating the need to borrow on overdraft, the company has saved itself £43,660 on each year's export sales. This would substantially increase profits.

Option 2

Costs to be funded £2.4 million

Credit taken 90 days

Credit granted 111 days

Net funding period: 111 − 90 = 21 days

Cost of funding = £2.4 million x 21/365 x 0.08
                = £11,046

In other words, by agreeing to sell on credit, the company must accept that its bank interest costs will rise by £11,046 per year.

So how does the company make its choice? On a simple cost basis, the first option is infinitely preferable and will be good for profits. But the company may find that it cannot get foreign customers to agree to such terms. In such cases, there is a *trade off* between the gross profit contributed by the export sales, and the additional costs incurred to fund those sales. Each case needs to be reviewed separately, using cost benefit analysis.

The above illustration shows that payment methods are important in addition to credit/settlement terms for export sales. There are only a limited set of choices open to exporters for payment terms; these are as follows:

Bank draft

This is relatively low risk as it means that a bank is guaranteeing payment, but as the bank is usually the importer's bank, there may still be a problem of access to the required foreign exchange.

Cheque

A slow payment method, which is also subject to the risk of non-clearance. Commercial banks also charge premium rates for clearance of a foreign currency cheque.

Electronic Funds Transfer (SWIFT)

SWIFT stands for Society for World-wide International Funds Transfer. The transfer operates for the movement of funds between member institutions, which are the main commercial banks. Exporting companies can receive instant payment from overseas, paid direct into their bank account, but the way the system works requires that both importer and exporter have access to member banks. The cost of SWIFT is relatively high when compared with other payment methods.

SHORT-TERM BORROWING TO FUND EXPORT SALES

As can be seen, and has already been suggested, some forms of payment will take longer than others. The exporter kept waiting for the money must find a way of raising short-term finance for export sales. At the simplest level, the finance could be in the form of a bank loan or overdraft, to cover the time until payment is received. More commonly, exporters turn to specialist sources of finance which include:

- export houses
- discounted bills of exchange
- forfaiting
- factoring
- countertrade
- leasing
- advances against collections.

It is not uncommon for large exporters to combine these sources of funds, according to needs at any particular point in time.

The specialist meaning of these terms is important to understand.

Export Houses

Export houses may act either as export agents or as export merchants. The agent may act on behalf of foreign buyers, seeking overseas suppliers for specified goods or services, or on behalf of the exporter, seeking out overseas buyers. A merchant acts independently, buying items from the exporter for onward sale. In representing an importer, the agent takes responsibility for ordering and the organisation of delivery. When representing an exporter, the agent may serve as the only route in to some foreign markets.

The benefit of using an export merchant is that such an arrangement reduces the credit risk of the exporter, as he now only risks non-payment by one party (the merchant) rather than a full array of foreign customers.

Discounted Bill of Exchange

A bill of exchange, as explained earlier, is a promissory note. When the note is drawn against a credit-worthy party, it may be possible to sell the bill on in the financial markets.

The bill of exchange is sold to convert a future cash flow into a current cash flow, and as a result it will be sold at a discount to its face value. The rate of discount will be determined by three things:

- the length of time to maturity, i.e. when payment is due
- the credit rating of the importer/acceptor of the bill
- the terms of the bill: with or without recourse.

FORFAITING

Forfaiting is the purchase at a discount of trade debt or receivables without recourse to the seller.

Forfaiting is a form of finance most commonly applied to sales contracts where payment is not required for at least six months or more. Consequently, it is often associated with sales of capital items, for which payment is made in a series of stages over a time scale of up to five years. For example, suppose that an exporter has sold a machine for which payment is expected at four six-monthly intervals, the first of which is six months after delivery. The cash from the sale is thus VERY slow in coming through. If receipt of the future payments could be guaranteed, then the exporter could sell on those payment obligations and raise cash immediately.

Forfaiting works via specialist companies, who are prepared to buy overseas promissory notes or bills of exchange at a discount. The risk of collection against the note is thus transferred to the forfaiter, with the result that forfaiting is both easier and cheaper to arrange if payment of the foreign debt is guaranteed. Any such guarantee will come from a bank and a note guaranteed in this way is described as 'avalised'.

The Head of National Westminster Bank's Forfaiting Unit has been quoted as arguing that 'Forfaiting should be as good as a cash sale to an exporter ... There is no risk to the exporter – it is the forfaiter that takes the risk – so there is no need for credit insurance.'

This is all very well, but it is nonetheless the case that forfaiting is a non-starter when the importer, his bank or his country is not viewed as credit worthy. In such circumstances the exporter will never find a forfaiter willing to buy the promissory notes.

In recent years, the markets within which forfeiting firms are prepared to operate have been extended. For UK exporters at least, it is now possible to raise forfaiting finance for markets previously viewed as high risk, such as Vietnam, Hungary and the Lebanon.

Given that forfaiting is a means of effectively eliminating the credit risk for the exporter, it is to be expected that the cost of the finance is relatively high. The general view is that it is not cost effective for deals with a value of less than £20,000. For deals of larger value, it is a useful source of finance to consider, because it offers companies the opportunity to grant flexible payment terms to the overseas buyer, whilst knowing that the sales proceeds can be encashed immediately through a forfaiter. The flexibility of payment may serve to boost overseas demand, which could not otherwise be accessed.

Factoring

Factoring works by the exporter selling the responsibility for overseas debt collection to a factoring company.

This is a very popular source of export funding in the USA and Canada, and its popularity in Western Europe is increasing rapidly. Export factors operate in the same way as factors for domestic sales, and the service provided may be recourse or non-recourse in nature. If the debt cannot be collected, but the factor remains liable to the exporter for the sum due, the agreement is referred to as non-recourse. If a debt is bad and the exporter accepts responsibility for it, then the deal is termed as being 'with recourse'.

In addition to the debt collection service, the export factor may provide other services such as loans against invoices, and credit risk insurance.

Loans against invoices allow an exporter to collect cash before the due date as per the invoice. The factor takes on responsibility for collection on the due date, but will pay cash against that collection. The cash paid is less than the invoice value, with the rate of discount being determined by the time delay before due payment and the credit rating of the importer. The result is that factoring is very similar to forfaiting. The key difference is one of time. Forfaiting is useful for medium or long-term contracts, whereas factoring is aimed at meeting short-term cash needs.

Countertrade

Countertrade is essentially a variation on bartering where the countertrade takes the form of a counterpurchase, such that an agreement to sell to a country is set alongside a deal to buy from the same nation.

Strictly speaking then, countertrade is not a form of finance, but it is particularly useful for companies dealing with purchasers which are subject to tight foreign exchange controls such as the Eastern European nations, or the less developed countries.

For example, the CIS may be prepared to sell graphite if the graphite shipment can be used in payment for computer hardware, which is in short supply in the CIS.

The complication of financing through countertrade is that it is cumbersome to administer, as deals are unlikely to be perfect matches in terms of value. The result is that companies can find themselves left with supplies of goods that are foreign to them in more than one sense of the word. The foreign exchange risk is then replaced with the risk of being able to convert the countertrade items into real cash.

Leasing

The exporter arranges for a leasing company to effectively act as intermediary, and sells the capital equipment for cash to the leasing company, having previously arranged for the importer to take out a lease with the same concern.

For exporters, leasing is most commonly used as a source of finance when the sale involves capital goods. The effect of the deal is to release cash faster, easing the credit strain on the exporter. When the leasing company is based outside the buyer's country, the arrangement is referred to as cross-border leasing. Large exporters frequently establish subsidiary leasing companies, because the leasing arrangements help to boost sales, whilst at the same time their ownership of the leasing concern allows them to keep the profits earned from the lease agreement as well. Rank Xerox is one example of a company which operates in this way.

Advances Against Collection

Advances against collection mean that a company can borrow money from a bank, with the loan secured against the receipts from an export sale.

This source of funding can only be used when there is an agreement for a bank to collect the documents and payment relating to an export sale. Banks will often offer a loan in advance of the money to be collected, up to a maximum of 90 per cent. The arrangement is easier to obtain when payment is due in the seller's domestic currency. When the collection is denominated in a foreign currency, the bank takes on a foreign exchange risk in addition to the credit collection risk; this may not be viewed as acceptable.

The published accounts of companies do not give the reader any insight into either the payment terms or financing methods used for export deals. This is unfortunate, as the financial effects of the different alternatives can be profound.

When there are with-recourse agreements, e.g. discounted bills, these may appear in a note to the accounts under the heading of contingent liabilities. The sum shown is the extent to which it is deemed possible that the company may become liable for sums not collected on with recourse bills which have been discounted. Such sums may, however, refer to either domestic or foreign bills, and so separating out the export finance element is impossible.

SHORT- AND MEDIUM-TERM FINANCE FOR FOREIGN TRADE

The financial markets are usually seen as divided into two categories: the money markets and the capital markets. The money markets deal in short- or medium-term sources of finance, and the capital markets are concerned with long-term funding.

The money markets with which this text is concerned, are those used in international business. The areas of particular interest are the Eurocurrency, and Eurocommercial paper markets. Interestingly, the Euro prefix does not specifically imply a market located in mainland Europe. Euro... simply means that the money has been deposited or raised outside its country of origin. A US dollar deposit account held in Japan would give rise to the term Eurodollars! This can be a little confusing to the uninitiated.

Eurocurrency

Eurocurrency is the term used to describe a short-term deposit or loan in a currency other than the domestic currency of the location. The minimum size of deal on the market is US$ 1 million. The opportunity to borrow or make foreign currency deposits over a short time frame is particularly attractive to multinational companies that may be dealing in a large number of different currencies on a regular basis.

The Eurocurrency market developed rapidly, alongside the expansion of world trade, but owes its origins to US investment in Europe in the 1950s. Dollars began to be both deposited and borrowed in Europe, and a market developed for lending and borrowing across national frontiers, but over time the number of currencies which were used for transactions in the market increased to include most major European and world currencies.

The main users of the Eurocurrency market are banks and multinational companies, and so the large-scale growth in international investment flows has led to a huge expansion of the Eurocurrency market over the last twenty years.

The attractions of the Eurocurrency market are threefold:

■ international companies can deal with a range of currencies that match their trading and investment needs

■ transactions can be arranged with ease because the market operates outside national regulatory boundaries. This gives added freedom to market users

■ Interest rates which are more attractive than their domestic equivalents. Deposit rates tend to be higher, and loan rates lower than the domestic markets because the eurocurrency markets are deemed to be riskier, and so preferential terms are required to draw investors.

The *Financial Times* publishes a daily table of Eurocurrency interest rates. The layout is as shown in Table 6.2.

Case example

A German company has received US$ in payment for goods shipped to a customer in Ohio, but the company treasurer knows that a US$ payment will have to be made in 90 days for components bought from a US supplier. Rather than incur transaction costs in converting the dollars back to Euros today, and then buying dollars again in three months time, the money can be placed on deposit in the Eurocurrency market. Using the rates shown in the table below, the interest rate received in this case would be equivalent to 6 per cent per year.

Table 6.2   *International Money Rates*

March 16	Short term	7 days notice	One month	Three months	Six months	One year
Euro	$4^{13}/_{16}-4^{3}/_{4}$	$4^{13}/_{16}-4^{23}/_{32}$	$4^{27}/_{32}-4^{23}/_{32}$	$4^{25}/_{32}-4^{3}/_{4}$	$4^{11}/_{16}-4^{9}/_{16}$	$4^{17}/_{32}-4^{13}/_{32}$
Danish Krone	$5^{1}/_{2}-5$	$5^{13}/_{32}-5^{5}/_{32}$	$5^{7}/_{32}-5^{1}/_{16}$	$5^{3}/_{16}-5^{1}/_{16}$	$5-4^{27}/_{32}$	$4^{27}/_{32}-4^{11}/_{16}$
Sterling	$5^{5}/_{16}-5^{3}/_{16}$	$5^{7}/_{16}-5^{11}/_{32}$	$5^{1}/_{2}-5^{13}/_{32}$	$5^{7}/_{16}-5^{11}/_{32}$	$5^{11}/_{32}-5^{1}/_{4}$	$5^{5}/_{16}-5^{3}/_{16}$
Swiss Franc	$3^{13}/_{32}-2^{29}/_{32}$	$3^{15}/_{32}-3^{13}/_{32}$	$3^{1}/_{4}-3^{5}/_{32}$	$3^{15}/_{32}-3^{3}/_{8}$	$3^{3}/_{8}-3^{9}/_{32}$	$3^{7}/_{32}-3^{1}/_{16}$
Canadian Dollar	$4^{31}/_{32}-4^{27}/_{32}$	$5-4^{7}/_{8}$	$4^{15}/_{16}-4^{13}/_{16}$	$4^{11}/_{16}-4^{19}/_{32}$	$4^{9}/_{16}-4^{7}/_{16}$	$4^{17}/_{32}-4^{13}/_{32}$
US Dollar	$5^{1}/_{2}-5^{7}/_{16}$	$5^{1}/_{16}-4^{31}/_{32}$	$4^{31}/_{32}-4^{29}/_{32}$	$4^{7}/_{8}-4^{3}/_{4}$	$4^{23}/_{32}-4^{21}/_{32}$	$4^{5}/_{8}-4^{17}/_{32}$
Japanese Yen	$7/_{32}-1/_{8}$	$3/_{16}-1/_{8}$	$9/_{32}-5/_{32}$	$3/_{16}-1/_{8}$	$5/_{32}-1/_{8}$	$1/_{4}-5/_{32}$
Singapore $	$1^{1}/_{8}-1$	$4^{9}/_{32}-4^{1}/_{16}$	$3^{7}/_{16}-3^{1}/_{4}$	$2^{29}/_{32}-2^{23}/_{32}$	$2^{27}/_{32}-2^{5}/_{8}$	$2^{25}/_{32}-2^{19}/_{32}$

Short-term rates are call for the US Dollar and Yen, others; two days' notice.

Source: *Financial Times*, 18 March 2001

The Table shows the broad range of currencies available in the market, which extends beyond the EC currencies that might be expected.

Since January 1999 the single currency has reduced the number of currencies quoted, because member countries now trade/borrow/invest in Euros instead of their domestic currency. As a result, the demand by multinational companies for short-term deposit or loan facilities in currencies such as the French franc or D-Mark has effectively disappeared.

The Eurocurrency market divides into lenders and borrowers. Firms with a short-term cash surplus in, for example, French Francs, will be lenders. Those with a short-term cash shortfall, will be borrowers in the market, and to understand the data in the table it is important to recognise that for each currency and time frame two interest rates are quoted. For example, the Swiss Franc rates for three months are shown as $3^{15}/_{32}-3^{3}/_{8}$. The *first* rate is the *annual* percentage rate that will be charged for a three-month Swiss Franc loan; the *second* rate is that which will be paid for a three-month deposit denominated in Swiss Francs. Needless to say, it is always the case that the borrowing rate exceeds the deposit rate, and the difference between the two rates is called the 'spread'.

It is noticeable that the annual interest rates shown in the table vary, both across currencies and across time, and it is important to understand the implications of such variations. The rate of interest associated with transactions in any particular currency reflect the state of the specific underlying economy and domestic interest rates. Consequently the interest rate for the UK at between 5 and 6 per cent is significantly higher than that of Japan at less than 1 per cent. This reflects the desire by the Japanese government to use low interest rates to stimulate the economy after its financial crises in the late 1990s.

Differences in interest rates across currencies might tempt company treasurers into seeking to borrow where interest rates are at their lowest in order to save money. If, for example, interest rate are 4 per cent lower in Switzerland than in the UK, then on a three-month £1 million loan, this would seem to suggest that interest of [£1m x $^3/_{12}$ x 0.04] or £10,000 could be saved. In practice this is not the case, because the exchange rate between the Swiss Franc and Sterling will reflect the interest rate differential. In other words, if the equivalent of £1 million was borrowed in Swiss Francs, then by the time the loan came to be repaid, the Sterling value of the loan would have risen by the equivalent of 4 per cent per year. This means that there is usually no real saving to be made from seeking out the low interest rate currency for a loan. (The use of foreign currency deposits/loans to hedge foreign exchange risks is discussed in the section on money market hedges in Chapter 7.)

The differences in interest rates across time reflect two things:

- higher rates associated with lengthier transactions reflect the fact that longer time frames imply greater risk

- market expectations of future interest rates.

For example, the short-term (overnight) rate for a Euro deposit is shown as $4^3/_4$, but for six months this falls to $4^9/_{16}$, a drop of just less than one quarter of one per cent. The market therefore expects interest rates in the ERM area to fall slightly during the early months of the year 2001.

Key Features of the Eurocurrency Market

- Short-term loans /deposits only

- Interest rates may be fixed or variable

- Variable loans are subject to roll-over, i.e. rates are re-set at regular intervals

- Interest is paid gross

- Low transaction costs which mean lower loan rates, and higher interest rates on deposits

- Loan sizes exceed those available in domestic markets. Syndication of loans is common

■ No reserve requirements for banks operating in the market. Banks can thus lend out 100 per cent of deposits

■ Speed of operation; loans can generally be arranged much quicker than in domestic markets.

Eurocommercial Paper

Eurocommercial paper is a market in which companies arrange short-term loans from non-banking institutions, with the loans denominated in a currency which is not that of the nation of issue. Loans are raised via the issue of short-term 'notes', and because of the resulting credit risk for the note purchaser this facility is only available to blue chip corporations. In the UK the Bank of England specifies the asset backing required for companies wishing to issue commercial paper in the domestic market.

The reasons for borrowing outside the banking sector are lower costs and greater flexibility. The system works as follows:

1 A company agrees an underwriting facility for note issues with a bank or syndicate of banks. This means that the bank agrees to purchase any notes which the company fails to sell in the open market.

2 A maximum borrowing facility is agreed, and the company may issue notes up to the limit of this facility. The value and timing of note issues is not controlled except via the borrowing facility.

3 Interest rates on the notes are variable, and dependent on current market rates. The maturity date of each issue is set for a period of between one and twelve months.

4 Banks sell the notes to investors on behalf of the company, and the underwriting facility is used to take up any shortfall.

The major benefit of the commercial paper market, as already suggested, is its flexibility. Companies can choose when to make a note issue, and can be guaranteed access to the required funds. In addition, the option to select maturity dates means that it is possible to take advantage of interest rate trends to minimise the cost of borrowing. For example, if long-term rates are moving down, funds could be raised via monthly note issues which are renewed until rates hit the low point.

The major problem with the market is that it represents a source of finance only available to prime borrowers. The vast majority of medium sized companies will be unable to use the commercial paper market, and their borrowing costs will consequently be higher.

Eurocredit Market

The term Eurocredit is applied to medium–long-term bank loans issued to companies in a currency other than that of the country where the issue originates. As with the other Euromarkets, access to such loans is of most interest to companies which are investing abroad and wish to raise finance denominated in the currency in which they will be receiving revenues. Demirag and Goddard[3] estimate that the average period for such loans is usually eight years, but the interest rate charged is subject to regular review as most loans are on a 'floating' rate.

LONG-TERM FINANCE: THE INTERNATIONAL CAPITAL MARKETS

The international capital markets can be clearly divided into two, the bond and equity markets, because in seeking to raise long-term finance company directors face a choice between these alternative sources of capital.

Companies are free to choose the debt:equity mix in their capital structure, and the proportions will tend to vary over time. Debt is attractive as a source of finance, because it is cheap relative to equity; the drawback is that it results in commitments to pay interest which may be difficult to meet in times of weak trading conditions. Conversely, equity creates no such commitments, but is relatively expensive. The international bond and equity markets serve the needs of companies as they manage the debt:equity mix, to suit the specific financing requirements of world-wide operations.

International Bond Markets

A bond is an issue of long-term debt, which may or may not be irredeemable. Most company issues are redeemable, which means that the issuer repays the nominal value of the bond to the holder, at some future point in time. The repayment date may be specified at the time of issue, or redemption may be at the discretion of the issuing company at some time between prescribed dates.

The language of the bond markets is a little specialised and it is useful to come to grips with some of the terminology before looking at the detail of how the markets work.

Terminology in the Bond Markets

Straights: Bonds which pay a fixed rate of interest

Floating rate notes (FRNs): Medium-term bonds on which the interest paid varies in line with LIBOR (London Inter Bank Offer Rate). FRNs usually specify a minimum rate payable, which is the coupon rate. Prices are generally quoted in US dollars.

Convertibles: Bond issues which are available for conversion into equity in the future. As with FRNs the price is usually quoted in US dollars.

The international bond market is used by governments and companies to raise loan finance in a non-domestic currency. There is a general principle of matching in financing, which suggests that the time scale of funding for a project should match that of the project. This means that the primary use of long-term bond money is for capital investment. In the case of public sector institutions, the money raised will be used for such things as infrastructure development. For private sector companies, the capital needs will take the form of investment in foreign subsidiaries, or purchase of equipment for overseas plants.

Bond issues may be Foreign Bonds or Eurobonds. A foreign bond is one which is issued in a domestic capital market foreign to the issuing company, for example, a US company issuing a bond in the Paris market. A Eurobond is a bond offered for sale simultaneously in a number of different countries, in a currency other than that of the country of issue.

Mini Case Study

In 1999 the German telecommunications and engineering conglomerate Mannessmann issued a Euro3 billion ten-year bond, to help finance its purchase of o.tel.o, a German telephone business, and also to buy out Olivetti's share of a joint acquisition of two Italian telecom businesses, Omnitel and Infostrada.

The bond issue is particularly interesting because it was denominated in Euros and was used to buy companies in two European states, Germany and Italy. It is illustrative of many deals in the international bond market, which is increasingly being used to fund cross-border mergers and acquisitions.

Both Foreign and Eurobonds usually mature in ten to fifteen years' time, and the very large issues will usually be syndicated, so that a group of financial institutions jointly bear the risk of underwriting the bond issue. A large secondary market exists for high quality bonds, and prices are readily obtainable through the financial press, from data supplied by the International Securities Markets Association.

The Eurobond market, in common with the other Euromarkets, is growing very rapidly. Some of the growth can be explained simply by increased international investment activity, but it is also a consequence of the simultaneous expansion of the swaps market. For example, a straight Eurobond denominated in Yen could be swapped for a Swiss Franc floating rate bond, if the foreign exchange needs of a company so required it. (Refer to the chapter on foreign exchange risk to check how swaps work.) It is estimated that well in excess of half of Eurobond issues are made with the intention of using them in a swap arrangement: either a currency or interest rate swap.

In the first six months of 1999, new corporate bonds worth Euro149 billion were issued in the European market, compared with Euro74 billion for the same period of 1998[5]. The 1999 market has also experienced a change in the mix of currencies in which the bonds are denominated, as is shown in Table 6.3 below.

Table 6.3   *Euro Market Bond Issues: 1998/1999*

1st Six Months 1998: Total Issues: Euro 74 billion		**1st Six Months 1999: Total Issues: Euro 148.9 billion**	
Currency	% of total	Currency	% of total
EMU member currencies	26.35	Euro	52.25
Sterling	13.24	Sterling	9.00
US Dollar	56.76	US Dollar	35.26
Other	3.65	Other	3.49

Source: *Euromoney*

The most noticeable change shown by the table is the increased preference for Euro denominated bonds at the expense of the US dollar and sterling. The dollar seems to have been sidelined as the currency of choice, even for companies outside the Euro-zone. This suggests two things:

- confidence in the single currency within the capital markets

- the driving force behind the issues is intra-EMU investment, particularly mergers and acquisitions.

The growing significance of cross-border investment within the European region was discussed in some detail in Chapter 2, and the trends within the capital markets serve to further confirm the importance of this investment pattern.

Table 6.4   *Examples of Recent Eurobond Issues*

Company	*Issue size*	*Purpose*
Vodafone AirTouch (Telecommunications)	Euro1.5 billion	Refinancing of a loan to support Vodafone's Acquisition of AirTouch in 1999
Carrefour (Retailer)	Euro1 billion	Re-finance 1998 purchase of supermarket chain Comptoirs Modernes
Saint Gobain (Glass, ceramics, building materials)	Euro1 billion	Re-financing plus funding of small acquisitions in USA, Europe and Brazil
North West Water	Euro500 million	Investment in renewal of pipelines/sewerage infrastructure
Ford Motor Credit	US$8.6 billion	Re-financing of existing debt and reduction in debt costs

Although the Ford Motor Credit issue shown above was a dollar issue, the company is expected to make its first Euro issue in 2000 because, as Dave Cosper the Treasurer explains, 'issuing in Euro can allow Ford to achieve a large distribution (i.e. access a larger number of buyers) and not only in Europe. Over time the Euro will have a strong demand in Asia. Asia investors who are large investors of dollar bonds will be soon looking for diversification, and the Euro will provide an alternative currency.'

In 1989, the World Bank successfully issued the first Global Bond, which was simultaneously offered for sale in Europe and the USA. In recent years, although such bonds are still rare, their issue has spread to the corporate market. For example, the US chemical group Du Pont is about to issue its first global bond for US$2 billion, spread over 5 and 10 year maturity periods. The growth of global bonds has been helped by the increasing integration of international capital markets, as discussed at the start of this chapter, although it is still too soon to describe the markets as fully integrated.

Equity Markets

Over the last twenty years there has been a very noticeable trend amongst institutional investors to wish to increase holdings of foreign assets in their portfolios, as a means of reducing the volatility of investment returns. This willingness to buy equity globally has been greatly aided by improvements in information technology and telecommunications, and increased freedom of international capital movements. The annual rate of growth in international equity trading during the 1980s was approximately 18 per cent, and more than 10 per cent of all equity trades were with a nonresident party. The scale of foreign deals varies between the different major stock markets, with London being the major player.

In 1992, foreign turnover as a percentage of the daily average reached 6.8 per cent in New York, 8.5 per cent in Zurich and 43.2 per cent in London.

Running parallel with the demands from investors to buy foreign stocks, has been a growth in demand from companies seeking a quotation on foreign stock markets. It is still true that many companies prefer to seek their initial public offering (IPO) on their domestic exchange, be it Madrid, Paris, Frankfurt or London. The domestic investor knows the company better, and there is a general perception that a higher price can be obtained for the stock. The only exceptions to this occur when an issue by a large company may drain liquidity in the local market, and so even the initial sale occurs overseas. One example of the latter was the IPO for the African mining company Ashanti Goldfields. The market value of the shares offered for sale was too high for the local stock market in Ghana, and so the company launched their shares in London instead.

Domestic quotations are frequently followed some years later with a foreign launch. This approach was adopted by Deutschetelekom, whose IPO in the German market in 1996 was followed by an Euro11 billion Europe-wide equity sale in June 1999. Multi-country share offerings remain difficult to organise, because Europe has not yet harmonized the rules on share issuance, but they are a very useful way of rapidly ensuring that a company's shareholder base is pan European.

The number of foreign companies that are listed on the key stock markets of the world is shown in Table 6.5.

Table 6.5   *Foreign Stock Market Listings*

	Number of Foreign Companies Quoted			
	1986	1989	1992	1998
New York	63	86	120	391
NASDAQ	244	286	261	441
London	584	599	522	466
Tokyo	52	116	117	n/a
Paris	195	223	222	183
Hong Kong	7	14	27	n/a

Source: FIBV

The figures clearly show that London continues to be the leading market, but that there is a general world-wide trend towards growth of foreign company quotations. The attraction of London is usually attributed to the lack of attractiveness of both the USA and Tokyo. Companies seeking a US listing must submit to the draconian SEC regulations, and the costs of maintaining a stock market quotation in Tokyo are very high.

Nonetheless, it is quite common for large companies to have a dual listing on the London and New York exchanges (either NYSE or NASDAQ). Examples of US companies which are also quoted in London are:

- AT & T (telecom)
- Colgate Palmolive (household goods)
- Ford Motor (vehicle manufacturer)
- Philip Morris (tobacco)
- Texaco (oil).

The list clearly shows that all economic sectors are represented, but it also suggests that dual listings are perhaps best suited to the very large transnational corporations.

All foreign companies which are seeking a US market quotation must register under SEC regulations, which many view as being the world's most stringent. One requirement is for filed accounts to be prepared under US GAAP (generally accepted accounting practice). Some major companies such as Ciba Geigy and BASF are unwilling to seek US stock market quotations because they do not wish to jump through the hoop of revamping their accounts in accordance with US GAAP regulations. Others, such as Daimler Benz are prepared to undertake a reconciliation of their accounts.

One way in which a company can raise equity capital in the USA before commencing full trading on the New York Stock Exchange, American Stock Exchange or NASDAQ is via the issue of American Depositary Receipts or ADRs. An ADR is a certificate which indicates ownership of a foreign stock. US banks purchase ADRs direct from the issuing company and sell them on to investors. Over the last twenty years the list of ADRs has been growing rapidly, and examples of company equity which is available via ADRs include:

- Porsche (Germany)
- Nokia (Finland)
- Phillips Lamp (Netherlands)
- Jardine Matheson (Hong Kong)
- RyanAir (Ireland)
- WPP (United Kingdom).

One of the main reasons for an ADR issue is if a European company is acquiring a US company. The Daimler-Benz purchase of Chrysler in 1998 was fully funded with ADRs, as was a large portion of the purchase of AirTouch by the UK company Vodafone. As with the bond market, we see that activity in equities is greatly affected by merger and acquisition activity.

The purchase of ADRs by US investors allows them access to foreign stock holdings, but as technology improves and the world moves closer to standardised trading systems, their appeal might be expected to diminish. By the end of 1998 only 23 per cent of total US investment in European equities was in the form of ADRs, with the rest held in local currency form[4]. This raises a general question as to the scope for further internationalisation of equity trading. The statistical evidence points to a world in which equity investors are buying foreign stocks and an increasing number of companies are seeking foreign market listings, but the twin obstacles of regulatory differences and alternative trading systems need to be tackled before the equity markets can truly be described as global.

Strategic Tax Planning

Tax planning forms a part of the overall financial strategy of a company, and so has primarily long-term implications for company funding and cash flow. Tax planning will cover a number of areas, including investment decisions and pricing decisions. For international companies engaged in foreign direct investment, the planning will also cover location decisions and transfer pricing policies.

The link between taxation and financial strategy is as follows:

- National rules on, for example, tax relief for capital investments may vary. The precise terms of relief may alter the net present value of a proposed investment, and so influence the choice of location.
- The rules on which costs are allowable against tax will differ between countries. This can mean that it is advantageous to locate heavy cost operations in specific locations.
- Tax payments have cash flow implications, which will alter the net present value of any future investments. At the same time, the precise cash flow pattern will influence the short-term borrowing needs for the company, and hence the overall cost of capital.

In seeking to minimise its world-wide tax liability, a company may wish to manage its internal pricing system in such a way as to maximise the profits earned in low tax rate countries. The extent to which it is possible to pursue such a policy will depend on the precise terms of international tax agreements between the countries involved.

Mini Case Study

A Japanese company recently purchased four aircraft at cost of $170 million, which it then leased on to Indian Airlines. The objective was to take advantage of the depreciation allowances available on the aircraft, which could be used to reduce the company's tax bill. At the same time, Indian Airlines benefited from the deal, because the ten-year lease agreement was at a lower cost than would have been possible using loan finance.

All in all then, tax can serve to significantly influence both the cash position and the return on capital of a company. In the light of this, it is useful for managers to understand some of the basic thinking behind international taxation in the world today.

Taxation of Foreign Earnings

The tax effects of foreign operations are dependent on the format of doing business in any particular location. A useful way of classifying alternative formats distinguishes between doing business *with* versus business *in* a country.

In dealing with, but not in, a country, a company is selling goods or services to an overseas buyer without undertaking the risk of any direct foreign investment. At the simplest level, this means straightforward exporting, but as the amount of trade increases, it might also include franchising or selling under licence.

The tax effect of such dealings is that the company will be liable to pay tax on its overseas profits, but to whom? The answer is dependent on where the earnings originate.

In the case of the exporter, the general rule is that even when sales are made via a local agent, the tax on earnings is due to the company's domestic government. The critical factor is WHERE the contract is made. If orders are always referred back to the parent office, then no foreign tax liability is likely to arise.

In contrast, in the case of both licensing and franchising, overseas tax liabilities will arise. In both situations, royalty payments are made from the overseas operator back to the parent company, and tax is due on these payments. If a company paid foreign tax on income received from royalties, and then incurred domestic tax liabilities on those same earnings, it would have been subjected to double taxation. This is deemed to be potentially damaging to trade, and so many countries now operate double taxation agreements. A double taxation agreement is an agreement whereby the liability to tax from foreign operations is the subject of a treaty between two or more countries.

The precise terms of these agreements will vary quite widely, and in planning for tax a company must pay close attention to the fine detail of tax treaties. In many cases, double taxation agreements also include specification of the terms under which tax paid on overseas earnings can be offset against the domestic tax liability on those same earnings. The extent of relief granted may vary between individual countries, and it may be that individual governments will not grant full relief when the foreign tax rate exceeds the domestic one. Suppose that the tax rate in Country X is 60 per cent and so tax due from royalty payments equals £600,000. In Country Y the tax rate is 30 per cent, and the government may limit the tax relief available to £300,000, i.e. the tax rate chargeable on domestic earnings. In such a situation, the company has still incurred some double taxation.

In addition to the taxes on earnings, a company will need to consider the rules on indirect taxation, such as value added tax (VAT). The VAT rules vary widely between countries, both in terms of the rates applicable, and the breadth of goods and services on which the tax is chargeable. In the light of this, it is best to consult experts in one of the international accounting firms. All such firms have specialist taxation departments which will advise on such issues.

As might be expected, the tax considerations for companies with direct investments overseas, i.e. doing trade *within* a country, are more complex in nature. Individual nations vary in the fine detail of their legislation regarding the basis on which a company is regarded as being 'resident' for tax purposes. In general terms, however, resident is used to describe a business which has a permanent establishment in a particular country. Permanent establishment is defined in the OECD model tax treaty as 'a fixed place of business through which an entity wholly or partly conducts its operations.' The place of business may be a showroom, storage facilities, manufacturing operation or distribution point, but national tax rules will dictate the tax position of each type of establishment.

Radebaugh and Gray[5] suggest that two styles of taxation legislation can be identified in relation to the earnings of foreign corporations: the territorial approach, and the world-wide approach.

The territorial approach takes the view that earnings should be taxed in the country where it is earned. Hong Kong is one country which adopts this approach, which means that for a German company with a branch in Hong Kong, the branch earnings would be viewed as liable to Hong Kong tax. In contrast, the world-wide approach which is adopted in the UK and the USA, taxes companies on all earnings, regardless of whether they originate from domestic or foreign operations. This approach leads to the problem of potential double taxation, as in the case of licensing and franchising companies. The way in which the tax bill is reduced is via similar use of taxation treaties which offer credit against tax paid overseas.

So far, there has been an assumption that the principles of taxation are reasonably common world-wide, but this is not in fact the case. A number of tax havens exist, which are used for tax planning purposes. Examples include Bermuda, the Channel Islands and Gibraltar. Some of these countries offer zero or very low rates of tax to foreign companies; others, such as Luxembourg act as centres for foreign holding companies. It is naive to think that tax can be avoided by registering in a tax haven and using that company as a vehicle through which to pass the bulk of company income. National governments are all too aware of the potential losses to revenue that would result, and have responded by introducing restrictive legislation. In the UK, for example, the controlled foreign companies legislation regards income earned in a tax haven as attributable to UK shareholders, unless specific conditions are met. Such legislation severely limits the usefulness of tax havens in tax planning.

SUMMARY

The aim of this chapter has been to introduce the role of the finance function in an international company, describe trends in the international financial markets and outline the main sources of finance for international companies. Managers cannot plan foreign operations without the knowledge that the required funding will be available when needed. The type, cost and scale of funding for foreign ventures differs, however, from that available for domestic operations. In this chapter we have looked at each of the sources in turn, ranging from short-term forfaiting, for example, through to global equity issues. Each type of finance has its place in the funding portfolio. In addition, the company finance director must be aware of the different tax rules for each country within which his business operates. By using such knowledge to the company's advantage, it may be possible to boost earnings per share.

In planning the financing of operations and the sourcing of profit world-wide, however, it must always be remembered that financial strategy is just one part of overall corporate strategy. The truly successful company makes sure that the two are never divorced.

CONCLUSION

Establishing a strategy for getting access to the money needed for international business is the first important role of the finance function. The second role is to make sure that in raising the funds, and in engaging in business transactions overseas, the financial risks to the company are managed carefully. This means paying particularly close attention to the question of foreign exchange risk, which is the subject of the next chapter.

References

1 Reed, H.C. (1989) 'Financial Centre hegemony, interest rates and the global economy', Chapter 16 in *International banking and financial centres*, eds. Y.S. Park and N. Essayyad, Kluwer Academic, Boston, MA.

2 Dicken, P. *Global Shift: transforming the world economy*, Chapman Paul, London

3 Demirag, I. and Goddard, S. (1994) *Financial Management for International Business*, McGraw Hill 1994

4 Bank of England (1993) *Cross Border alliances in banking and financial services in the single market*, Bank of England Quarterly Bulletin, August 1993 pp.372–378.

5 Radebaugh, L. and Gray, S. (1993) *International Accounting and Multinational Enterprises*, 3rd Edition, Wiley and Sons

Further Reading

References (3) and (5) above are useful textbooks, which look in some detail at international finance issues. Additionally, publications from specific markets are also useful, for example, London Stock Exchange booklets published in the UK. Journals which regularly feature articles on issues of international finance include:

Bank of England Quarterly Bulletin
Euromoney
Journal of Banking and Finance
Journal of Money Credit and Banking
Journal of International Business Studies
Journal of International Money and Finance
The Treasurer

Unless you are studying a finance or accounting degree, however, you may find that some of the terminology used in these journals is difficult to understand. In addition, for practical examples, and up to date market reports, there is no substitute for the financial newspapers such as the *Wall Street Journal* or *Financial Times*.

TUTORIAL EXERCISE

Students should bring to the tutorial a range of articles extracted from the latest week's copies of the business pages of the broadsheet papers such as *The Times, Daily Telegraph, New York Times, Le Monde, Corriere della Serra,* and the *Financial Times*. The articles should detail either investments by companies in overseas locations, or funds raised by them in the international financial markets. A tutorial discussion can then be built around the content of the articles, covering issues such as the size of the investments/issues, location, currency used etc.

ESSAY QUESTIONS

1 The chapter suggests that the financial markets are confident about the future of the Euro. Is this confidence working to raise the value of the currency relative to other major currencies such as the US dollar, and if not, why?

2 If the United Kingdom remains outside the Eurozone, does this make it a less attractive place for foreign direct investment?

3 Discuss why the internationalisation of the financial markets is a vital prerequisite for the internationalisation of business generally.

Case Study: The Impact of the European Common Currency on the Banking Sector

This case study assumes a basic understanding of the idea of the common currency.

Introduction

A survey carried out by the EU Banking Association suggested that the transition to the common currency (EMU) will have a substantial impact on the international strategy, funding methods and markets of the major European banks. At the same time, the changeover is expected to generate substantial extra costs for banks.

This case study looks at the ways in which banking are affected as the currency and money markets adapt to the new 'Eurozone'.

How Banks Have Been Affected

The adoption of the common currency has not been universal across all EU countries, as the level of political and commercial support for the move varies widely. The result is a two-tier banking system, with the banks from non-integrated countries seeking to maintain market share and profit margins in a transformed marketplace. A comparative advantage may be gained by banks that act quickly to take advantage of the changes wrought by monetary union.

Specific ways in which monetary union affect the banking sector include:

1 Cost increases

Large costs resulting from a need to implement the technical changes associated with the Euro, e.g. alterations to clearing systems and preparation of new Euro chequebooks / transfer forms.

The exact costs of such changes are difficult to calculate as the level of use of Euro denominated bank accounts amongst private (retail) customers has not yet been assessed. In the meantime, the dual currency basis for operations further increases costs until the final changeover date and introduction of Euro coinage and notes.

2 Elimination of markets

Foreign exchange trade between member countries has effectively disappeared, as export sales are denominated in the common currency. This has affected both the cash and derivatives (swaps and options) markets in European currencies, leading to lost revenue for banks.

For example, trade customers in the Eurozone no longer need to hedge a currency risk in the French Franc, because the invoice is in Euros.

3 Disappearance of local credit and money markets as sources of finance for overseas trade/investment

Local markets are no longer required, as Euro-wide funding sources are available for use with zero currency risk.

Implications

The domestic marketplace for banks within the Eurozone has been be redefined as the common currency area, rather than in terms of national boundaries as at present. The result has been increased competition in the banking sector, accompanied by an increase in the level of cross-border merger and acquisition activity. Banks operating outside the common currency area face potentially higher funding costs, partly due to currency risks, and consequently lower credit ratings. One view is that they could end up simply as credit rating agencies.

Source: This case study is based on an article by J. Gapper entitled 'Europe Faces ECU 225 million bank charge', published in the *Financial Times*, Sept 20 1994

CASE STUDY QUESTIONS

1 Should governments intervene to help the banks meet the costs of moving towards a common currency?

2 What are the implications for bank customers in the UK, if the UK chooses to remain outside the single currency?

3 Would non entry into the Eurozone threaten the future of London as the banking centre of Europe?

CHAPTER SEVEN

Foreign Exchange Risk Management

LEARNING OUTCOMES

After reading this chapter you should be confident that you are able to:

- Describe the financial risks involved in foreign trading and investment
- Explain how economic and monetary union in the EU and the single currency will affect foreign exchange risks for companies operating in member countries
- Describe the basic method of operation of the spot and forward markets
- Explain how hedging might be used to reduce foreign currency risks experienced by a company that trades overseas
- Trace the effect of foreign trading activity on working capital management

The list of objectives is fairly extensive, and covers areas of some complexity. You may therefore find it helpful to study the chapter section by section rather than at a single study session.

INTRODUCTION

You may recall that in the chapter on international strategy, that the overwhelming reason for choosing to internationalise operations was to increase corporate growth potential and profit. Expansion into foreign markets offers new opportunities but also creates more risks, particularly financial ones, and it is the task of accountants and corporate treasurers to advise on how to reduce those risks.

Some indication of the nature and extent of the financial risks that are encountered can be gleaned from study of the annual reports of international companies. The quotations given below are typical of the type of commentary that may be found in such reports.

> 'The Group seeks to cover exposure to exchange rate fluctuations on trade receivables and payables – provided that the costs of doing so would not, in the opinion of the Directors, be prohibitive'
>
> John Laing plc, Annual Report 1998, p.24

In other words, exchange rate movements can affect the size of payments both to and from overseas. If sums that a company may expect to receive fall because of a change in the exchange rate, then it will find that its profits are squeezed if costs remain unchanged. It may be equally likely that an exchange rate movement leads to a rise in the prices the company has to pay for overseas components, and this would also lead to a fall in the profit margin if selling prices are fixed. What makes this particularly worrying is that the direction of change in the exchange rate is uncertain, and totally outside the control of the individual company.

As the quotation above indicates, the company also faces additional costs if it chooses to eradicate the uncertainty of such fluctuations by covering its exchange rate exposure in the financial markets. 'Hedging', as this is called, costs money. In simple terms then, exchange rate changes are of importance to company revenues and costs, in other words their overall profitability.

This is clearly demonstrated in the following extract from the 1998 annual report of Dorling Kindersley Holdings plc., a publishing group which produces reference books, CD-ROMs and videos for sale across the world:

> 'Turnover in the rest of the world (i.e. excluding the UK and USA) reduced by 2 per cent with licensing revenues declining, principally due to the sustained strength of sterling combined with the economic problems in the Far East'
>
> Dorling Kindersley Holdings, 1998 Report and Accounts, p.2

The importance of exchange rates is reinforced four pages further on in the report, when in the Operating and Financial Review it is noted that:

> 'Sterling strengthened further in the year against all major currencies and, given that 73 per cent of the Group's revenues arise in overseas markets, the impact on both reported revenues and profits was significant.'
>
> Dorling Kindersley Holdings, 1998 Report and Accounts, p.6

This brief but simple comment says a great deal, and forcefully reiterates the influence of exchange rates on financial performance for all companies engaged in international business.

This chapter deals with the measurement and control of the financial impact of international operations, with specific reference to exchange rate risks. The financial impact is measured in terms of the effect upon the key financial statements, that is, the profit and loss account, balance sheet, statement of recognised gains and losses, and cash flow. Exchange rate risks are classified under the headings of economic, transaction, and translation risks. Control of the impact is assumed to operate via the use of hedging techniques, the most important of which are described in some detail.

THE FINANCIAL RISKS OF INTERNATIONAL TRADE AND INVESTMENT

It is common practice to summarise the financial risks of foreign trade or investment under three headings:

- Economic Risk
- Transaction Risk
- Translation Risk.

The headings are useful because in combination they illustrate that foreign involvement affects all of the financial statements of a business. Additionally, the effects are both short term and long term in duration.

Economic Risk

Economic risk occurs when there is a risk that actual and forecast cash flows will differ as a consequence of exchange rate movements. This is important because, according to finance theory, the present value of a company's future cash flows can be used to determine its market value.

Stock markets world-wide are continually revising their valuation of quoted stocks; the overall market value of a company is the value per single unit of equity multiplied by the number of equity shares in issue. The current value of each share is computed by discounting the future cash flows that will accrue to that share. The cash flows are generated by the company in the course of its business, which will be transacted in a variety of different products and also various market locations. As a general rule, as the value of forecast cash flows rises, so too will the value of the company.

The value of future cash flows is dependent upon a variety of factors both internal and external to the company, one of which is exchange rates. The quoted extract from the report of Dorling Kindersley Holdings contained comment on the detrimental effect of economic problems in the Far East: the 'Asia Crisis' of the late 1990s. During the crisis the value of some currencies, notably the Japanese Yen, declined dramatically, and this affected the cash flows of companies engaged in trading with Japan.

As suggested above, the term 'economic risk' is used to refer to the impact of exchange rate movements on cash flows and cash flow forecasts. When the cash flows are below those expected, the share price of a company will fall, or vice versa. This means that if a company is trading in an environment which is subject to high levels of economic risk, i.e. very volatile currencies, theory suggests that this will have the effect of making its share price more volatile. In practice, most companies will hedge the exchange risk in a number of ways, and so the share price effect will be reduced, but Directors need to be aware that economic risk *can* affect share prices.

For example, suppose that a US-based company exports 85 per cent of its turnover to Italy, and the Italian Lira is depreciating relative to the US Dollar. There is a risk that even if Italian sales grow rapidly over the next ten years, profit and cash flow will not, because the Dollar value of those earnings is falling. The fall in the dollar value is purely a consequence of the relative depreciation of the Lira, a factor which is external to the company but nonetheless affects the company's market worth.

In order to reduce share price volatility and minimise the economic risk, many companies respond by choosing to both buy and sell in a number of different countries, thus creating a 'portfolio' of currency exposure. The hope is that over the long term, gains in cash flows from one currency will serve to offset losses in cash flows in another currency, thereby reducing the overall economic risk.

It is important to remember that economic risk is concerned with long-term uncertainties. This means that it is very difficult to measure, but does not mean that it can be ignored. At the same time, stock market investors are frequently accused of being short-termist in their requirements, and if this is the case then they may not place great emphasis on the level of economic exposure.

In contrast, it *is* certain that investors attach great importance to the performance of a business as revealed in its profit and loss account. For this reason the transaction risk associated with foreign trading is particularly important.

Transaction Risk

Transaction risk is a simple concept; it describes a risk that arises because most goods and services are sold on credit. If the deal is undertaken in a currency other than that of the seller, then the seller may find that changes in exchange rates mean that the sum received differs from that expected. A short illustration is useful to show how the risk arises.

Deere and Co. is a well known US-based agricultural and industrial equipment manufacturer. Suppose that they receive a contract from a German wholesaler for 200 tractors, at a price of Euros46,000 each. The exchange rate on the date of issue of the invoice is 1Eur = 0.92USD. The invoice is paid three months later, when the exchange rate is 1Eur = 0.90USD.

At the exchange rate prevailing at the invoice date, the dollar value of the invoice is:

46,000 x 200 x 0.92 = US$8,464,000

At the exchange rate prevailing at the date of payment, the dollar value of the sum received is:

46,000 x 200 x 0.90 = US$8,280,000

The second figure is US$184,000 lower than the first. Few companies can afford to see the cash flow from a single sale fall by such a large amount, even if they trade on high gross margins. Sometimes exchange rate movements can turn a profitable deal into an unprofitable one. Transaction risk therefore affects the profit and loss account, and reflects the impact of short-term movements in exchange rates. For example, in its 1998 annual report, the sports retailer JJB Sports reported a fall in profits of £103,000 caused by exchange rate movements. For this reason transaction risk is the exchange risk which is generally regarded as being the most important, and is most frequently hedged. The alternative forms of hedging are discussed in the next section of this chapter.

Translation Risk

There is a fundamentally important link between the profit and loss account and the balance sheet. When a company earns a profit, and chooses to retain some of that profit rather than pay it out in dividends, the retention adds to the capital base of the company, and therefore facilitates the purchase of more assets. Profit is thus a means of strengthening the balance sheet.

If profit is earned overseas, and used to buy foreign assets, then at the end of the accounting year, when the financial statements are prepared, the value of those foreign assets will need to be 'translated' into the domestic currency of the parent company. There is a risk that, year on year, the value of those assets will change purely as a consequence of changes in exchange rates. It is this risk which is referred to as translation risk.

> Translation risk is the risk that foreign held assets (or liabilities) will change in value from one year to the next, purely as a result of exchange rate movements.

If the risk relates to a change in values, it follows that the values may go up or down. As the definition shows, the variation in value relates to both assets and liabilities, and so a drop in the value of a liability might be regarded as good, whereas a fall in the value of an asset might be viewed as bad. In the case of Morrison Construction plc., a UK-based company, the 1998 annual report shows a £35,000 increase in the company's net debt, caused purely by exchange rate movements. Similarly, in the notes to the 1998 accounts of Dorling Kindersley Holdings there is shown an exchange rate adjustment which results in a drop of £103,000 in the cost of, and depreciation charged on, tangible fixed assets. This is equivalent to saying that these assets cost less, but are also now worth less, purely because of the movement in exchange rates. This change in value does not matter, however, because it is not converted into a cash loss until the assets in question are sold. The term given to such changes in value is thus an 'unrecognised' or 'unrealised' loss/gain (as appropriate). The extent to which a company is exposed to translation risk is determined by the difference between the value of overseas assets and liabilities. This is illustrated in Figure 7.1.

Figure 7.1   *Positive versus Negative Translation Exposure*

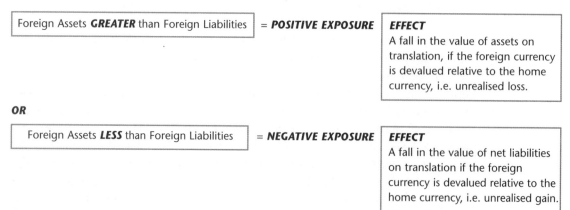

A simple way to reduce translation risk is therefore to match foreign held assets with liabilities denominated in the same currency, so that the balance sheet impact of changes in exchange rates is eliminated/mimimised. This form of hedging is known as matching, and is explained in detail later in this chapter.

It is important to understand that translation risk is concerned with a change in the accounting value of assets or liabilities, and this does not imply a *real* change in cash flows. If exchange rate movements result in the post translation value of a foreign held factory site changing from £3 million to £2 million between 1992 and 1993, the drop in value may reduce the asset base on the balance sheet, but it does not involve any cash flow. The 'loss' is therefore unrealised. Similarly, any increases in the value of foreign assets, when caused solely by changes in exchange rates, represent unrealised gains.

As translation risk does not affect cash flows, the general view is that it is not necessary to hedge such risks. The logic for this goes back to the finance theory stated earlier, that the value of equity (individual or total) is dictated by the present value of future cash flows. Hence it is only necessary to hedge those foreign exchange risks which affect cash flows.

The fact that there is no associated cash flow, no realisation of gains or losses, and no need to hedge, may lead companies to take the view that translation risk can be ignored. This would be wrong. Some measure of the value of overseas earnings and the associated capital investment is regularly required for financial reporting purposes. In addition, both management and investors need to be able to assess profitability and return on capital for the overall business. Consolidated accounts drawn up using translated figures are needed to enable such assessments to be made. This means that for practical purposes management need to be aware of translation risk, and its impact on the key accounting ratios in the consolidated accounts. At the same time it is not a risk which needs to be actively managed.

Accounting rules vary from nation to nation in respect of the way in which balance sheet values should be arrived at for the purposes of year-end translation. There are two main alternative choices regarding the exchange rate that should be used for the purposes of translation. These are explained below:

Closing Rate Method: the balance sheet values are translated using the exchange rate prevailing at the time that the balance sheet is prepared.

Temporal Method: The rate used is the one prevailing at the time the asset/liability was acquired.

These are a simplified view of the alternatives available. Accounting conventions within different countries actually give rise to more than two alternatives but the accounting complexity of them is outside the scope of this book. The end of chapter references can be used to find texts that describe the fine detail of accounting for foreign exchange transactions, and consolidating the accounts of overseas subsidiaries. Such texts also deal with the important issue of how to account for foreign exchange gains or losses; for example, should they be written off immediately, or dealt with via the reserves?

It is important to note that these rules should be viewed as country specific, e.g. SSAP20 is used in the UK, and this differs in a number of respects from FASB 52 which is applied in the USA. Once again, however, these financial accounting details are beyond the scope of this book.

THE IMPACT OF EMU AND THE COMMON CURRENCY

In January 1999 a common currency was introduced, which can be used for commercial transactions across a total of eleven European countries within the European Union. The common currency is the Euro, and the member countries of EMU are:

- Austria
- Belgium
- Finland
- France
- Germany
- Republic of Ireland
- Italy
- Luxembourg
- Netherlands
- Portugal
- Spain.

Note that not all members of the European Union are also members of EMU. The non-member countries (Greece, Denmark and the United Kingdom) are non-members because they have chosen not to have their national currencies locked to the Euro at a fixed rate established in January 1999. This is largely because the use of a common currency, in addition to a fixed exchange rate, requires acceptance of the principle of a common monetary policy, common interest rates and a European Central Bank. It is expected that referendums will be held in the non-member countries to determine whether they will become full members of EMU in the future.

The introduction of the Euro in 1999 was confined to the money and financial markets, but it is intended to bring in notes and coins in 2002. The three-year intervening period allows time for both businesses and individuals to familiarise themselves with the Euro, alongside the continued dismantling of barriers to cross-border capital movements.

From the perspective of foreign exchange risk, the concept of a common currency is very attractive, because if eleven countries conduct transactions in the same currency, then all types of foreign exchange risk are eliminated: economic, transaction and translation risks. This will lead to savings for companies in these countries, who are no longer having to pay transactions costs to convert from one currency to another. Writing in the *European Business Journal* in 1998, Malcolm Levitt estimated that the value of the eliminated transactions costs would amount to 0.4 per cent of the Gross Domestic Product of member states.

The largest savings are going to accrue to businesses in the member countries which choose to transact all of their business in Euros, and hence eradicate all of the costs of currency exchange. For the UK and the other non-member countries, these savings will only be available if they decide to switch to using the Euro, instead of the domestic currency, as the base currency for all transactions. In the meantime, and regardless of location, companies have been forced to spend large sums of money on new accounting, billing and IT systems in preparation for the introduction of the Euro.

The extent of foreign exchange exposure which a company will face in what is being called 'Euroland', is dependent upon their scale of use of the new currency. This may range from isolated transactions, such as payment of an invoice which is denominated in Euros, to maintenance of a Euro bank account through which both payments and receipts are processed, or full use of Euros for all domestic and European transactions. The more popular the use of the Euro as a currency for invoicing and payment, the greater will be the opportunity cost of continuing to use any other currency.

There is growing evidence that even small businesses which sell only into the domestic market may still be affected by the common currency. Writing in *Management Today* in early 1999, Alexander Garrett indicated that companies such as Siemens, Rover and ICI have made it clear to UK suppliers that they will be conducting business in Euros from 1999 onwards. This means that a London-based firm supplying components to the Rover factory in Coventry, may receive its payment in Euros and not in sterling. The additional costs of converting the payment back into sterling (which may be significant for small businesses), and hedging the transaction risks, will reduce profits.

For the larger multinational companies, with operations spread across the whole of Europe, it makes most sense for them to simply convert to Euro operations, which ignore the existence of national currencies in Euroland. ICI has already indicated that if the Euro proves to be a success, then it will move towards the use of the Euro as the base currency. This is regarded as a potentially vital move in order to protect competitive position, because currency conversion can add 3–4 per cent to costs, thereby making a company's prices uncompetitive compared with the rest of Europe. The conclusion is thus that the single currency offers huge potential benefits, but only to those businesses that use it to the full.

HEDGING FOREIGN EXCHANGE RISK: GENERAL ISSUES

In Chapter 5 on corporate strategy, it was suggested that in undertaking foreign operations, companies face a trade off between risk and control. This trade off can be particularly well applied in the context of foreign exchange risk. The exporter encounters a transaction risk which can be hedged by dealing in a variety of currencies to create a portfolio effect. At the opposite end of the control spectrum, the company which owns overseas investments has to accept the additional translation risk. Both parties will experience economic risk. This means that ALL companies engaged in international operations need to decide on the extent to which they wish to actively protect themselves against foreign exchange risk by hedging. The term hedging refers to any facility which is used with the express purpose of reducing risk.

A hedging facility may be organised internally by a company, or may be organised by making use of external markets, such as the forward currency markets. Hedging is used to reduce a variety of different types of financial risk. Here we are solely concerned with foreign exchange risks.

If hedging is used to reduce risk, then the Treasurer of any international company faces something of a dilemma. Should the hedging strategy be comprehensive and cover all risk, or should it be selective? Each hedge has an associated cost, and so by choosing to hedge only key contracts or exposure above a certain value, there is the potential to save money. Most companies choose selective hedging, on the grounds that full cover would be prohibitively expensive and complex to organise. One difficulty, however, is that in making selections of deals to hedge, the company faces the risk of effectively speculating in the currency markets.

Suppose, for example, that large receipts are due which are denominated in Japanese Yen, and the Yen is a currency that is strengthening relative to the domestic currency of the parent company. The company treasurer might decide that it is pointless to hedge a receipt in a currency that is getting stronger: this is the opposite of the example given earlier (Deere & Co.). What is happening here is that the Treasurer is seeking to reduce the risk by speculating that the Yen, the currency receivable, will continue to strengthen. If the currency in fact falls in value, then profits will be reduced.

The boundary between speculation and selective hedging is somewhat difficult to draw. A common way of distinguishing between speculation and protection against risk is to look at the whether the foreign exposure relates to commercial transactions. It is to be expected that companies will wish to manage currency exposures arising out of their normal trading activity. If foreign exchange dealing extends beyond the scale of those transaction exposures, then the likelihood is that the Treasury department is engaging is some speculative activity.

In most Western nations, accounting rules limit the ability of companies to speculate on currencies in this way. In the UK, for example, company law limits the activities of a company to those listed in its Articles of Association. This means that active participation in the speculative buying and selling of foreign currencies would be, at least, frowned upon and, at worst, illegal.

Checks will be made by the auditors in respect of the activities of the Treasury operation, but ultimate responsibility lies with the internal management.

As already suggested, the aim behind hedging, in contrast to speculation, is the reduction of risk. The extent to which risk needs to be reduced in the context of foreign exchange management, should reflect the level of risk viewed as acceptable elsewhere within the company. Different managers and investors groups will have different appetites for risk, and higher risk levels imply greater share price volatility and uncertainty regarding earnings per share. The company's approach to foreign exchange management should reflect its tolerance for risk and the overall objectives of investors. Risk averse management should not seek to make profits out of its currency dealings – merely to bring the financial risk down to tolerable levels.

In the light of this it can be argued that there is a need for disclosure of exchange management policies in annual reports. This would then allow investors to make informed judgements as to whether they were happy with the risk profile adopted by a company. Those who wish to avoid investing in companies that view Treasury departments as profit centres could do so, and the cost centre versus profit centre approach to currency management would be brought out into the open. Indeed in the

UK, the Accounting Standards Board's view is that companies should include a description of their approach to foreign currency management in the Operating and Financial Review.

Some companies do in fact already declare their policy, as illustrated by the extract from the annual report of John Laing's given below:

> 'Group Treasury provides a service to the corporate centre and to the operating divisions to enable risk to be managed at the lowest possible cost. Treasury is not a profit centre.
>
> John Laing plc., Annual Report 1998, p.24

Such a statement is far more enlightening than the usual note that appears in the accounts, which simply informs the reader that the local accounting standards have been followed in preparing the accounts.

In the light of the increasing complexity of many financial instruments, and the problems that they create for financial accounting, it seems reasonable to hope that the number of companies making such declarations as part of the standard reporting system will increase.

Before considering the detail of alternative hedging methods it is worthwhile recalling the key points covered so far:

■ Currency values' changes create a financial risk for international companies.

■ The risk may take the form of:

Transaction Risk;
Translation Risk;
Economic Risk.

■ Hedging can be used to reduce risk, and the primary concern of management is to reduce the risk to future cash flows, as these determine the value of the company.

■ Transaction risk is concerned with short-term cash flows.

■ Translation risk is concerned with the value of balance sheet items.

■ Economic risk deals with long-term cash flows.

■ This means that risk which is given most attention in hedging is transaction risk.

■ The introduction of the single currency will eliminate the foreign exchange risk between member countries.

HEDGING FOREIGN EXCHANGE RISK: THE DETAILS

In seeking to protect itself from transaction risk, a company may apply a variety of different hedging techniques, either in isolation or in combination. These are detailed below.

Invoice Currency

At the simplest level, an exporter can pass the risk of a change in the exchange rate over to the foreign buyer, by invoicing in the exporter's own currency. Needless to say, it is likely that the buyer will not take on the currency risk without some compensation, perhaps in the form of discounted prices. Even this simple form of hedging therefore has a cost.

Matching

Transaction risk only arises when there is a mismatch in respect of in the *net* value of receipts or payments in foreign currencies. This means that if, for example, a Singapore-based company knows that it needs to make a payment of $US20,000 in three months' time it faces the risk that the value of the payment when expressed in terms of $Singapore may change over the three-month period, and may increase. If, however, the company organises its operations such that it has invoiced a foreign buyer in US dollars, and is due to receive $US20,000 in three months' time, then there is no net exposure. The risk has been fully hedged. Matching can be applied to receipts and payments to or from both external or internal suppliers or customers. It is therefore particularly useful for large group organisations where there is a large volume of inter-group sales in a variety of different currencies. Such matching may be quite difficult to organise in practice, as it requires that both the time-scale and the value of deals are matched. Where the match is not perfect, any outstanding net exposure can then be hedged using external markets.

Matching is also used to reduce translation risk exposures, via the matching of assets and liabilities in a common currency. For example, the construction and engineering company John Laing plc. declared in their 1998 annual report: 'The US$ denominated assets in the US housing operations are matched by US$ denominated borrowings in order to minimise the effect of exchange rate movements on net assets.' By borrowing dollars, they are ensuring that if the sterling value of dollar assets reduces because of changes in the dollar:sterling rate, they will also benefit from a fall in the sterling value of the dollar borrowings. If the assets and liabilities are of similar size, the net exchange rate impact on the balance sheet is then zero.

Netting

This is effectively an extension of matching, but applied only to sales between companies that are part of the same group. For example, suppose that a UK site of Akzo Nobel Chemicals supplies a Dutch group member of the pharmaceutical division of Akzo. Some weeks later, there is a reverse sale, from the Dutch company to the UK company. It makes sense for the two transactions to be netted off, with only one payment of the net amount being made. Such an arrangement is known as bilateral netting.

In particularly large concerns, the process may be extended to become multilateral netting. Suppose that we increase the number of deals taking place within Akzo. A third Dutch member company supplies a UK subsidiary in Akzo's coatings division.

The result is two-way currency flows between several member companies in the Akzo group. By centralising the foreign exchange dealings the currency flows can be netted in aggregate instead of bilaterally. Multilateral netting works by means of each member company regularly reporting all foreign currency payment and receipt balances to a central treasury division. The division is then responsible for netting off the flows in each currency, and instructing individual subsidiaries on the net sums to be paid or received. Figure 7.2 illustrates how netting can be used to reduce the required number of foreign exchange deals.

Figure 7.2   *Multilateral Netting*

Net receipts due	$US net payments due				
	US	Switzerland	Australia	Germany	Total
US parent	Nil	12,000	450	6,500	18,950
Swiss subsidiary	4,000	Nil	2,000	750	6,750
Australian subsidiary	100	5,200	Nil	800	6,100
German subsidiary	500	200	6,000	Nil	6,700
Total receipts	4,600	17,400	8,450	8,050	

This means that net transactions can be calculated as follows:

US Parent

Due to pay $18,950 to other group companies, and receive back $4,600. A net payment of $14,350 is thus required.

Swiss Subsidiary

Receipts due total $17,400 and payments total $6,750, giving net receipts of $10,650.

Australian Subsidiary

Receipts due sum to $8,450 but payments amount to $6,100 leaving a balance of $2,350 receivable.

German Subsidiary

Due to pay $6,700 but receive back $8,050 giving net receipts of $1,350

Note that the sum of net payments exactly equals net receipts, i.e.

The US parent is a net payer of a total of $14,350

The subsidiaries are net recipients of

$10,650 + $2,350 + $1,350 = $14,,350

The result of netting is that only three payments are required; the parent company needs to make a payment to each of the subsidiary companies. This is much simpler than the original position, in which each individual concern would have paid each other party. The total number of payments without netting would have totalled twelve.

The reduction in the number of payments required results in lower banking and dealing costs, so that investors in the group will benefit from higher reported profits.

The Electrolux Group is one example of a company which uses multilateral netting to reduce dealing costs. The Group's Annual Report for 1993 indicates that 80 per cent of commercial transactions in foreign currencies relate to inter-company deals. The netting is used to reduce internal exposure and also 'enables the remaining currency flow to be continuously monitored.' By centralising transactions, the company is always aware of the scale and direction of its currency risk, and control of that risk is thus made easier.

A further advantage of centralised hedging operations is that the average size of deal is larger, and this allows companies to negotiate preferential terms when compared with the charges levied for multiple small transactions.

Leading and Lagging

When an importer needs to make a payment in a currency that is expected to strengthen, it is in his benefit to buy the foreign currency as soon as possible. The converse is true when the currency of payment is expected to depreciate in relative terms. The following example illustrates the process.

Example

A Portugese manufacturer sells shoes to a Norwegian importer to the value of Escudos 500,000. The current exchange rate is Esc24.36/N.Kr. The exchange rate in three months' time is expected to be Esc24.46/N.Kr.

This means that the Portugese currency is expected to weaken over the period, and it would be in the interests of the Norwegian importer to delay purchasing the required Escudos until immediately before payment is due.

By expressing the value of the import bill in Norwegian Kroner, the benefit is clearly illustrated.

Value of import bill at the current exchange rate

= 500,000/24.36
= 20,525.45 Norwegian Kroner

Value of import bill in three months' time

= 20,441.537 Norwegian Kroner

Leading or lagging is thus the process of managing the timing of purchase of a foreign currency payable, to take advantage of expected changes in exchange rates. Leading implies buying earlier, and paying the associated bill earlier, and lagging is the opposite.

Forward Contract

So far in discussing changes in exchange rates it has been assumed that it is possible to forecast the exchange rate in say, three months' time. This idea is not so fanciful as it may at first appear, because markets do exist to trade in currencies at an agreed rate, at a future point in time. These are the forward markets and they perform a useful function in serving the needs of both speculators and hedgers. In this chapter their role in providing a form of currency hedge is examined.

A quick reference back to the example in the previous section on leading and lagging should provide you with the answer.

A company needs to be reasonably certain of the trading margin on a deal, particularly if the market is highly competitive and so margins are narrow. The forward markets grant the opportunity for buyers and sellers of currencies to be certain of the value of a transaction. So how does the forward market work?

Not surprisingly, a price has to be paid for the certainty associated with a forward deal. The annual percentage cost of each forward rate is usually quoted alongside the rate. The exchange rates quoted are determined by the relative interest rates in the respective countries. The theory of exchange rate determination assumes purchasing power parity and interest rate parity, and freely floating exchange rates.

Table 7.1 is adapted from the layout for foreign exchange rates as used by the *Financial Times*.

Table 7.1   *Spot and Forward Exchange Rates against the Pound, October 1999*

	Closing Mid-Point	Bid/Offer Spread	One Month Rate	Three Months Rate
Belgium (B.Fr)	62.3677	342–011	62.2173	61.9414
France (FFr)	10.1415	360–469	10.117	10.072
Spain (Pta)	257.242	104–380	256.622	255.484
Canada (C$)	2.4354	338–369	2.4339	2.4297
Singapore (S$)	2.7948	931–964	2.7879	2.7735
Australia (A$)	2.5111	086–136	2.5099	2.5069
Taiwan (T$)	52.5755	579–930	52.6088	52.703

Once the terminology is understood, the mechanism of a forward contract is relatively easy to understand. The mid point figure is the mid point between the bid (buy) price and the offer (sell) price for the currency. For example, the exchange rate for French Francs/£ Sterling is shown above as 10.1415. This is best described as the 'average' exchange rate at close of trading the previous day. In order to determine the precise rate for buying or selling the currency the bid offer spread information has to be used.

For the French Franc the spread is 360–469. This means that the buy rate is 10.1360 and the sell rate is 10.1469.

This can be proved by taking the average of the two figures, and checking that this equals the mid point figure.

Proof

(10.1360 + 10.1469) / 2 = 10.1415

The spread between the two rates is the dealer's profit. It means that when selling French Francs, you need to give the trader more Francs per £1 sterling than you receive Francs when selling Sterling. This concept should be familiar to anyone who has sold foreign exchange when returning from an overseas vacation.

The closing rate given in the table is the current exchange rate, but the forward exchange rate is also quoted for both one and three months hence. The forward rate is simply the rate at which the market will buy or sell currency at a fixed point in the future. Most forward deals cover a three-month period as common trading terms grant the purchaser ninety days' credit. This allows a trader to hedge using the forward market by taking out a forward contract at the same time as the original transaction, e.g. shipping of exports is completed. A contract to buy or sell in the forward market is binding, and gives the company the advantage of being certain of the cost of the deal. The contract specifies the amount of currency being bought or sold, and the delivery date for the currency.

For example, suppose that a UK electrical chain bought supplies of video recorders from Taiwan. The invoice is for T$500,000, and is payable in three months' time. From Table 7.1, the three month forward rate for Sterling against the Taiwanese $ is T$52.703/£. The rate quoted is a mid point rate, and it would be necessary to confirm the buy/sell rates via a bank or foreign exchange dealer. In this case the supermarket has to pay T$ and so is a buyer of the foreign currency. Suppose that the three month buy rate is confirmed as T$52.690/£, the sterling value of the payment can now be calculated.

Sterling value using the forward rate
= 500,000/52.690
= £9,489

This compares with a value at the current exchange rate
= 500,000/52.5579
= £9,513

The Taiwanese dollar would appear to be depreciating relative to sterling, so that the value of the sum payable is falling. In such an instance, the buyer has two options:

■ decide to risk not taking out a forward contract in the hope that the dollar will depreciate more than the forward market implies, thus further reducing the sum payable;

or

■ choose to buy the currency forward to create certainty with regard to price. This may be particularly important to retailers, who may have already sold the goods before payment is finally made.

An understanding of whether the currency due to be paid or received is expected to weakening or strengthening is vital to the development of a coherent hedging policy. Where the currency payable is weakening, an importer may decide that hedging is unnecessary (as suggested in the earlier discussion). Conversely, if a currency payable is strengthening, a forward contract to buy that currency will be useful to limit the increase in value of the sum due. The opposite would be, of course, the case for exporters.

In practice this means that many multinational companies which have large foreign currency exposures have in-house forecasting units whose task is to predict future exchange rates. Where there are continually changing currency exposures, the short-term forward rate may not be of as much importance as the longer term trend in the rates. Forecasting such trends would, however, be the responsibility of the company, as a maximum of one year rates is available in the market.

It is important to note that forward rates are not shown for all currencies, for example the Argentinian peso, or the Brazilian dollar, although the number of currencies for which a forward market operates is continually increasing. For those currencies not quoted in the *Financial Times*, rates may be obtained direct from dealers for some, but not all currencies. This is because forward markets do not exist in all countries, particularly the small less developed nations, where foreign exchange is in scarce supply.

One of the unfortunate effects of hedging using the forward market is that it 'locks the company in' to the forward rate, and if sales are being made in a currency which is declining in value, i.e. depreciating, then even though the hedge protects the sterling worth of the receipts, it cannot protect against the depreciation, which will be built in to the forward rate. Dorling Kindersley Holdings suffered from precisely this problem in 1998 because they adopt a policy of fully hedging revenues via forward contracts. In the Operating and Financial Review section of their report and accounts, it is pointed out that the average hedged rate for Deutschmarks was DM2.8/£ in 1998, compared with DM2.3/£ in 1997. This drop in the value of the hedged receipts resulted in a £1.4 million drop in profits. The report acknowledges that 'such hedging brings certainty of sterling equivalent cash flows, but cannot protect the group against absolute adverse exchange rate impacts on earnings.'

Money Market Hedge

A money market hedge makes use of differences in interest rates between countries, which are not fully reflected in the forward exchange rates. If the currency markets are operating as perfect markets (in the economic sense), the cost of a money market hedge will exactly equal that of a forward market hedge, and so users will be indifferent between them.

A numerical example is the simplest way to illustrate how such a hedge works. A US company has sold goods to the value of DM25,000 to a German importer, and expects to receive payment in three months' time. Market information on interest rates and exchange rates is as follows:

Deutschmark loans	4.2%pa
Deutschmark deposits	3.5%pa
US dollar loans	6.75%pa
US dollar deposits	6.25%pa

Spot rate $/DM1.828
3 month rate $/DM1.818

The mechanism of the money market hedge is to borrow the currency due to be received, convert it at the spot rate back to the company's domestic currency, and place it on deposit until payment is received from the importer. When payment is made, the sum received is used to pay off the loan.

Step One

The payment due is DM25,000 and this will be used to repay the loan. The sum borrowed, at a rate of 4.2 per cent per annum, must therefore equal DM25,000 in three months' time, inclusive of interest charges over the period.

$$\text{Three month interest rate} = 4.2 / 4 \%$$
$$= 1.05\%$$

Sum to be borrowed is thus:
$$25,000 / 1.0105 = DM24,740$$

Step Two

The loan proceeds are converted at spot back to US dollars.
The dollar value is as follows:

$$= 24,740 / 1.828$$
$$= \$13,553$$

Step Three

The dollars are placed on deposit for three months, and earn an interest rate of 6.25 per cent per annum. This is equivalent to 1.5625 per cent over three months.

At the end of three months the value of the deposit is equal to:
$$= 13,553 \times 1.015625 \text{ dollars}$$
$$= \$13,765$$

Step Four

The Lire is taken off deposit when the loan has been paid off from the proceeds of the sale.

By use of the hedge the company has guaranteed for itself the receipt of a sum of $13,765 in three months' time.

This hedge is a direct alternative to a forward market hedge, and the company will select the hedge which yields the highest proceeds.

At the rates shown above, the value of the forward deal would be equal to:

$25,000 / 1.818 = $13,751

This is very close to the money market hedge value, and any difference in the value of the proceeds from a money market versus a forward hedge implies imperfections in the currency markets. The imperfections will be very short lived, and large companies will regularly monitor the relative worth of the two types of hedge, in order to take immediate advantage of any such imperfections.

Options

An option is similar to a forward contract, insofar as it represents an agreement to buy or sell currency at some time in the future. The difference is that an option does not have to be exercised, whereas a forward contract is binding. The purchaser of an option must therefore make a decision as to whether or not to exercise a specific option.

An option which confers a right to buy a fixed amount of currency at a pre-set price is a call option; one that confers a right to sell is a put option. The option works by the parties agreeing an exercise price; this is the exchange rate agreed for the currency if the option is exercised. There is a charge made for the option itself (the option premium), and this is paid upfront regardless of whether the option is exercised. The result is that the maximum cost of the hedge is the premium cost. Options are particularly attractive in situations in which there is some uncertainty regarding a transaction. The potential deal can be hedged at a cost equal to the premium charged, and then if the deal stalls no more expense is incurred and the company is not locked into a currency deal as would be the case with a forward contract. Alternatively, if the transaction does go ahead, the company has the opportunity to exercise or not exercise the option depending on the prevailing spot rate.

Options usually last for a period of three months, and over that time the spot price may vary both above and below the exercise price. The exchange rate variation represents a risk for the option buyer. If the option is a call option, then the risk is that the option exercise price will exceed the spot price for the currency. When this is the case, it is preferable to buy the currency in the spot market rather than exercise the option. In contrast, if the option is a put, then the concern is that the spot rate will be below the option exercise price. In this instance, it is again preferable to deal in the spot market rather than exercise the option.

Swaps

A simple currency swap takes the form of an agreement to exchange payments in one currency for payments in another. Frequently, swaps are arranged because a company wishes to expand in a country in which there are foreign exchange restrictions, or the local currency is non-convertible. Assume a Swedish company wishes to invest in construction of a manufacturing plant in Poland, but does not wish to directly exchange Swedish Krona for Polish Zloty. Polish banks are likely to be in need of hard currencies and so a swap should be relatively simple to arrange.

The swap works by means of the Swedish company depositing Krona in a Swedish bank, to the credit of the Polish bank. Simultaneously, the Polish bank places Zloties on deposit in Poland, in the name of the Swedish company. Over the period of the loan, the Swedish company pays interest on the loan in the Polish currency direct to the Polish bank, and the Polish bank makes interest payments in Krona to the Swedish bank. When the swap period expires, the respective currencies are repaid by the two parties.

The effect of the swap is to eliminate the long-term currency risk because the investment has effectively been financed by a Krona investment. There remains, however, a currency risk relating to the interest payments, and it is advisable to hedge these separately if possible.

Swaps are particularly attractive forms of hedge because they are often cheaper than conventional hedges. In addition, they represent a form of off-the-balance-sheet finance, and offer access to capital funds in countries where currency controls may be very tight and exchange rates volatile.

Currency Futures

Currency futures have declined in popularity in recent years, and are now traded on only a limited number of exchanges. The main market is the International Money Market based in Chicago.

A future is an obligation to buy or sell a fixed quantity of a commodity at some future point in time. The original futures markets dealt in commodities such as grain or soya beans, but the financial futures markets developed when it was recognised that currencies or interest rates are simply special types of commodities. The buyer of a futures contract is required to make a deposit equal to between 1 and 5 per cent of the contract value. Whilst on deposit this sum cannot earn interest, and so the lost interest forms part of the cost of this type of hedging instrument.

Currency futures are sold in blocks, e.g. Sterling futures are traded in £25,000 blocks. This means that to hedge a transaction of, say, £30,000 a single future contract would be bought. This would leave £5,000 unprotected, and a different form of hedge would need to be taken out to protect this balance. The fixed contract sums are an important disadvantage of futures deals.

If a currency is strengthening, the value of a futures contract denominated in that currency will rise. This means that if an importer faces a bill in the strengthening currency, if the position is unhedged the value of the bill will increase over time. If, however, a futures contract has been purchased, the gain in value of the contract will serve to offset the 'loss' from the increased bill value. It is very unlikely that the futures gain will exactly offset the exchange rate loss, but the mechanism does offer some protection.

THE IMPACT OF INTERNATIONAL TRADE ON WORKING CAPITAL

One of the risks of trade in general is the credit risk. With the exception of the retail trades, goods are sold on credit, and terms are set for the future payment of the invoice. The selling company thus needs to have the capital to offer such credit, and the greater the delay in receiving payment, the greater the funding that is required.

When overseas sales are involved, the complexity of agreeing that deliveries are complete and satisfactory and the general problem of distance often means that credit is granted for longer periods than would be usual for domestic sales. Collection of foreign debts is also more difficult and more costly, adding further to the working capital requirements.

A number of other factors serve to increase the financial risk of international sales when compared with domestic sales. Overall selling costs are likely to be higher, e.g. advertising and promotion, delivery costs, foreign exchange hedging charges. All of these cost increases add to the working capital needs of a company.

Higher working capital requirements mean higher financing costs for the business. This means that both operating *and* financing costs tend to increase as a company internationalises its operations. Needless to say, there will be a point at which scale economies take over, and costs flatten out, but in the intervening period companies need to remember that deciding to trade overseas will add to costs and capital funding needs. Both of these constitute additional financial risks, on top of the purely foreign exchange risks dealt with so far in this chapter.

SUMMARY

The aim of the chapter was to look in detail at the additional financial risks faced by companies that choose to trade internationally.

The risks can be categorised under the headings of transaction, translation and economic risk, but the type of risk faced is to some extent dependent on the nature of the international involvement. The foreign exchange exposure of a business which owns several foreign subsidiaries differs from that of an exporter.

Companies are primarily concerned about the effect of changing exchange rates on cash flows, and a variety of hedging techniques are employed to reduce exposure to exchange rate volatility. The extent to which hedging instruments are used, and whether companies should merely seek to reduce risk or should engage in currency speculation is a matter of debate. There seems little willingness on the part of companies to reveal to shareholders the nature of their foreign exchange management policy, although pressures are increasing in this regard.

CONCLUSION

The overall conclusion must be that internationalisation serves to substantially increase the financial risks faced by companies. In determining corporate strategy, therefore, management need to be aware of these risks, and confident in their ability to manage them. Then, armed with the funds for expansion, and the knowledge to limit financial risks they can address the next area of functional management – how to find a market for their products abroad. International marketing is thus the subject of the next chapter.

Additional Reading

Jacques, L.C. (1981) 'Management of Foreign Exchange Risk: A review Article', *Journal of International Business Studies*, Spring/Summer 1981, pp.81–103

Shapiro, A.C., (1989) *Multinational Financial Management*, 2nd Edition, Allyn and Bacon

Ross, D., (1988) 'Managing Foreign Exchange Exposure: Economic Exposure', *Accountancy*, March

Demirag, I. and Goddard, S., (1994) *Financial Management for International Business*, McGraw Hill

TUTORIAL EXERCISE

Students should use the *Financial Times* share service to obtain (free of charge) three sets of company accounts and find out all the ways in which the respective companies are exposed to foreign exchange risk, e.g. by overseas sales, ownership of foreign assets, foreign borrowings etc. Class discussion should address questions such as 'how much do they tell the investor directly about this exposure? Is it obvious, or do you have to search for it? Which companies are best at informing their investors?'

ESSAY QUESTIONS

1 Should investors be kept well informed about the foreign exchange and Treasury management policies of publicly quoted companies?

2 Explain why a company needs to be more conscious of its transaction exposure than its translation exposure.

3 Is the forward rate of exchange a forecast or best guess at the future spot rate?

4 Should foreign exchange rate speculation be made illegal?

Case Study: Foreign Exchange Management in the UK Post Office

Every time a letter or parcel is posted overseas, the postal services of two nations become financially intertwined. A letter sent from Australia will bear the stamp of that country, but if it is delivered to Los Angeles, the US postal service will have provided a service for which it may expect payment from the Australian postal system. The effect of this is that postal services world-wide are subject to foreign exchange exposure in the same way as any company with international dealings.

The post office in the UK is a net exporter of mail. Foreign postal administrations provide, in total, more services for delivery of mail than the UK Post Office provides delivery services for those foreign administrations. The result is that the UK becomes a debtor to the overseas delivery services, and the debts are delivered in a variety of currencies. The average sterling value of the sum payable at any one time is approximately £90 million, but this is subject to seasonal variation.

THE BILLING SYSTEM

The unit of account used for the billing of international delivery services is the Special Drawing Right (SDR). This is made up of a basket of currencies combined in predetermined weightings. The currencies which compose the SDR are the French Franc, US Dollar, Japanese Yen, Sterling and the Deutschmark. The foreign postal company can specify the precise currency (out of the basket) in which payment is required, but the bill will be expressed in SDRs.

Payment is due three months after receipt of the bill.

FORECASTING THE LEVEL OF FOREIGN EXCHANGE EXPOSURE

The extent of exposure is measured by the value of the net sum payable overseas at any one time. The responsibility for forecasting this value lies with the line management responsible for the provision of foreign postal services: International Mails. This is equivalent to the marketing and purchases departments of a manufacturing concern taking joint responsibility for forecasting the net value of imports/exports.

Forecasts are based partially on historical trends of bills received, but this presents a number of problems. One major difficulty is that it is not uncommon for creditors to delay over a year before billing the Post Office.

FORECASTING EXCHANGE RATES

In order to design a hedging programme, the Treasury department need to know both when payments are due to be made and the likely exchange rates which will prevail at the time.

The forecast is for the £/SDR exchange rate on specific dates. The delays in receipt of bills and the additional payment delay mean that the Post Office is seeking to hedge its transactions twelve to eighteen months ahead. Forecasts so far ahead into the future are likely to suffer a certain amount of inaccuracy.

The risk of inaccuracies is tackled by seeking to forecast trends and directions in exchange rates rather than the precise rates at any single point in time. The approach simplifies hedging procedures because if, for example, it is believed that the SDR will appreciate, it is beneficial to lead the payment by buying at current exchange rates. The problem of the approach is that the longer the time horizon for the forecast, the greater the likelihood that a currency rate may be volatile. Over some months there may be appreciation, but this could be followed by a long period of depreciation. This was the case with sterling during 1991/2. In the latter part of 1991 sterling appreciated rapidly. In early 1992 values stabilised, and then Black Wednesday marked the start of very rapid depreciation.

Mitigation of the risk of inaccuracies in exchange rate forecasts is done by using a mix of hedging techniques to give a flexibility of approach.

HEDGING POLICY

To avoid any risk of being accused of currency speculation, the Post Office has a policy of only hedging foreign exchange exposures created by trading.

Bills are issued in SDRs but the currency of payment will vary. This means that the requirement is to hedge against SDR/£ exchange rate movements.

The hedging instruments used are spot purchases, forward contracts, and options. Stop loss triggers are also used to limit losses where necessary, and in a similar vein the strategy is designed to take advantage of opportunities created by sterling appreciation.

PERFORMANCE MEASUREMENT

The effectiveness of hedging strategy is measured in terms of cost effectiveness. This reflects the strategy of viewing the role of foreign exchange management as risk reduction and not currency speculation. The Treasury function is thus viewed as a cost centre and not a profit centre.

Costs are compared to budget, and performance is also evaluated by comparison with two simple alternative policies: all spot or all forward purchases. The performance results are then used as an aid to the development of future hedging strategy.

CASE STUDY QUESTIONS

1 What are the advantages and disadvantages of giving line management the responsibility for forecasting net payables and exposure?

2 Is it beneficial or detrimental to the Post Ofice that bills are received up to fifteen months late? Alternatively, is the net effect dependent on other factors, and if so what are they?

3 Would it be impossible to use the chosen hedging instruments without information on the anticipated schedule of payments and receivables?

4 Explain why the hedging relates only to the SDR/£ exchange rate, and not to the individual currencies in which payment is made.

CHAPTER EIGHT

International Marketing

LEARNING OUTCOMES

This chapter looks at the inter-linked decisions that companies have to make in establishing an international marketing plan. By the end of the chapter you should be able to:

■ Describe how market segmentation can be used to identify potential international markets

■ Outline the methods used to research and screen overseas markets

■ Explain the alternative entry routes for international markets and the factors determining their selection

■ Discuss how companies decide on product, pricing, promotion and distribution policies in international markets

INTRODUCTION

Kenneth Ohmae[1] argues that the success or failure of a business in the twenty-first century will depend on whether it can compete effectively in world markets. Any entrepreneur knows that marketing is central to success, but if the market is international, then the problems of customer targeting, market segmentation and market servicing are substantially increased.

Achieving success in moving from a domestic into a world marketplace requires, as suggested by this chapter's objectives, that companies work through a number of inter-linked decisions. To view the entire globe as a potential market is an unmanageable idea for most businesses, and they need a means of narrowing down the options to a number of potentially viable alternatives through the use of market segmentation techniques. Once potential national markets have been identified, more detailed research combined with a screening system can be used to create a shortlist.

Figure 8.1   *Shrinking the World*

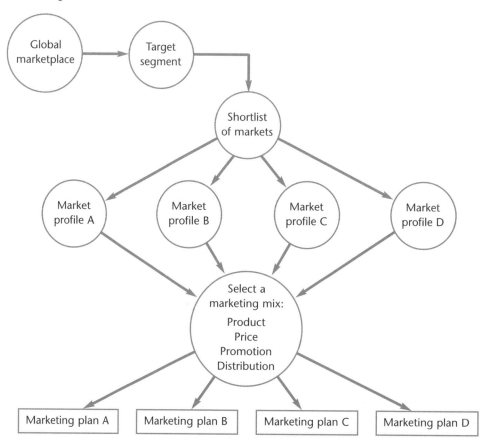

Figure 8.1 above illustrates the collection of stages involved in creating an international marketing plan, and this chapter details the stages in turn. The company moves from a position where, in theory, there is a global marketplace, to one in which segmentation and research has helped to identify target countries. Plans can then be drawn up to meet the specific requirements of each of these markets.

In this way the construction of a marketing plan is broken down into distinct sequential stages. Identifying target markets is the first stage in the process. The next decision that is required is to choose from an array of alternatives – from simple direct exporting through to direct investment – relating to routes of market entry. At this stage, the decisions change to focusing on the needs of the individual market, and policies relating to product specification, pricing, promotion and distribution must all be specified. A formal marketing plan can now be written for each target location, but it is useful to review performance against the plan on a regular basis. In this way, policy mistakes can be identified quickly, and the plan amended accordingly. Failures in international marketing can often be explained by failure to be methodical in approaching the key questions of: where to sell, what, and how? By looking at each stage of the process in turn, we can see that a methodical approach may be time consuming, but each stage adds value to the process. We begin by looking at the potential for global market segmentation.

MARKET SEGMENTATION

The term market segmentation refers to the way in which a market can be subdivided into a number of component parts. Understanding the make-up of the components is useful to the international marketer because it is not possible to meet the needs of all customers all of the time. Niche submarkets can be useful for small firms trying to find a way in to a market dominated by large players, and they can also be used to extend product life cycles in new geographic locations.

There are a variety of different ways in which markets can be segmented; indeed, ingenuity in segmentation is an important ingredient of marketing success, but the key tools used to identify submarkets that are of particular relevance for international marketing include:

- culture
- geography
- socio-economic groups
- consumer behaviour – attitudes, tastes, level of brand perception, motivation, responsiveness to
- technological change.

It is helpful to look briefly at each of these in turn.

Culture

In Chapter 4 you saw how the world can be subdivided into a series of cultural groupings, and cultural attitudes can have a substantial effect on the willingness of a market to respond to new product offerings. Think about your own buying habits and it is easy to see that the food we eat, the clothes we wear, the way we spend our leisure time and the style of our homes and furniture are all subject to strong cultural influences.

It is also useful to remember that cultural differences do not always match political boundaries, as in the case of Spain, for example, where the Basque population have a separate cultural identity from their fellow Spaniards. The former USSR is another example of a strange overlap between political and cultural boundaries. Similarly, in Belgium, the Flemish- and French-speaking regions have distinctive cultural characteristics. In contrast, although Monaco and France are politically separate units, they share a common culture. International markets can therefore be usefully subdivided along cultural lines, and the justification is that it is likely to be easier to sell a standardised product into markets which are culturally similar.

Geography

Geography is a very simple way of dividing the world into a series of smaller grouped markets. One simple approach would be to see the global market merely in terms of the continental groupings of Europe, North America, Latin America, Asia, Africa and Australasia. In practice, this subdivision may be over simplistic for marketing purposes however, because a common geography does not necessarily imply a common set of tastes/market requirements. For example, the North American market can readily be subdivided into Canada and the USA, because of cultural differences. The strong British influences within western Canada, and the French influences in the east of the country serve to further segment the market. Similarly American citizens on the eastern seaboard regard themselves as very different from say, Californians or residents of the southern states of Texas or Arizona.

Geography can also be helpful as a way of dividing the world into different climatic zones. This is particularly important for products such as cars, where it is imperative to change the product design if it is to function in a different climate zone. For example, air conditioning units in passenger cars are fitted as standard for the US market, whereas in the UK they come as an optional extra in many makes of vehicle. Changing product designs to suit different climates is potentially very expensive, and adds to the complications of international marketing.

As suggested, geographic segmentation is usually only a starting point for specifying different potential markets, and it is usually combined with other market characteristics such as socio-economic attributes or language. The chocolate confectionery market is a good example of one in which geography is an inadequate means of segmenting the market. Within Europe, there are clear differences in taste and consumption patterns for chocolate. Chocolate products consumed in the United Kingdom contain a higher fat content and are sweeter than those eaten in mainland Europe. At the same time, Southern Europeans eat less 'block' chocolate than Northern Europeans, even though they have an equal preference for bitter chocolate. An alternative way of segmenting the European market would be by product type: count-lines, such as Snickers/Mars bars, versus children's products such as Kinder eggs, or gift products like Black Magic or Ferrero Rocher.

Socio-Economic Groups

The amount of wealth and the social composition of a population, such as the age structure, racial mix and family size and life style all serve to affect patterns of consumption. For example, products such as fast food items like burgers or pizzas will tend to be in higher demand in countries where there is a relatively high level of disposable income, and the large majority of the population are working and looking for time-saving opportunities in their consumption habits. Alternatively, in low income areas, products such as cigarettes may be in demand, but they are bought in single units rather than in the packets of twenty familiar to Westerners.

Ideally, the market researcher wants to be able to identify the particular socio-economic group that is most likely to purchase a given product. Information collected in the domestic market may help, but unfortunately it cannot be guaranteed to be accurate. For example, in Western Europe Mercedes cars are popular amongst the higher social classes, who view them as high quality vehicles which are also something of a status symbol, indicating success. In Greece and Turkey, the cars are primarily owned by taxi drivers, who value their size and reliability. If Mercedes tried to market their cars for use as taxis in the UK, for example, they would struggle to succeed, because the market's perception of the vehicles is fundamentally different, and the London taxi cab design is well entrenched as the UK's idea of the appropriate vehicle.

Consumer Behaviour

The factors that attract consumers to different products, and the way in which people react to issues such a technological change can vary quite widely, and these can be used as tools for market segmentation. The teenage market is a clear case of a specific consumer group, with readily identifiable patterns of behaviour, and in fact age is a very important determinant of buyer behaviour. Using the music market to illustrate the differences, CD singles are primarily purchased by the 13–22-year-old age group, and virtually never bought by the over-50 age range. Similarly, the massive growth in the market for bottled beers in recent years has originated in the 18–25 years' age group, whereas older consumers continue to drink draught products. In marketing parlance, distinguishing between groups in this way is termed segmentation by usage. Pareto Law suggests that between 15 and 20 per cent of consumers will be responsible for over half of total purchases of a product, and so being able to target high usage segments in a market is a vital ingredient of success.

One element of buyer behaviour which has become increasingly important in recent years is that of attitudes towards branded goods. Some people may be indifferent between branded and own brand products whilst others may only purchase the branded items. In some instances, the brand is the central factor in market success. When McDonald's opened their first restaurant in Moscow in the 1990s, the queues were huge, despite the fact that the food had to be paid for in difficult to obtain hard currency, and the price was very high relative to local wage rates. The appeal was in the US brand, and so the product succeeded. If the idea had been franchised out and sold under a local name, the story is likely to have been very different.

The international marketer therefore needs to understand what is driving the demand for a product, and look for markets where similar behaviour is exhibited, in order to maximise international sales.

Technological Change

Both markets and individual consumers can be differentiated in terms of their openness to new products and technologies. Some consumers ('leaders')will pay high prices to be amongst the first owners of the latest technology, whilst others ('laggards') will only purchase a product when it is entering the mature stage of its life cycle. In a similar manner, but on an international scale, technologically based products are sold in different national markets at different times, so that an item that might be viewed as outdated in the USA is seen as innovative in poorer less developed countries.

Cameras are a good example of this phenomenon. Video cameras were first launched in Japan and South East Asia, but rapidly spread to the USA and Europe. As the world market for the cameras increased and became more competitive, and customer sophistication increased, older heavier cameras began to be discarded in the original markets, but simultaneously the rich consumers of economies in South America and Asia wanted to buy into the technology. For such markets, the product had become affordable because volume production and technological developments had reduced both production costs and prices.

Understanding the opportunities for segmenting the world markets according to adoption rates for new technologies is of major importance to manufacturers of consumer durables.

Once a market has been segmented, there remains the question of what to offer and how to promote, price and distribute the goods or services. In particular, companies have to choose between a standardised, differentiated or concentrated marketing strategy. In an international context, the strategy which is chosen can be used to distinguish multinational from global corporations.

The global corporation seeks to maximise profits by standardisation, treating the whole world as a single market. In contrast, the multinational company opts for differentiation, changing its marketing mix* to suit the specific needs of individual segments. Concentrated marketing refers to a strategy in which a company selects specific market segments. Ignoring the rest of the market, it tries to achieve maximum market penetration by focusing its efforts on a much reduced number of potential customers who are targeted using a standard marketing mix.

Concentrated marketing is representative of a risk averse approach to entering the international marketplace. It may be possible to identify foreign markets where tastes are very similar to those of domestic customers, and so the additional effort and cost required to gain overseas sales is minimised. As experience of international markets is gained, the area of concentration can be widened, and perhaps some differentiation introduced if desired.

For the more ambitious company, looking to gain fast growth of international sales, the choice between the polar extremes of standardisation versus differentiation is fundamental. Amending any, or all of the dimensions of the marketing mix to suit the needs of individual markets will cost money, and so from a financial perspective standardisation is more attractive. The question is, will it work?

STANDARDISATION VERSUS DIFFERENTIATION IN MARKETING

The chief proponent of a standardised approach is Levitt[2]. In Chapters 2 and 3 you have seen how the international business environment is changing as transportation costs have fallen rapidly resulting in much greater levels of international travel, and technological improvements in communication have increased the amount of information available about foreign places and cultures. Writing in 1983 Levitt argued that such changes have led to a homogenisation of markets, as people across the world have increasingly common tastes. In such a world, the global marketer can act 'as if the entire world (or major regions of it) were a single entity; it sells the same thing in the same way everywhere.' By taking advantage of the similarity of tastes, a company can sell standardised products across the world, and gain competitive advantage

---

* The term 'marketing mix' refers to the combination of product, price, promotion and distribution policies used to introduce a product into a market.

through exploiting economies of scale so that it earns a reputation as the lowest cost producer of high quality goods. The consumer benefits from the lower costs via reduced prices. In such a scenario, the optimal marketing strategy is to sell a standardised product through a standardised marketing programme, *but* the scenario assumes homogenised tastes.

Examples of companies which have adopted this approach include Levi-Strauss, Coca Cola and McDonald's. In each case, the brand name and the associated image are important contributors to the global success – everybody recognises the name and knows what to expect from the brand. Even so, these companies have been unable to entirely standardise their products across the entire world. For example in Scandinavia McDonald's found that it needed to sell beer in its outlets to match local habits and tastes, and in India they needed to provide burgers made of lamb instead of beef to comply with the Hindu religious beliefs.

If companies with brands and marketing power as big as these need to adapt to local needs then it may be that standardisation cannot work, and Levitt has got it wrong. In fact, Levitt did not suggest that total standardisation was the ideal, merely that it was advantageous to focus on the similarities between markets rather than the differences, on the grounds that differentiation would add to cost. It is worth remembering that even though in theory a wide geographic spread will result in a greater number and extent of marketing mix differences, the differences might not be immutable.

Maximising the opportunity to standardise, and taking advantage of the resulting cost savings, whilst at the same time being sensitive to local requirements is to 'think global' and 'act local', as proposed by Quelch and Hoff[3], but this is far from easy in practice. There is a fine tightrope to be walked between the two extremes of approach, and care must be exercised to avoid imposing standardisation where it will not work.

The Parker Pen Company is a good example of a case where an attempt to introduce globalised marketing failed quite quickly. Parker launched its campaign in 1984, based around a common advertising theme 'Make your mark with Parker' which featured the Parker logo. Unfortunately, the plan turned sour, was halted in 1985, and a year later the company's writing division was sold off in a management buy-out. Parker's national subsidiaries and distributors had argued that the national markets needed to be differentiated but Parker headquarters suggested that common advertising did not preclude such flexibility. The example clearly illustrates the huge practical difficulties of determining what to standardise and how much.

WHEN CAN STANDARDISATION WORK?

Overall, the primary attraction of standardisation lies in the fact that it both simplifies the task of international marketing but also reduces costs. It is therefore useful to look at the market conditions which favour a standardised approach.

Industrial Products versus Consumer Products

There is evidence to suggest that it is easier to sell standardised industrial products rather than consumer goods. The first reason for this, put forward by Sandler and

Shani[4] is that business to business sales depend upon functionality of design rather than aesthetics. Samiee and Roth[5] also suggest that the development of industrial products requires greater levels of capital investment and so when they are produced in larger volumes then scale economies can be substantial, helping to reduce prices. Industrial customers can then take advantage of these lower prices and pass them on to end-consumers in their own products.

An example of an industrial product where standardised marketing is potentially possible is the supply of machines to vehicle manufacturers for use in testing vehicle emissions. Under environmental protection legislation many countries require vehicles to perform within clearly specified limits for exhaust fume emissions, and so manufacturers are anxious to ensure that new products meet the regulatory requirements. The chassis dynamometers used for the emission tests will be not be produced by the vehicle manufacturers themselves, but purchased from specialist engineering companies such as Froude-Consine. The same basic design of testing equipment can be sold to various different vehicle manufacturers throughout the world as a standardised product, because the need is for efficiency of operation, not manufacturer specific design. Customer taste is unlikely to vary for such products.

Companies that make consumer goods rather than industrial goods will find that five key factors favour the adoption of standardised marketing. The five factors are as follows:

■ *Customer segmentation*

As already suggested, it is possible to segment a market in a number of different ways, but there is evidence that where products are aimed at having universal appeal amongst a very specific group of consumers, then it is feasible to standardise the marketing. For example, the teenage market is clearly targeted by Levi-Strauss in their latest design of 'engineered' jeans. Teenagers do not want to wear the same design of jeans as their parents' generation, and so the product is differentiated to suit teenage taste. At the same time, teenagers have grown up in the 'homogenised' world described by Levitt, and their tastes are broadly similar around the globe. A standardised marketing campaign can thus be used for such products. Goods for conspicuous consumption – such as high-priced cars like the Aston Martin or Ferrari, or watch brands such as Rolex – are also suitable for standardisation.

■ *Universal needs*

Levitt suggested that standardised marketing is most suited to products for which there is a universal need and, comparing consumer durables and non-durables, the consistency of need is more applicable to durables. Quelch and Hoff[3] therefore argue that companies should not try and sell standardised versions of products such as cosmetics or food, but should instead concentrate on applying the approach to items such as white goods (refrigerators, washing machines, etc.), furniture, or vehicles.

The international furniture company IKEA illustrates how this approach is applied in practice because the company carries a standard range of furniture items in all of its stores, but varies its ranges of non-furniture items such as fabric goods and gift-ware to suit local taste.

■ *Stage in the product life cycle*

In the early years of a product life cycle a company can benefit from first mover advantage and lack of competition. In such a situation it is possible to retain a standardised product because consumers are seeking the new technology rather than sophistication of design. In the later stages of the life cycle when the level of competition has increased, consumers may become more discriminating and there will be a need to differentiate.

The personal CD and mini-disc market is illustration of this. When personal mini-disc players were first launched, they were relatively small compared to CD players and held more music, so that they had immediate consumer appeal on the basis of these two technological advantages. Consequently standardised marketing was suitable. Within twelve months, however, new producers had moved in, and the emphasis was on attracting customers via product differentiation, such as recordable versus non-recordable/battery life/size and weight, etc.

■ *Short technological life*

The example above also illustrates the view of Samiee and Roth[5], that standardised marketing is well suited to products that have a short technological life. In new technologies where the cost of design change is high there is a need to maximise the returns from such products, before market share is forfeited in favour of the next technology. Maximising returns and minimising costs can best be achieved through standardisation, and so there is a tendency for products in markets where technologies are changing rapidly to be standard in format. The APS and digital camera market is another example of this type of scenario. Canon cameras are universal in design, and marketed universally. When technology progresses, the company launches new products in markets where the technology is relatively mature, but continues to market the older technology products in less sophisticated markets. As such, there is standardisation of approach for the individual products, and global branding for the full range of Canon products.

■ *Global branding*

In the case of mini-disc players the manufacturers, such as Sony, Sharp, Panasonic and JVC, extended their product ranges to meet changing consumer needs, as did Canon with their camera designs, but in both instances the companies were still able to employ standardised marketing campaigns for their brands. Geiser[6] believes that global branding is a vital ingredient for standardised marketing. A global brand can be used to define consumer expectations, linking the brand image to specific product types and quality images. If successful, the desire for the brand can then overcome any desires for localisation. The universal success of brands such as Calvin Klein and Ralph Lauren Polo Sport are evidence of how fashion items need not be localised. Targeted at the 14–25 year age group, these brands have created a desire for brands *per se*, almost regardless of other product characteristics.

It is clear that a great deal of understanding of market characteristics is required before it is possible to begin to determine the extent of standardisation which might be feasible. Such information can only be acquired through extensive market research, which will then enable a company to hone down its choices of potential markets to manageable proportions.

THE CASE FOR MARKET RESEARCH

In practice, however, not all companies will undertake research before entering a foreign market. Some may be drawn into a market by impromptu orders from a foreign customer, whilst others may go into a market purely on a hunch. Ellis and Williams[7] cite the case of Mappin and Webb, a London-based high class jewellers. The company's choice of Prague as the location for its first store in mainland Europe was explained by the chief executive : 'I've got a good hunch about Prague. It's new, it's enterprising, people are making money.' Clearly not all international marketing decisions are based on rational analysis.

In undertaking market research a company needs to consider two related issues – the absolute size of the market and the environmental factors that might affect a market's profitability. Market size is the primary determinant of potential revenue, and its calculation is essentially an issue of data collection and analysis, taking into account any economic and cultural factors which might affect demand. The logic for environmental scanning is that in entering a new market, a company wants to ensure that it is operationally feasible to reach the potential customers, and that institutional or legal requirements will not make it difficult to earn a profit. In this respect, environmental scanning takes into account the operational issues relating to the relative costs of operating in a given market, and the availability of resources as well as aspects of political and legal infrastructure. Linking marketing and operational issues in this way makes use of the ideas presented in Chapter 5, when corporate strategy was broken down into its functional components. A central theme of this book is the need to be permanently conscious of functional interdependencies in order to be successful in managing an international business.

Estimation of Market Size

In collecting information about potential market size, it is important to bear in mind that research can be expensive, and that ultimately only one or two target markets will be selected, so collecting information on all possible options is impractical and financially irresponsible. If a company has a 200-item product portfolio, and it is believed that the products could potentially be marketed in 200 countries of the world, this gives an array of 40,000 possible options. Clearly it would take months of work to appraise each of these separately, and so a scanning system must be devised to bring the choices down to more manageable proportions. One way of doing this is to use ideas such as those presented in the last section of this chapter, to select out the products which are most easily sold in standardised form. A second filter could then make use of international statistics to shortlist the potential markets for these products.

A variety of international bodies collect statistics on economies around the world, which can be used to collate information about income levels, import and export patterns, inflation rates, exchange rates, demographic patterns, educational levels, family size, labour costs, natural resources, and a whole array of economic and social data which may influence the size of a potential market. The most useful sources of such statistical information include:

- United Nations, and its subsidiary bodies such as the World Health Organisation
- International Monetary Fund
- Organisation for Economic Cooperation and Development (OECD)
- World Trade Organisation
- European Union.

The statistics produced by these bodies are particularly useful to researchers because they are collected and presented in a consistent form year on year. Obtaining comparable figures can be very difficult when looking for information on many different countries, but by using internationally collated statistics one can be certain of their comparability. The one problem that can arise with global statistics is that the collection and tabulation takes a long time, and so they are often two or three years out of date when they eventually get published. Nonetheless, they are incredibly useful for comparisons on a global scale, and if you look back at Chapters 2 and 3 you will see that a lot of the tables on international trading patterns and foreign direct investment have been compiled from data published by these bodies. The large international institutions also produce written reports on topical issues which may also be useful for market research purposes.

Using the international comparisons to filter out a limited number of possible markets, researchers can then progress to the collection of more detailed market information from specialist sources. For statistical information about a particular country, the national statistical office is a useful place to start. Most governments operate some form of service, but the quality of the data may vary widely across the world. Data collection is expensive, and its analysis and presentation requires a certain amount of educational ability, and so the quality of information available in many of the poorer countries of the world can be either limited or inadequate for company requirements.

Another potentially useful source of information is trade associations or (in the UK) Chambers of Commerce. These organisations will include members who have specialist knowledge of particular markets and possibly direct experience of a particular locality, and they often maintain databases of contact addresses and sales figures which can be very useful.

International accounting and consultancy firms such as Price Waterhouse Coopers or Cap Gemini, as well as the international divisions of banks and government agencies, may provide information in the form of market analysis reports, or country analyses. As such concerns will cover a wide range of clients spanning a large number of different industry sectors, these reports may be fairly generic in nature, but they will still contain more detail that the bare international statistics. Additionally, it is possible to buy information on particular countries/sectors/markets from specialist information agencies such as Reuters.

Last, but by no means least, the Internet can be an invaluable source of information for basic research purposes. Many information providers post data on their websites, but will offer more detailed data in return for a subscription. One difficulty with using the Internet, however, is that the technology allows sites to track the users who have logged on; and if a company is seeking information about a commercially sensitive proposal it may not wish its identity to be known. Care must therefore be exercised to ensure that such problems are avoided.

Collecting the statistics is only the first stage in the estimation of market size. The next stage is to modify the statistics to take account of social and cultural factors. As we have already seen, language, customs, religion and tastes will all affect attitudes towards a particular product. In practice, a company is likely to start from a point of trying to identify the markets requiring the least amount of differentiation, and so one approach is to take each dimension of product, price, promotion and distribution, and score a country in terms of its perceived openness to standardisation.

For example, market characteristics could be scored on a scale of 0–10, with higher scores indicating greater ease of standardisation. If a benchmark score of six is specified as indicating standardisation is acceptable, then it is possible to select all countries/markets with a score of six or above, and devise a common marketing campaign for all those locations.

By this stage in the research process company managers have a list of countries and the associated market sizes together with a judgement as to the scale of differentiation required for each one. A ranking of, say, the ten best options is therefore now possible.

Environmental Analysis

The final part of the selection process involves consideration of the environment of the shortlisted markets, to see which locations pose the lowest risk, the easiest operating environment, and hence the greatest potential profit. Political, institutional and competitive factors all affect potential profitability and risk, and language, geography and costs help determine the ease with which operations can be established and maintained. It is helpful to look at each of these in turn.

Political factors, such as the stability of the current leadership, and the absence of racial, tribal or social unrest can significantly affect the attractiveness of a market. The communications 'revolution' means that it is usually the case that the whole world is aware of problem regions. In the year 2000, for example, managers would have known that Kosovo, Serbia, Chechnya, Fiji, Sierra Leone and Sri Lanka were all suffering from either social unrest or outright fighting because of political problems. More difficult to identify are the potential problems. The financial markets are particularly sensitive to political problems, and so the major credit rating agencies such as Standard and Poors all produce what they call sovereign ratings, which are a measure of the credit rating for a nation state. These ratings are a good reflection of the general level of stability in a country.

The importance of politics goes beyond just the issue of potential unrest, however, because the state of relations between two nations or two cultures can affect the willingness of consumers to buy from a foreign supplier. For example, a well known UK-based supermarket chain suffered problems when it opened a branch in Egypt. Egypt's population is predominantly Muslim, and the supermarket came under attack from activists who claimed that in selling Western products it was threatening the Muslim cultural heritage, and locals were asked to boycott the store. It would have been very difficult to predict such an attack, because although there are clearly cultural differences, Egypt is not viewed as politically unstable. Furthermore, Western products sell very well in other Muslim states such as Oman, Saudi Arabia and Dubai.

Political regulations or 'red tape' can also create problems for companies. Operational efficiency can be dramatically undermined if the regulatory framework is complex, in respect of obtaining manufacturing licences, processing imports or compliance with local tax regulations. Government may also impose rules on foreign companies relating to the use of local labour instead of expatriate managers, the proportion of local content in products, and the ownership of foreign-held assets; many countries require that a certain percentage of equity is locally owned. At the same time, regulations may restrict the ability of a company to repatriate revenues and profits from a foreign market. Unless it is willing to invest in the locality over the very long term, such regulations may make it too risky to move into such a market.

The greater the degree of political intervention and risk of social unrest, the higher the risks of entering any particular market, and the lower the expected profit. In the light of this, it is useful to try and generate a score for political risk, which can be used to rank the market choices.

The institutional framework in a marketplace can also affect its relative attractiveness. The institutional framework includes, for example, the distribution network, and the ownership of the media. Centralised media ownership, for example, makes it much easier to promote products on a national scale. In China, the media is very fragmented and regionally focused, and this works to increase advertising costs. Conversely, in Europe, for example, the widespread ownership of satellite and cable television makes international, Europe-wide advertising easy to organise and relatively low cost per head of population.

National differences in distribution networks will be considered in some detail later in this chapter.

The competitive environment – both currently and in the future – affects the risk of being unable to gain or retain an adequate level of sales to be profitable. The competitive threat is likely to be linked to the legal and political environment, perhaps in terms of the government's attitude to monopoly power, or foreign direct investment, or rules on patents and intellectual property. For example, most of the rich developed nations have laws to regulate the power of monopolies and control anti-competitive practice. Moving into a new market where there is minimal regulation of anti-competitive behaviour can be risky, as 'unfair' tactics may be used by other companies to prevent newcomers seizing market share. Intellectual property rights affect the ability of a company to protect a competitive advantage which might arise from patents, licences or trademarks. Enforcement of such rights may be the only way of protecting a company's investment in product development costs. If companies are able to freely copy the products of other companies, without any control over breach of property rights, then the competitive environment is much more open, and it is harder to guarantee long-term profitability. Consequently, the risks of marketing in such locations are increased.

Factors such as a country's geography, language and infrastructure can be very important determinants of the financial viability and ease of operations in a given market. Geography can impede access to customers by making the distribution process difficult, and the problem can be compounded if a country's infrastructure is poor, so that transportation is slow and expensive. Language may also serve to restrict market access, particularly if there are regional or tribal languages which subdivide a country. In such situations, advertising, product literature and packaging may all need local amendments, so increasing the complexity of operations quite substantively. Whatever the cause, even if there are thousands of potential customers but they cannot easily be reached, this problem needs to be identified early on in the market research process.

Combining the various environmental influences to derive a ranking for the relative attractiveness of different alternative markets, a score for political risk, together with scores for ease of operations and market access, it is possible to obtain an aggregate, or weighted score for the market environment. Linked to the information about the ease of standardisation within any given location, a company's managers can now select their target markets.

The decision criteria and the scores, location by location, can be portrayed in grid form, using a framework such as that in Table 8.1

Assume that all factors scores are based on a scale of 0–10, with higher scores indicating increased attractiveness.

Table 8.1   *Market Selection: Sample Scoresheet*

Market size	Standardisation benchmark level of 60 indicates no need to differentiate	Political risk	Institutional environment	Competitive environment	Ease of market access: geography and infrastructure	Access to resources	Labour costs	Cost of capital and relative tax rate	Market size	Total weighted score
Factor weighting	40	10	2.5	5	5	5	10	2.5	20	100
Country X	7	6	5	3	7	7	3	3	6	595
Country Y	5	8	3	6	5	5	6	4	8	597.5
Country Z	7	6	5	4	5	4	8	8	6	637.5

The market score grid allows alternative countries to be scored against each of nine criteria, with the relative importance of the respective criteria being indicated by the weighting factor. In the sample grid, the ability to retain a standardised marketing mix is ranked as the single most important factor, with market size being ranked second. In contrast, a number of aspects are seen of very limited importance, such as the tax rate, and the institutional environment, and they are consequently given a very low weighting. The net result is that Country Z attains the highest weighted score. The particular weighting given to each element is likely to vary from company to company, as will attitudes to risk and the perceived causes of risk. For example, the low level of importance attached to the cost of capital and tax rate in the example above may be a consequence of the fact that the company in question is making a relatively small investment in the new market, and so these costs will be quite small. In the case of a business intending to invest several millions of dollars into a foreign marketing campaign, the cost of capital may be weighted significantly more heavily.

Clearly there are subjective judgements required when assembling such as score sheet, and so the results should be interpreted with caution. Nevertheless, it provides a way of accommodating the multiple considerations that need to be factored in to any decision about market selection, because it explicitly recognises the many things that can affect a market's riskiness and potential profitability. An additional advantage of this type of approach to country selection is that it provides a consistent method of approach which can be used repeatedly over the years. As lessons are learned, the benchmark scores for different factors can be altered, as can the weightings, but managers have the assurance that they know the basis on which a decision is being made, and can understand the underlying thinking.

Managers can now move on to the next stage of the marketing decision – the entry route in to the selected market.

MARKET ENTRY ROUTES

The term market entry route refers to the way in which a product is sold into a given market. In the case of overseas sales, there are a variety of different ways of gaining a foothold in the market, and it is helpful to rank the alternatives in terms of their relative level of risk. If it is assumed that managers act rationally, then having gone to the trouble of using a structured approach to market selection, it is reasonable to assume that they will want to minimise the risk of losing their investment and/or credibility in that market.

In ascending order of risk, the alternative entry options open to companies are as follows:

- Exporting – indirect
            – direct
- Overseas sales branches
- Management contracts
- Licensing
- Contract manufacturing
- Franchising
- Turnkey projects
- Joint ventures
- Foreign direct investment – Merger/acquisition of a local concern
            – buying in local expertise, sole ownership

In addition to thinking about the relative risk of the different alternatives, it is important to ensure that the company has the ability to fulfil its aims. Deciding to set up a wholly owned foreign subsidiary without having regard to whether you have the cash resources, skills and staff to run it is just stupid. Marketing decisions need to be assessed in the context of their operational implications, as has already been suggested.

Exporting

Exporting is a commonly used method of first entering a foreign market, because it provides a simple means of increasing sales, without any large-scale commitment of resources. However, exporting is not just for small firms – statistics show that it is a very important sales route for even the largest multinational and global companies. For each of the last ten years Britain's biggest exporter has been British Aerospace, which recorded export sales of over £6 billion in 1998, and an annual survey published by the *Financial Times* showed that over twenty companies had export sales in excess of £1 billion in 1998. Some of the biggest exporters are foreign multi-nationals which have established UK-based manufacturing plants, and then export the output from these plants. The US-owned companies of Compaq computers, IBM and Ford Motor Company are all examples of this phenomenon.

Indirect exporting is the 'gentlest' way in to foreign markets, because it does not require companies to engage in any face to face contact with overseas customers. At its simplest, indirect exporting works via a business selling its products to a domestic intermediary or agent, who takes on responsibility for finding overseas customers in return for a commission fee. For example, the large US department stores such as Saks and Maceys employ London-based agents/buyers to find suppliers for some products. A UK textile company may approach such an agent with a portfolio of designs, and if an order is placed, the invoice will be made out to the London agent, not the US store. Even though the products end up being sold in New York, the UK manufacturer has made the export sale in sterling, and dealt entirely with a UK buyer. For companies wary of the risks of foreign marketing, this offers a very low risk entry route, but it has the disadvantage that some of the profits from the sales are 'lost' through payment of the agent's commission. A similarly painless method of indirect exporting is by 'piggybacking', whereby your products are sold to a domestic company which owns foreign sales outlets, through which it sells on your goods. Toys 'Я' Us has helped some small toy manufacturers into exporting in this way, as they bulk buy goods for distribution to many different stores world-wide. Similarly, in the UK the Yorkshire-based company Peter Black that supplies Marks and Spencer with toiletries, cosmetics and footwear, will find its products on sale throughout Europe in Marks and Spencer stores, even though the orders were placed in the UK.

Direct exporting puts more pressure on the selling company, because they are now required to go out and find potential distributors and end-customers. There is also a need to get to grips with all the regulations and procedures that govern the export process, and set product specifications, prices and promotional campaigns that are suited to the target market. In order to reduce the learning curve involved in exporting for the first time, many firms use freight forwarding companies. These organisations will (for a fee) take responsibility for any and everything including insuring cargo, booking shipping or air freight space, warehousing, obtaining export licences where necessary, and managing the shipping documentation through to collection of payment. As with export agents, freight forwarders ease the administrative burden that might accompany exporting, but the result is that profits are also reduced.

The Leicestershire-based company Brush, and the Brussels-based ABB Alstom Power are examples of companies that are both involved in the direct export of power generating equipment such as gas turbines. As suppliers of high value industrial equipment, direct exporting is preferable to indirect for the companies because the direct contact with the end customer means that equipment designs can be refined to meet individual requirements where necessary, and long-term contracts can be agreed for maintenance and the supply of spares.

Overseas Sales Branches

Once export sales have become well established, and a company is able to feel certain that a market is expanding, it may consider increasing its investment in the country via the establishment of one or more overseas sales branches. Instead of operating through agents or distributors, the company invests in its own office, storage facilities and sales force in the chosen location. Needless to say, such investment will only be undertaken if there is seen to be strong growth potential in a region. At the same time, the increased fixed costs of such offices means that in the early months there may be a period when the profit from overseas sales becomes a loss, until the new break-even position is reached.

A small service company, Impact Development Training Company, based in the English Lake District is an example of a company that uses this type of arrangement. Impact offer adventure training and team-building courses for managers, and after twenty years of UK operations, they now operate in thirty countries around the world. Demand across the thirty countries is serviced from four non-UK permanent sales bases in Poland, Japan, Thailand and Italy.

Management Contracts

Another low risk form of overseas selling also relates to the service sector, with the use of management contracts. In the hotel business, companies often sign management contracts whereby they agree to manage a hotel on behalf of another business, whilst putting their own name over the door. Similar agreements are common in the cinema trade. When the property owner resides overseas, what is being exported is the service of managing the business, but it is a relatively low risk sale, because all of the end transactions are occurring in the domestic market, and the owner pays a management fee that is usually linked to sales receipts.

Licensing

This approach to entering a market works through a company selling a licence to an overseas party, which grants the right to manufacture/sell their product or service in return for annual fees. The licence may cover any or all of:

- manufacturing processes
- technical know-how and specifications
- patents
- the use of trademarks
- copyrights.

The annual fee paid to the licensor is usually calculated as a percentage of sales receipts. The use of licences can provide a means of entering a market which is otherwise difficult to access, due to problems of gaining entry to the distribution system, or tariff/quota barriers which prevent access via exports from home. Licensing can also offer valuable opportunities to local manufacturers and distributors that are keen to expand but lack the product lines to do so. If the licensee is already well established in the sector, it may be easy to gain rapid growth of sales.

The music business is an example of a sector where international licensing is relatively common. For example, UK record companies do not usually export CDs and tapes to overseas markets, but instead license a local manufacturer to produce and distribute the music on their behalf. In return for the granting of the licence, the UK company then receives royalties based on a percentage of the wholesale value of the sales. Similar such arrangements are used in publishing, where printed texts are not exported directly, but instead the copyright is licensed to a local company, and sales-based royalties are paid to the original copyright owner.

The investment and commitment required to undertake licensing is relatively low, but there are also some risks. In particular, there is the risk that once the licensee has the technical knowledge of the production process, and market information, they may cancel the licence and set up in direct competition. Even if the licence is retained in the long term, there is a risk that quality is difficult to control from a distance. The licence may be brand linked, and there is consequently a need to maintain consistency of quality, but without regular quality audits by the licensor, this may be difficult. The other downside to licensing as a market entry route is that it means that less profit can be made compared to that which would be possible if production was kept in the hands of the original manufacturer. As with many investments, some earnings are sacrificed in return for reduced risk.

Contract Manufacturing

Contract manufacturing works by a foreign company agreeing a contract with a local firm to manufacture items on their behalf, making to order as and when required. The use of such local contract manufacturers is becoming increasingly widespread, as multinational companies seek to optimise the geographic distribution of their production capacity across the world, so that they have easy access to all of their main markets. For example, in the semiconductor business, there are companies who specialise in the production of semiconductors for sale to other firms. Contract manufacturing differs from licensing in that although a local manufacturer is used to produce the item(s) to a defined specification, the company that has placed the contract retains control over the marketing and after sales services.

One of the aspects of contract manufacturing which makes it particularly appealing is that it is currently seen as an integral part of supply chain management. Large companies will maintain a list of 'approved' suppliers, whose ability to maintain quality standards has been verified, and will then put contracts out to tender from these suppliers. In the case of the US giant General Electric (GE), and increasingly in the automotive trade as well, the invitations to tender may be posted on the Internet. Product/component requirements and the design specifications are included in the tender document, and the purchasing company gains by being able to buy at the lowest possible price.

When the contract is for goods to be sold within the local or regional market area, a contract manufacturing arrangement means that a company does not have to concern itself with large-scale investment in manufacturing plant, but can instead concentrate its investment in marketing. The costs, and the risks will thus be reduced. The one potential problem with contract manufacturing is that of maintaining tight quality control in a geographically remote location.

A good example of a global company that makes extensive use of international subcontracting is Nike. Donaghu and Barff[9] point out that Nike do not own any integrated production facilities, but instead manage a network of subcontactors that specialise to a greater or lesser degree. In particular, Nike have two classes of production partners, the high volume producers of mass market footwear and 'exclusive' partners that are responsible for the top-end expensive products. The position of Nike in this scenario is essentially one of a merchandiser, with a 100 per cent market focus.

Franchising

International franchising is particularly appropriate to formulaic styles of products or services, which are sold under a well established brand. It is generally recognised that branding is an essential ingredient of franchising success.

Franchising works as a contractual agreement by which the franchiser who owns the business idea and brand, sells (franchises) the right to operate the business in a specified area, subject to compliance with prescribed modus operandi. The franchisee then pays a fee to the franchiser in return for access to the business, and the fee is usually made up of a fixed charge on signing the agreement, plus regular payments of royalties-based on sales. In many cases, the terms of operation of the franchise also require that inputs are purchased from the central franchiser. For example in the case of a pizza chain, the franchiser will require the owner of an outlet to buy all of the pizza bases and toppings from them. This requirement is a way of both ensuring consistency of product quality, and also increasing the franchiser's profits via markups on the ingredients sold on. Franchise agreements are usually highly localised, but a master franchise may be sold which covers a large region, e.g. France, and the owner of that agreement then takes responsibility and a profit share from sale of the more local agreements within the region.

The role of the franchiser is to provide guidance, training and support to the franchisees, who often see this as a low risk route into running a small business. In return, the franchiser receives the fee and commission income, together with the potential to gain rapid expansion of a business at very low risk. The biggest potential difficulty for the franchiser is that of successful co-ordination of a wide network of businesses, all with different managers. The brand needs to be protected if the overall business is to grow by attracting more franchisees, but there can be a tendency for managers to want to 'go their own way' if tight controls are not imposed from the centre. In the case of international franchising this risk is increased because cultural variations in management styles may greatly impede the use of a common approach.

Retailing and restaurant businesses are sectors which frequently use franchising as a way into new markets. For example, in retailing, the international furniture company operates a mix of company-owned and franchised stores. If you have visited one of their stores, you will have noticed that they all have a similar layout, carry common products and provide identical customer services such as children's play areas and a restaurant. In the catering trade, well known brands such as Pizza Hut, Kentucky Fried Chicken, Dunkin Donuts, McDonald's and Planet Hollywood are all franchised. Again, as a customer of one of these outlets you will recognise the consistency of the product range across all locations, the décor and layout, method of food preparation and style of presentation are all identical.

Turnkey Projects

Turnkey projects are common in the construction business, and the term is used to describe a situation in which a company agrees to build a large facility and bring it to the point of being fully operational, before handing over the key to the purchasers. Large-scale infrastructure or power generation projects are often built on a turnkey basis on behalf of foreign governments. For example, the UK company Hawker Siddeley has constructed a number of power stations in Sub-Saharan Africa on a turnkey basis. Less-developed nations may lack both the engineering expertise and the production capability for such projects, and so they employ foreign companies to complete the full project. Hydro-electric plants, dams and road building projects are all well suited to turnkey contracts. The advantage for the contracting company is that a typical project will have a very high value, and so they gain large foreign sales. The disadvantage is that there are substantial risks, primarily of cost escalation, when such long-term contracts are undertaken. The time taken to complete may exceed original estimates because of problems of regulation, red tape and poor infrastructure in the location, as well as potentially difficult climatic conditions which can hamper progress. At the same time, there is a need to ensure that the company receives payments on account as different stages of the work are completed. This may be difficult when an economy is short of hard currency, which is usually used for pricing in such contracts.

Joint Ventures

The term joint venture is used to describe an agreement between two or more independent companies to establish a separate company for the purposes of pursuing a particular business project. It is important to note that the joint venture stands as a separate business from those of the partner companies. International joint ventures are attractive because they enable a foreign company with limited knowledge of a local market, to link up with a domestic company that may have the required domestic expertise. Such a partnership helps to reduce the risk of trying to enter a new overseas market with restricted knowledge and resources. At the same time, by sharing the cost of the venture, the required amount of capital is reduced, and so it may be possible to set up several joint ventures to tackle a number of markets simultaneously for the same investment cost as one wholly owned direct investment in a single market. Spreading the markets in this way further serves to reduce risks.

Market exploitation is not the only reason for joint ventures, although it is the focus here because this is a chapter on marketing. It is useful to remember that three types of alliance can be observed, classified according to the reason for collaboration. The three types are research, technology and market oriented ventures. These categories recognise that companies can benefit from collaboration on a variety of fronts.

An example of a recent international joint venture is an agreement between BASF Coatings and Akzo Nobel, who plan to set up an automotive OEM coatings venture in Australia. The term OEM stands for Original Equipment Manufacturer, and so the venture is intended to offer sales, marketing and technical services to automotive manufacturers in respect of paint finishes for their vehicles. The venture is attractive to the two companies because BASF wishes to strengthen its share of the Asian coatings market, and Australia is a good base from which to do this. Akzo will benefit because its plant in Melbourne will manufacture the coatings for the joint venture. It is interesting that BASF have other joint venture agreements in the coating business in the same region, but to serve different market segments. They have an agreement with Wattyl Coatings, Australia's second largest paint company, for an automotive refinish facility (dealing with the supply of paint for accident repairs etc.) and another OEM venture with NOF Corporation in Japan. By creating a network of joint ventures BASF is seeking to make greater market inroads than would be possible with a single investment.

The critical factor influencing the success of a joint venture is selection of a suitable partner. Some writers have likened the relationship to a marriage, which has to be approached with extreme caution, and only agreed to when the two parties fully understand one another. In similar vein, many ventures end in divorce. Unlike marriage, some joint ventures are never intended as a permanent arrangement but are instead established with the aim of completing a single specific project such as the European Airbus. The Airbus project is a collaboration between a number of aircraft manufacturers from across Europe, aimed at designing and constructing the next generation of large wide-bodied passenger aircraft. The research and development costs of a new breed of airliner are huge, and outside the scope of any single company, so the joint venture has worked to facilitate a project that otherwise could not have started. This is another of the advantages of such arrangements.

Perhaps one of the more surprising facts about joint ventures, as illustrated by the BASF:Akzo example given above, is that the majority of them are partnerships between competitors. Dicken[10] cites research which showed that over 70 per cent of international alliances between 1975 and 1986 were made between two companies operating in the same market. He also notes the fact that companies are starting to form not just one but multiple alliances, such as is evidenced by BASF's approach to the Australian/Asian market described earlier. These multiple alliances are a characteristic feature of international business in the twenty-first century, and are leading to the new organisational structures that were outlined in Chapter 5.

Mini Case Study

Talisman Energy

In 1998 the Calgary-based oil company Talisman Energy entered into a joint venture agreement to extract oil from an area of Southern Sudan. There were four parties to the agreement: Talisman, and the government owned petroleum companies of China, Sudan and Malaysia. At the time, Sudan was a country at war, with the Islamic government from the north of the country engaged in battles with the Christian inhabitants of the south.

The joint venture caused anger amongst human rights activists because it was claimed that government troops had been responsible for expelling people from the area where the drilling was to take place, and that the royalties that Talisman was paying to the Sudanese government were helping to fund the war. At the same time the United Nations Commission for Human Rights expressed the view that the oilfield drilling was leading to human rights abuses and leading to increased fighting.

In defence of its position, Talisman argued that its presence was valuable to the locals, as it helped to fund health and education provision. In addition, it felt that the presence of a Western investor could be useful in reducing any local rights violations, because it would be recognised that any such abuses would be widely reported in the Western press. When news of the accusations reached the ears of company shareholders, two major pension funds sold their holdings in protest at the company's Sudanese involvement, and Talisman's share price became volatile.

Talisman remain involved in the project, but recognise the difficulties that joint ventures can bring. The political fallout from a poor choice of either location or partners can prove expensive in terms of shareholder support, and if the market really does not like the risks then a business can become vulnerable to take-over.

Source: *Financial Times*

Foreign Direct Investment

If trade barriers are strong, so that exporting is impossible, and it is difficult to identify potential local companies to use for production/distribution or both, a company may be left with no choice but to opt for direct investment in order to enter a market. In such a situation, the choice must be made between opting for a merger or acquisition of a local business, to buy in local expertise, or to go for sole ownership of a new venture. The choice is a strategic one, and is dependent upon a variety of factors. For example, purchase of a local company will mean that market access can be gained more quickly than if a new plant and distribution centre is established from scratch. It may also enable the company to enter the market via an already established brand. On the other hand, working with a local company might be seen as disadvantageous because it does not make clear the distinction between the foreign and local concerns, to facilitate differential branding.

In terms of relative risk, it is likely that acquisition of or merger with a domestic competitor is the safer option. The scale of investment is likely to be lower, and there is also the advantage that the concern is already up and running so there should be an immediately positive cash flow. This choice brings with it all the usual difficulties of mergers or acquisitions such as coping with the changeover of management, the elimination of duplicate functions and the introduction of common operating systems and corporate culture. Nonetheless, it is a market entry route that has proved attractive to a very substantial number of firms.

The UK-based building materials group Caradon, for example, recently entered the Scandinavian market via the acquisition of Eltek Fire and Safety, a Norwegian company that manufactures fire detection and alarm systems. The Norwegian acquisition complements the company's purchase earlier this year of two German electrical companies. Caradon's current strategy is to increase its presence in the world market for control systems for 'intelligent buildings', and these purchases serve this objective in two ways:

■ adding to the product portfolio and
■ broadening the geographic spread of the company's markets.

Expansion by foreign acquisition is not confined to the market for goods, as can be seen by the trend towards consolidation in the financial services sector. For example HSBC (Hong Kong and Shanghai Banking Corporation) now owns the former Midland Bank in the UK, and the Royal Bank of Scotland has a stake in the Spanish bank Banco Santander.

If the decision is to enter a market by establishing a brand new production and marketing facility, then the risks are high, as well as the costs. If one accepts the staged models of internationalisation, such a method of international expansion is the final stage of the internationalisation process. In practice, it is the case that for most industries the costs of setting up new foreign production facilities can only be justified if the target market is very large. For example, Japanese electronics companies have established a number of production facilities in the United Kingdom, such as NEC in Scotland and Fujistsu in the North East of England. These sites offer easy access to the large and expanding single European market. In similar vein, the choice of the East Midlands as the site for the Toyota Motor company's manufacturing plant can be explained by the location advantages it offered in terms of access into a wider Europe. As a general rule, therefore, the choice of direct investment from new as an entry route is comparatively rare, and tends to be associated with the larger, probably transnational organisations.

At this stage it is helpful to summarise the factors that might influence a company's choice of market entry route. These include:

- Attitude to risk
- Access to capital
- Current resources and resource requirements
- Management ambition
- Available opportunities
- Desired speed of market entry
- Requirements in terms of level of control.

How the final choice is made probably depends upon the nature of the opportunity. If there are lots of options, then a decision can be taken slowly and rationally, perhaps using a scoresheet similar to that used for market selection. Alternatively, a choice may emerge out of a series of discussions and 'gut reaction' to events. Every company will be different, as will the resulting level of success in gaining a share of the overseas market.

MANAGING THE MARKETING MIX

The final international marketing decisions that still need to be discussed are those which relate to the selection of the marketing mix for any particular market or group of markets. The four components of the mix are product, price, promotion and distribution, all of which require separate decisions. We can now look at each of these in turn.

Product Decisions

If managers have already gone through a detailed market segmentation exercise, prior to selecting their target market, it is likely that they have a very good idea of the degree of product modification that may be required to achieve market success. Nonetheless, as Majaro[11] points out, 'the product is the heart of the marketing mix. If the product fails to satisfy the consumer and his needs, no additional expenditure and effort on any of the other ingredients of the mix will improve product performance in the marketplace.' It is vital, therefore, that product decisions are carefully thought out.

When talking about a product, it is helpful to remember that there are several components to the package that makes up a product. These include its design, ability to perform the desired function, packaging, brand (where applicable) and after-sales service. Decisions on each of these components are best made with a particular buyer in mind, and the issue of standardisation versus differentiation can be answered *for that target consumer* in respect of each factor. The example of a US-based bridal wear company wishing to market overseas can be used to illustrate these ideas. In the USA, many brides still wear traditional-style white dresses, but if these were marketed in Japan they may cause offence, since white is the colour used to signify death – the colour of the design has to be altered for the new market. Equally, the market in the

Philippines might be very accepting of the white colour, but the dress sizes are likely to be too large. Filipino women are generally much smaller than their American counterparts. All of these factors need to be taken into account when targeting a particular market, and it should be borne in mind that any differentiation is likely to lead to an increase in costs.

A decision to modify, if made, is therefore based on substantial market analysis. For example, the chocolate that is on a Mars bar in the USA is not identical to that which covers a Mars bar for sale in Europe, and the reason is that consumer tastes in chocolate differ in the two markets. The US chocolate is not as sweet or as chewy as the European version. Mars will have decided to differentiate the markets only because it felt that the product could not otherwise succeed.

Apart from consumer taste, the other factors that need to be taken into account when making product decisions are:

1 Corporate objectives: Is the aim for short-term maximum profit or a steady long-term growth in market share? If objectives are short-term, the product should be marketed without amendment, to keep costs down.

2 Will standardisation of the product bring market demand down to an uneconomic level? Strictly speaking the markets where this might be true should have already been filtered out in the market selection, but asking the question again does no harm.

3 What resources does the company have to cope with the additional work created by differentiation? Product policies need to fit with corporate resources.

4 What would be the cost impact of product modifications on manufacturing, distribution, marketing and financing? If the cost impact is measured, then the return on investment with a standard product can be directly compared with the return on investment with a non-standardised version.

5 What impact might product changes have on the market profile of the product in other countries? For example, customers might start demanding modifications because they have seen them elsewhere and like them; this would raise costs. An example of this might be the way in which CD players are automatically installed in cars sold in some markets, but not in others.

6 Should a product be sold under a brand name, and should that name be global or local? Consumers in the industrialised markets are likely to be brand conscious and so the use of a known global brand name can enhance sales in this type of market. In contrast, where consumer markets are relatively undeveloped, there may be no gain in the use of the name, as it goes unrecognised. Equally, in terms of language, the brand name may not be well suited (or even offensive) to foreign customers. For example, the Spanish drinks company Gonzalez Byass, which has a substantial share of the UK market in sherry, also makes a brandy which is sold in

Spain under the name Soberano. It is difficult to imagine this brand name working successfully in England, because 'sober' implies a lack of alcohol.

Pricing Decisions

A combination of factors, both internal and external to the firm, will work to affect the price that can be charged for a product in different markets. The overall result of these multiple combinations is that it is generally impossible to apply a common world price (see Yip[12]). This leads to the problem of establishing prices for each individual or each group of markets, and the starting point for this process is likely to be the formulation of a range of possible prices along a spectrum such as that illustrated below.

Figure 8.2

Competitive price

Lowest price
Break-even or
minimum return
on investment

Highest price
'What the
market will
bear'

The spectrum of possible prices takes into account both cost- and market-based influences on price. At worst, the company needs to be able to either recover some of its costs or achieve a minimum return on its investment. At best, customers may be persuaded to pay very high premiums for uniquely desirable goods. In between, there will be the prices charged by competitors, and the managers need to select their position on the spectrum.

The choice will be determined in part by the overall product 'package' that has emerged from the product decision, and partly by competitive conditions in the target market. If, for example, the market is dominated by a single large player, then a company will generally need to follow the pricing policy of that leader if it is to have any hope of gaining a market share. In contrast, if the competition is weak, there will be greater potential for freedom of choice over the price. In deciding the price of equivalent goods sold by competitors it is useful to compare products in terms of all the components of the product mix, as already discussed. If the new entrant is offering more stylish design or a more advanced technology, then a price premium is probably acceptable, but it is important to compare like with like. The need for careful comparison cannot be overemphasised, because if a product is priced too low, then it may either damage the corporate image or lead to a failure to take profits that were available if the price had been right. This was true of the MGF sports car, which was sufficiently attractive at its UK launch price to generate a waiting list for vehicles. Some customers were then able to take delivery of the car, and sell it on in the second-hand market for a price greater than a brand new vehicle! At the right price, more profit would have been made.

The Daewoo range of cars is another example of international car pricing, but this time one which was more successful. The Korean car company's success in Europe is partly based on the fact that its vehicles were well engineered, having been developed in a joint venture with General Motors. Their design is traditional, probably slightly old fashioned in some respects, but they are supplied at a price which includes lots of extras such as sunroof, air conditioning, ABS brakes, mobile phones and a number of years servicing as standard.

Despite these add-ons, the price is slightly below that of comparably sized models from other European and US manufacturers which also charge extra for each additional facility. Daewoo has gained market share because they recognised that a least one part of the market was more sensitive to price than to design. This illustrates how the price and product decisions are closely intertwined.

Once a price has been determined which links price to the product specification, and fits the general market conditions, a number of other factors need to be considered. These are:

1 *Company objectives*

   As with the product decision, price will be affected by the objectives. A business may want to gain the maximum market share as quickly as possible, and in such instances it is best to go for a 'penetration' pricing strategy, whereby the price is set as low as is required to achieve the desired market share. Alternatively, if a product is highly attractive because it is currently unique, then a 'skimming' strategy could be adopted to sell at the highest price possible to early customers in order to maximise short-term profit and cash flow. Another strategy might be to seek to create barriers to entry so that no competitors can steal market share, and for this it would perhaps be necessary to sell products as loss leaders until the risk of competition has disappeared. There have been some suggestions that this was the approach adopted by Sega when it first launched its Master System in Europe; it is said that the retail price of the system was below its landed cost. In practice, the anti-dumping laws that operate in most industrialised countries would ensure that such a strategy could not be deployed, as it would be seen as a form of unfair competition.

2 *The legal and regulatory environment of the intended market*

   Price will be affected by rates of duty, and purchase taxes, but (as just indicated) there may also be legislation that defines and controls restrictive trade practices such as retail price maintenance, or sets rules on the need to display the price on the packaging, etc. In the United States, for example, companies are bound by the Foreign Corrupt Practices Act which forbids American companies that are selling abroad from making payments such as bribes in return for obtaining orders. In some countries it is almost standard practice for customers to ask a foreign supplier to quote an inflated price, and then pay the price differential into the personal bank account of a company official. In outlawing such actions, the

American legislation is promoting honesty in business dealings, but some US firms have complained that the act works to prevent them getting foreign orders.

3 *Economic conditions, particularly the forecasts for interest rates and inflation*

Where an economy is suffering from relatively high rates of inflation, a mechanism for regular price reviews will need to be put in place if profitability is to be maintained. Inflation will lead to increases in the cost of distribution, and the cost of capital in a market, but if prices remain constant then the margin will be eroded. In the early 1990s for example, when Mexico was suffering from rampant inflation, the local distributor of the Dulux brand of paint, made by ICI, was forced to implement monthly price adjustments, and gave up producing a price list because it went out of date too quickly.

In contrast, a stable economy will imply that prices are likely to change slowly, and market growth may also be quite slow, so the company will have to be patient in waiting for long-term profit.

An additional consideration is that economic conditions will have a direct impact on living standards, and on the consumer's ability to pay. Hexter *et al.*[13] cite the example of European companies trying to enter the Chinese market by selling bouillon and chicken powder in place of monosodium glutamate as a flavouring and thickening agent. The powder is priced at a 300 per cent premium over its local equivalent, and so even the richest Shanghai households find it difficult to afford. Such a pricing policy will severely restrict the speed of market adoption of these products.

4 *Exchange rates*

The relative strength of a currency is a reflection of the strength of the underlying economy, but from the point of view of the international marketer, it can help determine whether a market is profitable or unprofitable. Some protection from currency risks can be gained by pricing higher as the level of risk increases. For example, if a currency is weakening, the value of the net receipts when converted back to the exporter's domestic currency will be falling. In order to protect the value of receipts in the domestic currency, it may be possible to take out a foreign currency hedge (as described in Chapter 8) but raising prices in the overseas market will also help. The only time when this might cause a problem is if the foreign market is very price sensitive, and so sales are lost as a consequence of the price rise.

5 *Terms of sale*

The price shown on a price list, or quoted to a customer will often not be the price that is ultimately paid, and it is important to understand custom and practice relating to price negotiations in each different market. In the Middle East it is usual for prices to be negotiable, and so it helps to set an initial price above that which is required. In the USA such negotiation is less frequent, and prices are set accordingly.

Terms of sale also cover the credit terms granted to customers. As long as a debt is outstanding, working capital is required to fund it, and so the granting of extended periods of credit can be expensive. Some countries, such as the United Kingdom, have rules that grant small suppliers the right to charge interest on accounts that remain unpaid after a certain time period, and this helps to protect vulnerable companies. In establishing the selling price, account can be taken of the credit terms, so that if they are lengthy the price can be raised to cover the extra cost.

Having adjusted its initial price to take account of all of the factors listed above, managers should find that they will avoid a situation in which there are large price differentials across national boundaries. Such differentials are a threat to successful international marketing because they can lead to pressures from the 'expensive' markets for discounts and reductions. This is exactly what happened at the start of the year 2000 in the UK retail motor trade. Customers realised that they can obtain the same vehicle at a lower price from a dealer in mainland Europe, and so specialist shippers have set up what might be termed a 'grey market' in cars, exporting them from Europe into the United Kingdom. Avoiding large international price differences helps to eliminate the risk of such problems, thereby protecting the product and brand image.

Promotion Decisions

Promotion is all about communication – telling potential customers and the market in general about your products by the use of a words and visual imagery. The seller has a message which needs to be communicated to a target audience, and the communication is only successful if the message is understood. Understanding can be enhanced if the international marketer makes full use of the information collected in the original market selection process, to construct a market profile.

The promotion process can be subdivided into three distinct dimensions:

- Objectives
- Style of message, and
- Routes.

Objectives

It is easy to assume that the aim of product promotion is sales, but in practice the objectives may be a little more subtle than this. In fact, the objective when selling into a new market is likely to be very different to that sought in an established market. For example, iced coffee is a product which is consumed widely in the USA and certain parts of mainland Europe, but is still relatively unknown in the United Kingdom. In launching a campaign to sell such a product into the UK, the first consideration is to *inform* consumers of the existence of such a product and create an understanding of its characteristics, typical consumers and brand image. It may take some time to build up consumer understanding, and so in the initial stages of the product launch, sales are not the primary objective. Nestlé has recently launched a series of advertisements for its Nescafe Ice drink in England. The advertisement shows a young man lying back surrounded by ice, looking very content as he drinks a bottle of the iced coffee, and the tag line reads 'It's a state of mind.' Soon after the product was launched, a teenager 'rewrote' the tag line on one billboard in the centre of a large English city, to read 'It's a tragic state of mind.' The insert illustrates the view of just one consumer about the product (and the advertisement), but it illustrates the fact that it takes time to build up consumer confidence to the point at which they will make a purchase. In a new market, therefore, where a product is in the early stages of its life cycle, the main objective of promotion is one of creating consumer awareness and knowledge.

Of course, a company may be entering a foreign market which is new to them, but is already familiar with the product in general. In such cases, once a product is at or beyond the maturity stage in its life cycle, the primary objective of advertising changes to one of increasing sales. The emphasis is on maximising the revenue from the product before it reaches the end of its life, and so promotions seek to both boost current sales and extend the life cycle where possible.

In an international context, these differences in objectives mean that it is important to be aware of the positioning of a product in terms of its life cycle in each of the different markets. At one time, there were often significant time lags between the introduction of products into different countries, but this is no longer the case. Where differences remain, the objectives and hence the style of promotions must be varied across the locations, but in other instances the campaigns can be standardised. Consequently, for consumer goods such a Coca Cola or Reebok clothing and footwear, there is consistency of advertising on almost a global scale.

Style

The style used in communicating with consumers can vary widely, but again for international firms it is vital to pay close attention to the question of understanding. One obvious variation in style is the choice between the use of verbal or non-verbal messages, and it is tempting to believe that international advertising is best done via the use of visuals rather than the written word. This assumption oversimplifies the cultural divide between nations which, as you saw in Chapter⁴, extends well beyond the question of language. For example, some countries, such as Germany, demonstrate a preference for advertisements that provide facts, whilst others (such as the UK) use humour as a way of getting a message across. Attitudes towards the use of sex or sexual imagery in advertising also varies widely.

Majaro[11] cites the case of the famous Esso tiger as illustration of the problem of gaining global acceptance of visual imagery. When it was decided to use the tiger as a global brand image, it was realised that it would not work in some cultures where the tiger was regarded as too ferocious and so its looks were modified, with lengthened eyelashes and a general softening of its appearance to make it more toy like. The global advertising then proved successful.

If one accepts Levitt's view that products can be standardised on a world-wide basis, then so can promotion, and it is noticeable that advertisements are moving in this direction. In such cases there is marked tendency to use visual imagery as much as possible. For example, there is an Adidas television advertisement in which a lorry is driven into the centre of a city square, somewhere in Europe. From inside the lorry there are released hundreds of Adidas footballs, and members of the public begin to play with the balls. The only words in the advertisement are the Adidas logo and the tag line 'forever sport' which appears at the very end.

Where language is used in advertising or other promotional material, then in the international context great care must be taken to avoid cultural offence or the risk of mistranslation. One of the more frequently quoted instances of a product requiring re-naming to be sold abroad is that of the Rolls Royce model originally called Silver Mist. The model name was changed to Silver Shadow for export to Germany because in German *mist* means 'dung'. In this regard it is helpful to have material translated by someone familiar with the everyday language of the country, so that unnecessary formalities are eradicated, and the use of offensive slang is avoided.

Route

A company needs to be careful in selecting the route that it uses to promote its products, if it is to maximise its marketing success. There are four main routes to choose from, and each has advantages and disadvantages in relation to different types of products:

- Advertising
- Sales promotion
- Publicity
- Personal selling.

Advertising is used to describe promotions that use commercial media to send messages to the market. The media encompasses newspapers and magazines, mail-shots, billboards, commercial radio, television and the cinema. International marketing managers should be aware that the availability and usefulness of different classes of media will vary across countries, and they often reflect a nation's level of economic development. For example, billboards may still be the main route used to advertise in the rural communities of Africa and Asia, but television is probably the most popular advertising medium in the industrialised West. Again, the market profile should contain information on the local media.

Sales promotion involves promotion without the use of media, via trade shows, product demonstrations, and the issuing of samples. In-store sampling is a good way of introducing new food products to a new market, because people may be tempted to try a small taste, whilst being wary of paying for something they later find they do not like. Trade shows are a useful way of attracting the attention of new distributors or agents in a foreign market, particularly for industrial goods.

Publicity is more general in nature, and relates to the way in which no individual product or service is promoted, but media reporting of a company's general activities can help to build up the corporate image and ultimately help sales. The head of the Virgin group of companies, Richard Branson, is a person who is very good at finding ways of maximising the public profile of the group. His round the world balloon journeys are not advertising, but still work very effectively to remind people of the Virgin brand.

Personal selling tends to be used for products that are highly specialised or bespoke, and is promotion by means of presentations direct to potential buyers. This is commonly used for industrial goods, and is often a follow-up to enquiries that have been made at a trade show.

The mix of routes selected for any given market will reflect both the product type and the level of control that the company wishes to exercise over its foreign operations. Publicity and personal selling tend to be organised centrally, whereas sales promotions and advertising may need to be fine tuned to local needs, and so decisions are decentralised.

The last consideration in planning foreign promotions is legal regulation. Rules on labelling, trade descriptions, and the content of advertisements can vary, and knowledge of such variations is vital to the avoidance of expensive mistakes. In Europe, for example, there is an EU directive which prohibits companies from making medicinal claims in respect of food products. This means, for example, that a manufacturer cannot claim on packaging or in advertisements that a food 'helps reduce the risk of heart disease' or 'cures ulcers' etc. Any company wanting to launch a new food product in Europe needs to be ware of this regulation. Similarly, in France, Spain and Italy there is a total ban on cigarette advertising, whereas in the UK only television advertising of cigarettes is banned, but all advertisement must include a government health warning on the risks of smoking. The subtleties of international regulatory differences should be identified in market profiling, and if they are not, then major international agencies will be able to offer advice.

Distribution Decisions

Distribution refers to the route through which products progress from the original manufacturer to the end consumer. There are a number of different distribution channels that may be followed and these are classified as long or short depending on the number of stages involved. For example, a consumer goods manufacturer could choose the following route to distribute their products:

Manufacturer ⟶ Agent ⟶ Wholesaler ⟶ Retailer ⟶ Consumer

This is a relatively long chain, but in a new market it can be helpful because it means that the manufacturer passes on the risk of final sale to the intermediaries, and cash flow will not be subject to the delay of waiting for consumers to decide to adopt the product.

A much shorter chain is one in which the manufacturer sells direct to the retailer:

Manufacturer ⟶ Retailer ⟶ Consumer

This approach also has advantages, because the retailer is closer to the end customer, and so the time lag between production and final sale can be reduced. This is particularly important for products which have a very short life, such as high fashion items.

The shortest possible distribution chain is that of direct selling, whereby the manufacturer uses no intermediaries but instead deals directly with the end consumer. The computer manufacturers Tiny and Dell are examples of companies that sell in this way. Dell in fact used direct Internet selling of personal computers to revive its whole business, when it found that competition had eroded its sales and market share via traditional distribution routes.

The optimal type and length of distribution channel is determined, in part, by the type of product, as can be seen in the following Table.

Table 8.2   *Linking Product Types to Distribution Channels*

Product type	Key characteristic	Distribution channel
Complex consumer goods e.g. computers / electrical goods High value industrial goods	Requirement for after-sales service, and support	Short – either direct sales or manufacturer → retailer → customer
Fast-moving consumer goods	Competitive market environment and need for wide distribution	Indirect, via wholesaler, to ensure coverage of large number of outlets
Perishables, e.g. fruit and vegetables	Short shelf life	Short: direct or straight through the end retailer
Customised products e.g. bespoke software	Need to understand end-customer requirements	Short, preferably direct

Understanding the relationship between the type of product and the appropriate distribution channel is an issue which has to be decided for domestic as well as international markets, and so in moving into an international environment the manufacturer is likely to already have a reasonably clear idea of the distribution channels to be sought out.

One issue which affects international but not domestic operations, is the need to think about the geographic location of production plants and markets, so that an efficient distribution system can be established to link them. This aspect of distribution, commonly referred to a logistics, involves decisions about the best way of physically moving goods between locations rather than the way in which they are sold to the consumer. Consequently, although it has implications for marketing, it is viewed as an operations management issue and so is discussed in Chapter 9.

There is widespread acceptance in the business community that distribution channels tend to be highly specific to each country/region, and so understanding local custom and practice is vital to success. The first step in any international distribution decision is therefore identification of exactly what channels are available in any particular locality. This includes taking into account not just the physical existence of, say, a wholesaler network, but also the extent to which it is either owned by competitors or loyal to particular suppliers. For example, in many countries wholesalers will be required by manufacturers to sign exclusivity agreements, which mean that they will not market competitors' products.

Local Differences in Access to Distribution Channels

In the UK domestic paint market, the product is sold to the trade (professional painters and decorators) via specialist centres, whilst it is sold to the consumer through large retail 'sheds' such as B & Q and Sainsbury's Homebase. These sheds will usually stock the brand leader Dulux made by ICI, Crown (from the Dutch company Akzo Nobel) and own-brand goods, most of which are made by Kalon.

By way of contrast, the paint market in the USA is characterised by the fact that the paint manufacturers operate their own retail outlets. The company with the largest market share, Sherwin Williams, owns over 2,000 stores. This arrangement clearly makes it difficult for foreign manufacturers wanting to enter the US market. The UK manufacturer ICI dealt with the problem by purchasing (in 1986) a US manufacturer, Glidden, in order to gain access to outlets.

The high cost of buying another company in order to access distribution channels is obviously one which is only open to larger companies.

Source: *Financial Times*

The USA is the world's largest consumer market, and the example illustrates the fact that where the potential market is large enough, it may be worth a company investing in establishing its own sales and distribution network, but this can be very expensive. Equally, such investment requires resources which extend beyond just the finance, and so it is an option only open to big businesses.

Once a company has determined the ideal type of channel for distribution, and its availability in the country, there remain a number of other factors to be taken into account. These are:

■ *Level of control*

Shorter distribution channels increase the level of control over the marketing process, so the risks of, for example, a product's image being damaged by bad retailing is reduced. At the same time, a decision needs to be made about how much the company wishes to operate control of distribution from the centre as opposed to allowing local management of the issue. This will be determined by the company's overall strategy and the resulting structure, as described in Chapter 5.

■ *Speed of market entry*

Where there is an aim to move into a new market very quickly, there may be very little choice about the particular distribution channels to use. There will be insufficient time to establish new systems from scratch.

■ *Profit impact*

Assuming that a company wishes to maximise the long-term profits from a new market, it must look carefully at the cost and revenue effects of choosing different distribution methods. Long channels may be quite useful for cash flow, because the payment will not be delayed until an end sale is completed. At the same time, there is likely to be a lower credit risk in selling to an established agent or wholesaler. On the other hand, the profit margin is likely to be reduced as the distribution chain lengthens, simply because each party needs to make a profit. The volume of sales that can be achieved is also likely to be affected by the method of distribution. Market coverage by direct sales representatives may be small compared to what can be achieved by using a large established wholesaler or agent. Consequently, even though the contribution per unit sold is lower when using a wholesaler, the overall returns might well be much greater. All of these effects on cost and revenue should be quantified, and the resulting range of financial returns passed to the Board of Directors for a decision.

PRODUCT VERSUS SERVICE MARKETING

So far we have assumed that a common approach can be adopted in terms of international marketing, regardless of whether a company wishes to sell goods or services. This may slightly oversimplify the issues, and it is useful to look at the special factors that need to be taken into account when looking for overseas markets for services.

The first step is to return to the question of the potential to standardise, and in the case of service provision this is largely determined by the degree of judgement that is needed to 'fine tune' a service to meet individual customer needs. This is clearly illustrated in Figure 8.3 below.

Figure 8.3   *Customisation of International Services*

		Degree of customization of service characteristics	
		High	Low
Degree of judgement in meeting customer needs	High	Surgery Gourmet restaurant	Mass education
	Low	Hotel	Airline Fast-food restaurant

The Figure clearly shows that the potential to standardise is increased only as long as there is little need to explicitly acknowledge differences between individual customers in terms of their service requirements. An airline can be considered a 'service factory' because of its high levels of investment in aircraft and booking information systems with personal contact restricted to check-in and in-flight cabin services. This is vastly different from a solicitor's office, with its high levels of personal contact and comparatively low levels of investment in equipment. Alternatively, we may consider two companies in the same sector, using catering as an example. A fast-food outlet will employ more standardised materials and processes and operate a more restricted menu than a gourmet restaurant. The consequence is major differences in the product, process and delivery strategies for the serving of meals.

A failure to look closely at how localised a country's service requirements might be can perhaps explain why it is that fast-food outlets have successfully internationalised, whilst many retailers have not. Differences in cultural preferences, styles of shopping, product preference and quality standards will all affect consumers' attitudes to retailers. Consequently, there have been a number of high profile withdrawals from international retail expansion. Readers Digest, the magazine and book retailer withdrew from the Japanese market after a total of twenty-four years, of which only eleven had been profitable. Similarly, the UK retailer Marks and Spencer announced the closure of all of its European stores which have never been profitable. It may be that only standardised or highly branded products can successfully be retailed in the international market.

The central issue in successful international marketing of services is therefore good understanding of client needs: give the customers exactly what they want. This helps to explain why the large investment banks, professional accountancy and consultancy firms such as J.P. Morgan, Price Waterhouse Coopers and Anderson Consulting have been able to create a global presence. The clients of these organisations are primarily large companies which themselves have a global marketplace. Consequently the professional firms are merely 'following their clients' when they establish overseas offices, because the companies such as Microsoft or Ford will buy the service on a global contract, not on a country by country basis. As long as good client relations are maintained the contract remains in place and issues of standardisation versus localisation can all but disappear.

In conclusion then, the questions to be answered in constructing a marketing strategy are more or less identical for both products and services. The emphasis merely changes, with service providers needing to pay special attention to customer relations. Having addressed the question of where to sell, how to enter the market, and identification of product, pricing and distribution choices the international marketing plan is complete.

SUMMARY

The process of assembling an international marketing plan is a lengthy one, as reflected by the length of this chapter, but it can be broken down into a clearly defined series of stages. Failures in international marketing can usually be explained by a company's lack of systematic analysis of either market selection, market mix or both. For example, inadequate research on market size and cultural characteristics, may result in a failure to differentiate a product adequately. This in turn leads to high expenditure on promotion in order to gain just a small market share, and ultimately the company may find that it is not making a profit on its foreign sales. By viewing marketing as a series of incremental decisions, when problems arise the cause can be identified by working back through the system to trace the source of the mistake. As with most things, mistakes can be rectified, but the price can be high, both in monetary terms and in terms of corporate image. In the light of this, well thought out marketing strategies can be seen as fundamental to international business success.

CONCLUSION

At this stage in the book you have acquired a good understanding of:

- the external environment
- how companies internationalise
- the funding and financial risks associated with international growth
- the process of devising an international marketing strategy.

Unfortunately, however, knowing where you want to sell and what, is still not quite enough, because company managers still need to decide where and how the goods are to be bought, processed and distributed to the chosen markets. This is the task of the operations manager, and is thus the subject of the next Chapter.

References

1 Ohmae, K. (1989) 'Managing in a borderless world', *Harvard Business Review*, Vol.67, May–June, pp.152–61

2 Levitt, T. (1983) 'The globalisation of markets', *Harvard Business review*, Vol.61, May–June, pp.92–102

3 Quelch, J.A. and Hoff, E.J. (1986) 'Customising global marketing', *Harvard Business Review*, Vol.64, May–June, pp.59–68

4 Sandler, D. and Shani, D. (1991) 'Brand globally but advertise locally? An empirical investigation', *International Marketing Review*, 9, pp.18–31

5 Samiee, S. and Roth, K. (1992) 'The influence of global marketing standardisation on performance', *Journal of Marketing* (October), pp.1–17

6 Geiser, P. (1986) 'Global products, localised messages', *Marketing Communications*, 11 (December), pp.23–26

7 Ellis, J. and Williams, D. (1995) *International Business Strategy*, Pitman Publishing, London, pp.229

8 Donaghu, M.T. and Barff, R. (1990) 'Nike just did it: international subcontracting and flexibility in international footwear production', *Regional Studies*, Vol.24, pp.537–52

9 Dicken, P (1998) *Global Shift*, 3rd edition, Chapman Paul, London, p.228

10 Majaro, S. (1977) *International marketing: a strategic approach to world markets*, George Allen and Unwin Ltd, London, p.78

11 Yip, G. (1992) *Total global strategy*, Prentice Hall, Englewood Cliffs

12 Hexter, J., Perez, J. and Perkins, A. 'Gold from noodles', *The McKinsey Quarterly*, 1998, No.3, pp.59–73

Further Reading

Stonehouse, G., Hamill, J., Campbell, D. and Purdie, T. (2000) *Global and Transnational Business*, Chapter 7, entitled 'Global and transnational market servicing strategies', Wiley, Chichester

Root, F.R. (1987) *Entry strategies for international markets*, Lexington Books, Lexington

Meloan, T. and Graham, J. (1998) *International and global marketing, concepts and cases*, Irwin McGraw-Hill, Singapore

The following journals and trade magazines also contain useful articles on international marketing:

International Marketing Review
Journal of Marketing
Business Horizons
European Journal of Marketing
Journal of Marketing Management
International Journal of Advertising
Marketing Week
Marketing

TUTORIAL EXERCISE

Specify two products/product groups which you think can be virtually standardised on a global level, and two that you believe could never be standardised. Think about the last time that you visited a foreign country and think about whether these products were on sale there. Try and list ways in which either product specification, promotional methods, or prices differed from those in your home market and use this to reach a conclusion on the level of standardisation in the marketing of the products. If the products were unavailable, can you explain why this might have been the case?

ESSAY QUESTIONS

1 Is global branding the easiest route to successful global marketing?

2 Do you agree with Levitt's proposition that consumer tastes are being homogenised?

3 What effect might the growth of e-commerce have on international pricing decisions?

Case Study: Bulmers

Bulmers is a UK-based company pursuing the strategic objective of being an international drinks firm specialising in 'alcoholic long drinks.' The long drinks market includes beer, cider and spirits combined with mixers, such as vodka and lemon or gin and orange.

Historically, Bulmers began its corporate life as a cider brewer, and cider remains the company's most important product. The target age group of cider drinkers is 18–24, and over the years Bulmers has established itself as market leader in the United Kingdom, where it currently has a market share (for drinks bought in pubs/clubs/restaurants) of approximately 70 per cent. The core brand names of Strongbow, Woodpecker and Scrumpy Jack are familiar to the majority of young British adults. In addition to selling their own products, Bulmers own the UK distribution rights for premium bottled beers such as Amstel, Red Stripe and San Miguel.

Recognising the potential risks of concentrating on a single market, Bulmers has operated an international division for some time. The company has been selling into Australasia for over thirty years and, via exports, foreign distribution agreements and wholly owned subsidiaries, world sales now span over forty countries. Nonetheless, the company is still heavily dependent on the UK market for the bulk of its earnings.

In 1996–7 the UK beer and cider market began to decline, with year-on-year sales falling by around 3 per cent across the industry. The causes of declining sales were a combination of changing tastes, as wine consumption replaced beer consumption, and problems with a general reduction in the level of drinking outside the home. Bulmers faced a declining market for their core product.

The company's response was to seek to increase its overseas sales by building on its expertise as a cider brewer and the established UK brand strength. By the end of 1999 the company had four core strands to its international operations outside Australia. Within Europe, Bulmers owned Cidre Slassen in Belgium, which is the country's market leader in premium cider brands. Belgium is well renowned for its varietal beers and Slassen seeks to gain market share from beer drinkers by providing both traditional and flavoured cider products. In practice, the Belgian market is relatively small however, and 70 per cent of Slassen sales are exported to nearby border countries such as Germany and France.

In the rest of the world (excluding Australasia), Bulmer is seeking to expand in three key markets – the USA, South Africa and China. In the early–mid 1990s Bulmer's exposure to the US market was limited to the distribution of its Strongbow and Woodpecker brands through Guinness Bass Import Company. In 1998 Bulmers decided that it was time to invest directly in the USA and they purchased Green Mountain Cidery, owner of the Woodchuck brand, which had a 17 per cent share of the US market. This purchase was followed in 1999 by the acqusition of the Hard Cider Company, which is estimated as having a 50 per cent market share. At almost the same time, Bulmer agreed to shift the distribution of Woodpecker and Strongbow brands over to the Green Mountain plant, and in so doing they further increased the company's market share. The current rate of growth of the US cider market is approximately 20 per cent per year.

In South Africa, the world's second largest cider market, Bulmers has spent £1.2 million in the last twelve months on purchasing a company that owns three local cider brands.

Additionally, a joint venture arrangement has been agreed with the company's South African distribution partners, Bavaria Brau. The agreement means that cider brewing facilities will be transferred to a site adjacent to Bavaria Brau, who will take over responsibility for packaging of the drinks.

China is a new market for Bulmers. In 1999 the company entered into a joint venture (in which they provided £200,000 of working capital in return for a 65 per cent share) with San Kong, a local brewery. The agreement is for the construction of a cider plant in the southern city of Qufu. Bulmer's international director, John Harvey, describes China as a market with 'enormous potential for the development of alcoholic long drinks.' The aim is to pioneer a cider market, where beer is currently the most popular drink.

There are powerful reasons why the Chinese market is attractive to Bulmers, including:

- a young population when compared with established Western markets
- a tradition of consuming 'long' alcoholic drinks, particularly beer
- cider is a relatively low cost product, with potential mass appeal.

Unfortunately, a large number of companies, both Asian and multinational in origin, have also recognised the huge untapped potential of the Chinese food and beverage market. The difficulty that most firms encounter is that market potential is not necessarily converted into profits. A *McKinsey Quarterly* report has shown that pre-tax returns on investing in China can be low. The largest 2,500 joint ventures registered pre-tax returns of below 6 per cent in 1995. Overall, returns ranged from −36 per cent to +60 per cent and even the 200 largest concerns only managed pre-tax profits of 10 per cent after four years in China.

The statistics suggest that it is very difficult to make money in the Chinese food and beverage market, and the McKinsey researchers found that there are five factors that are critical to success:

1 Choice of product category
2 Pricing
3 Rapid building of scale
4 Investment in sales and distribution
5 Strong branding.

Product Category

In selecting product category, companies can choose between products which differ widely in their level/speed of consumer acceptance. In ascending order of acceptance the categories are:

- Existing products
- Direct replacement products, e.g. potato crisps instead of salt-flavoured snacks
- Bought products to replace home-made, e.g. soup
- Totally new products

Price

Pricing affects product affordability, which is a core determinant of sales volumes. In 1997 the average income in Chinese cities was around £35 per month (US$52), and so products sold at a price of 20–40 pence are readily affordable by the bulk of the population. When the price of a food or beverage rises above £1.40 then it become very difficult to sell.

Scale

There is evidence that larger producers are more profitable than smaller. Scale advantages arise because China is an expensive market to service because of its fragmented retail, distribution and media channels, combined with a geographically dispersed market with low spending power. Penetration of such markets requires investment in staff to build up sales and it is often cheapest to begin by marketing in just one region, and spreading out from this single base.

Investment in Marketing

The sheer size of the potential consumer market in China, combined with media fragmentation, has meant that advertising costs can be very high relative to sales. In the premium beer market where competition is fierce, McKinsey estimate that the average spend per drinker of $14 per year is equal to that in the USA. Launching a brand within just one region can be expensive when product testing and modification are taken into account. McKinsey estimate that expenditure of £1.5–£4 million is needed to launch a new brand in a single region. They cite the example of the Tingyi company, whose own brand of instant noodles has a 25 per cent market share by volume and 35 per cent by value. Establishing its market position required that Tingyi bought up one half of all the advertising in the instant noodle market during the first four years of the brand's life.

They continue to absorb 35 per cent of advertising in the segment, an amount equal to their percentage share of market value. The implication is that a prerequisite for success is investment in marketing rather than fixed assets.

Strong Brand

In common with many consumer markets China is highly responsive to branding. Western branded products can be used as status symbols if they are kept at affordable prices, but success requires that the brand profile is retained over the long term. The speedy growth of competition implies that being a first mover does not automatically grant the status of an unassailable brand.

Given the long list of criteria that determine success in the Chinese market, it is likely that as the twenty-first century begins, the senior management at Bulmers will be hoping that they have made the right decision in agreeing to the joint venture with San Kong.

Sources: http:/www.bulmer.com; Marketing, London, December 1999; Hexter, J., Perez, J. and Perkins, A., 'Gold from noodles', *The McKinsey Quarterly*, 1998, No.3, pp.59–73

CASE STUDY QUESTIONS

1 What potential problems might Bulmers face in pursuing global branding for Strongbow and Woodpecker?

2 How has their international growth to date helped to reduce the likelihood of such problems arising in practice?

3 Is it fair to assume that it may be possible (even easy) to convert beer drinkers to cider drinkers?

4 The joint venture in China offers lower risks to Bulmers than direct investment in wholly owned manufacturing facilities, but how might Bulmers have sought to penetrate the Chinese market with an even lower level of risk?

Operations and Supply Chain Management

INTRODUCTION

The central focus of this book is to analyse the way which the changing global environment has created challenges for companies engaged in international business. In becoming international in scope, companies face the very specific operational problem of ensuring that they can produce and efficiently serve all of their markets. The task of organising production and distributing goods to the marketplace has customarily been termed operations management, and this chapter aims to explain the various functions within operations management and the particular problems encountered when production units and markets are spread around the globe.

In the context of Porter's value chain, as described in Chapter 5, operations management straddles three of the five primary activities – namely inbound logistics, operations and outbound logistics, as well as linking in to the support function of procurement. Covering so much of the value chain, it is easy to see how important good operations management is to a business. In recent years, recognition of the need to integrate the different elements of operations management has led to some writers re-labelling it supply chain management (SCM), and SCM is now the common term used to describe the task of managing the various components of purchasing, production and logistics in combination rather than as separate functions.

Although there is currently no consensus definition of SCM, whatever the label given to the task, as Akkermans[1] *et al.* observe, 'supply chain management ... has become one of the top priorities on the strategic agenda of industrial companies', and current thinking suggests that effective management of the operations side of a business is a valuable way of obtaining a competitive advantage.

One reason for prioritising operations management issues might be this more explicit recognition of its vital role within the value chain. Another reason might be the effect of progress in information and transport technologies and the global liberalisation of trade and investment which, according to Vos and Akkermans[2], has added to the complexity of designing and managing supply chains. All of this means that it is a function which cannot be ignored in any discussion of international business.*

The first part of this chapter provides a summary of the scope of operations management irrespective of the international environment, and the techniques and strategies used by managers in this field. The following parts of the chapter use this foundation to explain the key operational decisions that need to be made in an international or global business, and the changing role of technology in those decisions. The final section looks at the way in which different forms of market entry – exporting, licensing, joint ventures, and foreign direct investment – all have specific operational implications.

THE PRACTICE OF OPERATIONS MANAGEMENT

As already suggested, operations management is concerned with the delivery to the customer of products of a required quality and appropriate volume, by the specified date. The products in question may be either goods or services, and the aim is to manage their production at an economic cost.

A good operations management system is defined by Thomas and Griffin[3] and Holmes[4] as one which ensures each of the following:

- high product quality standards
- flexibility of volume and product mix
- speedy and reliable delivery.

In achieving each of these objectives, operations management can be divided into the separate functions of:

- vendor management (for purchasing and inventory control)
- production management (for materials processing)
- distribution management (for product storage and transport)
- product delivery and support (for customer processing).

---

* For the purpose of consistency, and to avoid further debate on the terminology, the chapter will use the term operations management from this point onwards.

In practice, these various subdivisions (see Figure 9.1) are usually part of an endless chain of operations management from receipt of materials to customer supply, with data processing as a common supporting thread throughout almost all operations.

Figure 9.1   *Operations Conversion Process*

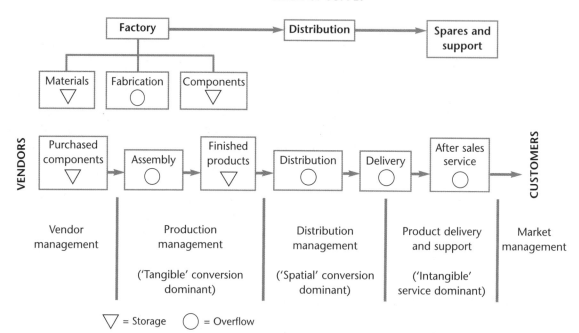

To remain competitive, a company must use its operational resources in a cost-effective manner, whilst retaining some measure of flexibility to meet changing market requirements in quality, technical sophistication, delivery and cost. The fundamental problems facing the operations manager can consequently be summarised as: **how**, **where** and **when** the product is to be made and delivered (see Figure 9.2).

The operations manager's task, according to Muhlemann et al.[5], can be summarised by 5Ps, namely:

- product
- process
- plant
- programmes
- people.

The quality, delivery and cost features of the *product* very often determine the choice and sequence of *processes* used in its manufacture or delivery. These processes need to be carried out in a tangible fashion using particular machinery and equipment housed and maintained in a *plant*, which may be a factory, office or restaurant. The flow of work or customers through the plant must be in accordance with particular *programmes* (i.e. timetables or schedules) to ensure timely completion according to delivery deadlines, consistent with adequate utilisation or 'loading' of the plant. The operation of the plant and development of programmes all require the participation

Figure 9.2   *Practice of Operations Management*

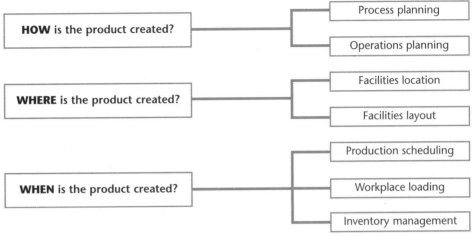

of people either as plant operators, clerical and service *personnel*, maintenance personnel, process technologists or managers.

The senior executive charged with operations management is therefore usually responsible for the utilisation of the majority of a company's physical and human resources (see Figure 9.3), and will have to cope with the market-related pressures for product quality and delivery, at the same time as financial pressures for cost control. He/she must also keep up to date with technological change in products, processes and procedures and the introduction of new products and processes.

Core Technologies in Operations Management

In recent years, certain core technologies have emerged which are having a significant effect on the development of manufacturing, and companies are now having to locate their assets in locations where they can gain access to these key areas of expertise. The core technologies are classified as:

- Advanced Materials
- Telecommunications
- Computerisation.

The first critical technology is that of advanced materials including composites, as many products operating in conditions subject to thermal and mechanical stress require the use of such advanced materials. Competence in the development and processing of these materials has consequently become a necessity.

The second core technology is that of telecommunications. Access to this technology ensures the rapid and accurate transfer of alpha-numeric and graphical data required for product and process development.

re 9.3   *Operations Management (Resources and Costs)*

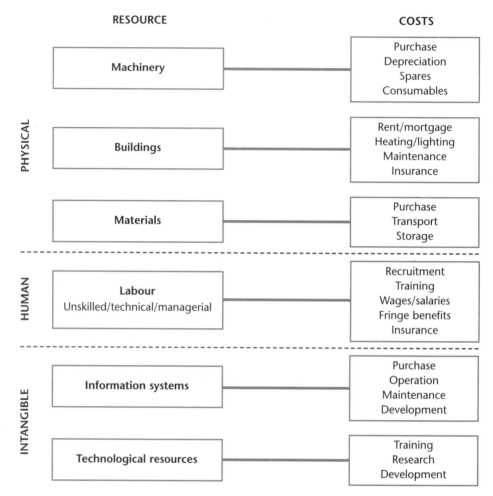

Computerization and the electronic components and subassemblies required for the design and manufacture of contemporary products form the third core technology.

Research indicates that Japanese companies have a clear competitive advantage in the development of many of these technologies, and it is therefore likely that these companies will continue to exert a dominant and growing influence in international markets. In the mid 1980s Japanese companies invested heavily in Research and Development. The fruits of this research are already evident in such areas as VLSI technology, robotics, optical and vision technology and ceramic materials for car engines, and it seems likely that Japanese technological dominance will increase rather than decline.

The levels of Japanese companies' research and development expenditure do not necessarily outstrip all of their European and American competitors in terms of expenditure as a percentage of sales or pre-tax profit, but Japanese companies do appear to be more active than their European counterparts in terms of total R&D expenditure. Sixty-five firms from Japan, for example, appear in the top 200 international companies ranked by total research and development expenditure, compared with forty-eight companies from the European Union, and seventy-two from the USA.

Much of American R&D has been directed towards military applications whilst Japanese firms tended to focus their R&D towards civilian applications. In many ways, therefore, Japanese companies may be even better technologically placed than their American competitors, and ironically Japan is becoming more dominant in remaining military markets as many of the civilian technologies which they have developed are now finding widespread military applications.

AN HISTORICAL PERSPECTIVE OF INTERNATIONAL OPERATIONS

International trade has traditionally taken place between different countries for reasons of comparative advantage in resource endowments. With the onset of the Industrial Revolution in the eighteenth century, international specialisation became more developed between the industrialising and the non-industrialising nations, and manufacturing capability consequently emerged as a factor in international comparative advantage.

The original pattern of European industry was one of initial domestic location, and subsequent investment abroad for materials extraction and product distribution.

As industrialisation gathered momentum, particular areas of technical competence began to emerge in certain industries in specific countries, but the further international specialisation of production was hindered by tariff barriers. As a result, foreign direct investment in either joint ventures or wholly owned subsidiaries began to emerge as a means of exploiting product and process technological know-how over a larger market, whilst simultaneously avoiding trade barriers. Growth from foreign direct investment was particularly evident in the United States, with its abundant natural resources, large and growing population, and a high rate of industrial development in both the manufacturing base and communications infrastructure.

The development of design and manufacturing technologies for mass production, combined with expertise in the branding and logistics required for mass marketing, resulted in American companies beginning to outstrip the growth rates of their European counterparts during the late nineteenth century. The high levels of expertise were evident in a wide range of industries from the process-based food and tobacco industries to metal-based consumer durables.

As the US domestic market began to mature in the first quarter of the twentieth century, American companies ventured into overseas markets using their technological advantages. This market penetration was achieved mainly through investment in developed European countries, coupled with logistical systems to support branding and other marketing strategies.

Following the devastation of much of European industry following World War Two, US companies was able to gain even further advantages through European location as access to markets were almost guaranteed during European reconstruction. American technology was also transferred to Japan to assist in the reconstruction of its war-damaged economy but as the reconstruction of European and Japanese industry progressed, their larger companies began to emerge as strong competitors to the American multinationals.

In more recent years, Japanese companies have been establishing a supremacy through high quality manufacturing, and targeting of resources into specific strategic technologies related to computers and advanced materials. Having achieved market dominance in these products, Japanese companies have located assembly plants in the major consumer markets of North America and Western Europe. These assembly plants, in their turn, have transplanted particular management practices and working procedures from Japan to America and Europe, and also attracted component suppliers capable of meeting stringent requirements for quality and delivery.

Furthermore, many major European and American companies have attempted to emulate Japanese production management practices to improve their competitiveness. There is a view that Japanese industrial competitiveness has been generated by the use of total quality management and just-in-time systems. The Japanese have also simplified the management of operations and inventories by concentrating on core operations and technologies, and establishing close contacts with a comparatively small number of supplier companies located at the top levels of a pyramid of vendors. Suppliers are selected on their capability to provide economic and timely delivery of subassemblies, components and materials. Note that this approach makes use of the theory of the value of networking outlined in Chapter 5. Access to new and efficient networks is particularly useful in offering a competitive advantage in complex product industries where relative materials costs are rising rapidly. It is apparent, therefore, that the management of operations has played a key role in international trade and technology transfer since the mid eighteenth century, but in recent years the emphasis has been on the importance of technological expertise in products and processes, and organisational innovation to competitive success.

INTERNATIONAL OPERATIONS MANAGEMENT STRATEGY

Operational Aspects of Competitive Advantage

Decisions on operations strategy are closely linked to a company's overall strategy and, in particular, the way in which a company is seeking to gain competitive advantage. Competitive strategy is influenced by the breadth of product range offered by a company, and whether it wishes to compete across a broad product line, or a specific segment or niche. This distinction between broad and narrow markets leads Porter[6] to the view that companies should seek to gain competitive advantage and market share by either seeking to be the lowest cost producer or through a product differentiation strategy.

Presenting competitive strategy as a choice between these two extremes is perhaps an oversimplification, because in practice many firms find that both types of competitive advantage are important. Sweeney[7] argues that world-class competitors now require a capability of high differentiation *and* low production costs. In addition, writers such as Stalk[8], Sweeney[9 and 10] and Spanner *et al.*[11] suggest that competitive advantage can also be gained via 'time based competition', that is, the speed at which new products can be conceived and delivered to the marketplace, and costs reduced by tight process management. The Table below, comparing Toyota with a US-based motor company, shows why Japanese companies have gained a strong reputation for time efficiency.

Table 9.1 *Time-Based Competitiveness (Japan and USA)*

	Toyota	**Detroit**
New product development	3 years	5 years
Production throughput time	2 days	5 days
Inventory turnovers	16/year	8/year
Dealer ordering	1 day	5 days

Source: *Bower and Hout*[12] (reproduced in Tunc and Gupta[13])

Making choices about the breadth of product range and target market, the extent of product differentiation, and rate of new product development will all have operational implications for how resources need to be allocated along the value chain. Market location needs to be taken into account when determining the location of production and distribution units. The product design may affect both location and choice of manufacturing systems if it requires access to specific supplies/labour or process technology. The use of new products to gain competitive advantage implies strong investment in research and development facilities and finally the expected volume of sales (and hence production) will also have implications for the type of production technology that may be selected.

All of this means an operations strategy tends to 'emerge' from the broader corporate strategy. It also implies that there are a number of separate, inter-linked operational decisions to be made. The first of these is the choice of location for each element in the production and distribution process and subsidiary choices for each location in respect of:

- The facilities (type, size and degree of specialisation)
- Capacity
- Technology.

In combination, these decisions are sometimes referred to as 'configuration'. The configuration of suppliers, production units and distribution facilities for a company defines, according to Dicken[14], the spatial distribution of its activities, and careful selection of the resource configuration can provide a competitive edge. The aim is to achieve a configuration that grants a competitive edge via quality, delivery or price.

Take, for example, the case of a textile manufacturer and retailer such as Benetton. In terms of just its European operations, the company needs to decide where to locate each of the following:

- Design facilities
- The plants that make, dye and cut the fabrics.
- Garment 'assembly' sites
- Warehousing for distribution
- Central support facilities, e.g. HRM, finance.

The location decision will affect the access to technology and labour skills and, most importantly, the overall cost of producing the goods and getting them to the marketplace. Having decided location, then the questions of facilities, capacity and technology must also be resolved. Configuring operations is not straightforward even when a company is only servicing a domestic market; but the problem becomes infinitely more complex in an international marketplace.

The second major issue to be resolved, once the configuration is determined, is that of co-ordination. How will the operations manager ensure that the workloads and scheduling of each separate geographic unit are co-ordinated so that the declared aims of getting the right mix and amount of products to the correct market at the correct time are achieved?

For example, it is no good a supermarket launching a special price offer on French white wines if they are unable to ensure that the French wholesalers can supply the required volumes, and that these volumes can be shipped, processed through customs, warehoused and then packed onto lorries for countrywide distribution. Customers do not want to find empty supermarket shelves labelled 'special offer' and be told 'sorry we have run out' when they have decided to make a purchase. This is a potential logistical nightmare, which requires extremely careful planning and control, and new technologies are becoming increasingly important in aiding the co-ordination process. Even something as apparently simple as e-mail can be an extremely useful tool in ensuring that distant suppliers are kept up to date on delivery requirements.

It can therefore be concluded that good co-ordination and good configuration are ways of maintaining customer goodwill and gaining a competitive advantage. Such an advantage can be preserved if decisions on these issues are supported by an infrastructure of an appropriately trained workforce, procedures for quality planning and control, systems for materials planning and control, and an adequate organisational structure.

We can now look in detail at the two core issues of configuration and co-ordination in terms of international operational decisions.

Configuration

As already indicated, a company's operational configuration defines the location of international operations, product sourcing and distribution options, and the facilities, capacity and technology to be allocated to each location.

Looking firstly at the location decision, Dunning[15] suggests that the choice will be affected by:

- Cultural issues
- Political conditions
- Costs of production and transportation
- Market potential and the competitive environment
- Access to resources.

Chapter 4 highlighted the cultural considerations that come into play when engaging in international business. Using a foreign supplier or distributor, whether an associate company or locally owned business, requires an understanding of the local culture, methods of working and business practice, and risks are reduced if there is minimal cultural distance between the two countries. Political conditions are most significant if a company has foreign-owned assets and there is a potential risk of expropriation, but even exporters may face political uncertainties that create difficulties in the processing of goods or payments.

In relation to the selection of locations for manufacturing units, McGrath and Bequillard[16] summarise the choices facing companies as:

- Home-country manufacturing
- Regional manufacturing
- Co-ordinated global manufacturing
- Combined regional and co-ordinated global manufacturing.

The choice will tend to complement the company's internationalisation strategy, so that if a company is taking a slow, low risk approach to internationalisation, it is more likely to choose to export, which in turn implies that domestic manufacturing is likely to be preferred. Regional manufacturing suits a strategy whereby a company is targeting a large regional market with a standardised product range. The car industry is an example of one which tends to use regionally-based configurations. Figure 9.4 illustrates how the Toyota Motor Company presents a format for the international division of car part manufacturing in the Asia Pacific region. The region is large enough to be treated as a self-contained market, and so the planning of parts manufacture and final assembly can be organised on a regional level. Toyota operates a similar system in Europe, where its assembly plant at Burnaston in the United Kingdom is supplied with parts manufactured at a variety of diverse locations, and the assembled vehicles are sold throughout mainland Europe. It is useful to note that Toyota chooses to create its regional structure around a market, in other words it is market-oriented production.

Ohmae[17] observed that many larger companies are now choosing to adopt a similar approach of locating their final assembly stages near to their largest market, since the unit labour costs for mass production industries is comparatively small, accounting for between 10 and 5 per cent of the total cost of the product. For example, the transport and insurance costs for product shipments of finished electrical products from South East Asia to the USA can account for 13 per cent of the free on board (FOB) costs, whereas the savings in labour costs may only be around 7 per cent. Consequently it makes economic sense for assembly to be closer to the market to save on total costs.

In some industries, production will be regionally clustered to take advantage of particular local resources/technology/institutions, and so the configuration is production rather than market oriented.

Co-ordinated global manufacturing assumes that a company is operating in a global rather than regional manner. That is, it may source, produce and distribute its products from anywhere in the world, and the combined regional-co-ordinated global approach works by some aspects of operations taking a regional focus whilst others are global in orientation.

Figure 9.4   *Plan for the Manufacture of Car Parts in the Asia Pacific Region*

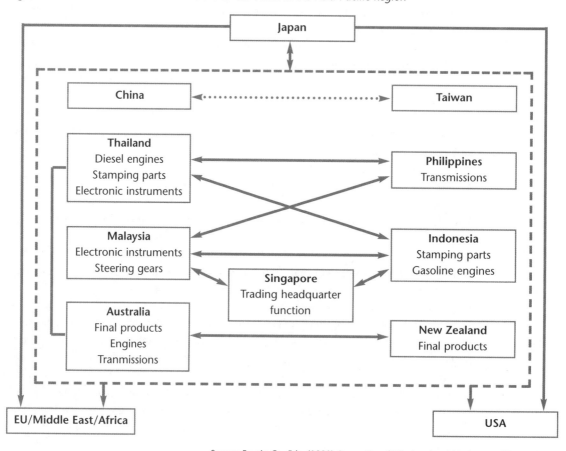

Source: Fourin Co. Eds. (1990) *Perspective of 90s decade world strategy of Toyota Group*
(Toyota Gurupu no '90 Nendai Sekai Senryaku no Tenbou: in Japanese), Fourin Co., Nagoya

In choosing locations for each stage of operations, the potentially conflicting requirements of proximity to markets and proximity to materials and other operating resources can be resolved by reference to relative costs. If materials and components are heavy, bulky, or otherwise expensive to transport, it is usual for the processing plant to be located near to materials' sources. If the finished product is expensive to transport to its market locations, however, because of such factors as fragility or lengths of distances, then it may be more appropriate to locate the manufacturing facility closer to the point of consumption.

If it is assumed that companies aim to maximise their profits, then it could be argued that the final choice of location for all of the different elements in the value chain should be the one that minimises the sum of manufacturing and transport costs, but there is some evidence that costs are becoming less important to location choice. Dunning[18] argues that over the course of the last thirty years the traditional criteria of access to raw materials or basic resources and lower labour costs have been replaced by a search for strong economies with good institutional facilities. That is, the search for access to strategic assets such as technical expertise or organisational competence now dominates the configuration decisions of many multinational companies.

This idea can be explained more clearly by looking back at Figure 9.4. In determining how to divide up the production of the different car parts across the Asia–Pacific area, Toyota has clearly paid attention to the political, cultural and cost characteristics of the different nations, but the strategic assets discussed by Dunning are also relevant. The parts which have the simplest technologies and are labour intensive are made in the locations that are least developed, such as Indonesia and Thailand. The primary advantage offered by such locations is access to low-cost labour and basic resources such as land. In contrast, the more complex components which require higher skill levels and perhaps greater investments in production technology are made in the more developed locations of Malaysia, Australia and New Zealand. The trading function is allocated to Singapore, a country with advanced communications technologies and one from which all of the subsidiary units can be served with ease. The Toyota example is a good illustration of a manufacturing configuration in which supplies of a range of components from low-cost locations are sent for finished assembly close to points of market demand, although some highly critical, expensive and sophisticated components may still need to be fabricated in OECD countries. This issue of the importance of technology to operations management in the twenty-first century will be considered again later in this chapter.

In selecting the exact countries and localities for each operational element, it may be useful for managers to employ a scoresheet approach, similar to that outlined in Chapter 8 for use in developing a marketing strategy. Alternative locations can be narrowed down to a shortlist on the basis of broadly-based information from public sources, and then compared on their scores in terms of core requirements such as availability of key resources, market proximity, production costs, political stability and cultural empathy. This will give the operations manager a basis for then moving to the second phase of the configuration decision process, when facilities, capacity and technology are determined location by location.

In many respects, in making such choices the operations manager will be faced by many constraints. If Country X has been selected as a site for component manufacture, then the technology and capacity aspects of the site will primarily be predetermined by the design of the product being made and the anticipated market size. Company strategy in respect of low cost versus differentiation is also likely to be relevant. Facilities in terms of land, transportation access, the need to provide after sales services etc., will also be dictated by other components of general strategy. This means that location is the most important consideration in determining configuration.

It is worth noting that service companies appear to be more flexible in their choice of locations. The core technology in many service operations is that of information technology, and the 'backroom' carrying out of the technical transactions can easily be separated from the 'front office' engaged in interfacing with customers. These two locations can then be connected by electronic means.

Avis Europe plc. car rental operations use a system whereby car hire centres may be either licensees or wholly owned subsidiaries, both providing an appropriate mix of product models and service tailored to particular market needs. These front offices, however, are fully supported by a global computer system for reservations known as the Wizard system.

(Source: Armistead[19]).

Co-ordination

Effective co-ordination of the various sites around the world requires that systems exist to ensure that goods or services are produced at levels which lead to the fulfilment of strategic objectives. Co-ordination is of vital importance because in practice there are likely to be regular changes in demand patterns, production capabilities, and hitches in supply. Co-ordination can be broken down into two main parts:

- Global versus local sourcing
- Control of the global 'pipeline'.

In considering global versus local sourcing, Ferdows[20] identifies a total of six alternative roles that can be played by foreign factories:

1 Offshore factory 2 Source factory	These categories are characterised by their usefulness because they offer access to low-cost inputs such as labour.
3 Server factory 4 Contributor factory	These factories are important because they are located close to national markets and offer a high level of customer service.
5 Outpost factory 6 Lead factory	These factories use the highest level of technology, which is usually available locally.

As the number of locations and the classes of factory types increases, the co-ordination problem becomes more complex: there will be more documentation to manage, more deliveries to process and potentially more national borders to cross. Good management systems are therefore vital to ensuring costs are kept down.

Work by Scully and Fawcett[21] has shown that many US companies do not pay close attention to the importance of co-ordination costs, and instead focus time on trying

---

Mini Case Study

The operations manager at Hanes Printables, a textiles division of the US-based Sara Lee corporation recently established a new production planning system to cope with a supply chain he described as 'too complex to manage'. The manager had to co-ordinate a chain of 4,500 supplier units, and fourteen apparel assembly (stitching and finishing) units spanning five countries. In addition to company-owned suppliers, Hanes had an agreement with National Textiles to supply ready-cut garment 'components'. National Textiles source (or knit) the fabric, dye and bleach it and then ship it to any of the Sara Lee apparel plants around the world. The knitting, dyeing and bleaching and cutting could all take place at different locations.

The aim was to devise a way of improving capacity planning and scheduling, so that stock levels were reduced and the company could accurately identify what could be delivered to customers.

Source: *Apparel Industry Magazine*, May 2000, Vol. 61, Issue 5, pp.31–38

to save production costs. This can sometimes lead to poor location choices, because where resource costs are low there may also be a poor infrastructure which creates high co-ordination costs. In cases where co-ordination is improved, such as the Sara Lee case cited above, the cost savings arising from reductions in global stock levels can be very substantial.

In deciding on global versus local sourcing, an operations manager also needs to consider the relative merits of centralisation versus decentralisation in respect of purchasing, stock management, transportation and materials handling, and information systems. The centralisation/decentralisation decision must often be made for very diverse product ranges serving geographically dispersed markets.

Centralised procurement

In considering the problem in respect of the purchasing of supplies, companies are looking at the relative merits of the economies of scale obtainable through centralised bulk purchasing versus the additional transport costs of moving inputs to the dispersed production or assembly locations. In addition, control over delivery times, input quality and supplier services is more easily managed in a centralised system. The control benefits take on increased significance as the cost of any production shutdown increases. The way in which some economies impose local-content rules on manufacturers will influence the purchase system that is selected and, needless to say, the ideal solution is dependent on the individual product, and the geographic location of both manufacturing units and markets.

The choice to be made is one of totally centralised purchasing for all key inputs, versus a structure which grants foreign subsidiaries or agents autonomy over part or all of the purchasing decisions. At the very extreme of the centralisation spectrum, is a system of global procurement which is centralised at world level through the segmentation of suppliers. Cisco Systems Inc., the US-based computer electronics company, uses this type of approach[26], utilising intranet links with its contract manufacturers and distributors to order systems which are then delivered direct to the end customer. Cisco sends order information to its contract manufacturers who in turn send on the details to the subassembly contract manufacturers. In this way, all of the procurement and management of orders is handled through what might be termed the 'first tier' contract manufacturers and, in the words of Cisco's vice president for supply management, 'we never touch 65 per cent of the units that go to our customers'. The contract manufacturer takes responsibility not just for the ordering of components and management of the assembly process, but also organising its delivery to the customer and payment of the distributor. From Cisco's point of view, the beauty of this approach lies in its simplicity, as all the task of co-ordination is passed down the supply chain, although the company admits that it can only be used for less complex products which require minimal configuration.

Internet technology has led to a massive growth in websites offering businesses the opportunity to invite tenders for supply of components/services. Such purchasing methods can save costs by enabling companies to take advantage of both the centralisation of the purchasing process and the increased competition amongst contractors. In the automobile industry, when Ford and GM were considering setting up a trade exchange for procurement, Goldman Sachs estimated that the cost savings that might accrue from such an arrangement would amount to around $1,000 per vehicle, or 6 per cent of the manufacturing cost.

58K.com is an example of an internet auction marketplace for print procurement. The site works as a 'marriage bureau' for buyers and sellers of print services, whereby the buying companies post details of available contracts on the web, and potential suppliers post anonymous tenders for the work. 58K.com makes its money by taking a 2 per cent commission on successful bids. It is not yet clear whether such sites will encourage further centralisation of procurement amongst multinational companies, or facilitate the process of decentralisation, because the system means that local contracts can be separated out on the sites and offered for tender independently. It is interesting that regulators, such as the Federal Trade Commission in the United States, are keeping a watchful eye on these Internet-based purchasing networks, to ensure that they do not lead to anti-competitive practices.

Inventory management

Centralisation of stock control and distribution is beneficial when tight management of deliveries into and out of stock is important. For example, in the UK retail trade, there is an increasing trend towards centralisation of stock holding. A food industry survey in 1992[22] revealed that 83 per cent of the goods handled by retail multiples used central warehouses for distribution. Control is particularly important where items display any of the following characteristics:

- high unit values
- technological sophistication
- vulnerability to deterioration in certain environments
- health and safety risks
- perishability.

Decentralisation of stock control, however, creates the possibility of locating the distribution points more closely to locations of customer demand, and also of setting ranges and levels of stock to match customer demand more closely as a consequence of increased customer contact. For example, the UK food retailer Tesco operates what it calls a Tie system whereby the company's main suppliers are linked directly into Tesco's own database. The suppliers actually pay Tesco to connect to the system, which enables them to monitor the demand for their products in Tesco stores, and update delivery schedules to minimise the risk of stock outs. Tesco gains from the system by needing to carry lower stock levels but maintaining customer service levels.

The advantages of both central and locally managed structures can be obtained through centralised buying and stockholding of nationally used items, together with local buying of items having their demand restricted to a particular location. Networked computer systems can be used to enable stock levels and demand to be monitored across all of the decentralised locations so that excess supply can be transported to points of high demand. The computer links can also work backwards down the supply chain, to suppliers. Surveys suggest that the use of such information systems to organise quick-response ordering systems can generate significant savings in stockholding costs. A central warehouse can be used as a hub in this distribution system, where items can be collected, re-allocated and distributed as required. This type of arrangement is used by Nike, the US-based sportswear and trainer manufacturer, to manage its European supplies. Nike has a central distribution hub in the USA in Memphis. In Europe, the company decided to establish a European distribution centre in Belgium, which will replace the twenty national and local warehouses originally used to service the Europe-wide market.

Another alternative is to cluster decentralised locations into 'areas'. In such cases, transport from a national centre to an area centre is achieved by one particular mode of transport, before distribution from an area centre to a local centre using another form of transport suited to lower quantities of material.

In international distribution systems, clusters of countries with transport linkages (e.g. the road network throughout the continental countries in the European Union) can be jointly served if there is careful selection of the location for the distribution depot. This may allow regionally centralised purchasing and distribution to be combined in one location.

Amongst smaller and medium sized companies, there is currently a trend towards the subcontracting out of distribution services, as companies find they do not have the internal systems to effectively manage the process in-house. For example, the UK-based fashion and fabrics group, Laura Ashley, has contracted out all of its distribution to Federal Express Business Logistics.

Contracting out benefits the company by enabling it to rid itself of the investment burden of warehousing whilst at the same time gaining access to logistics expertise. Against this, there is the loss of control risk that accompanies such an arrangement. For a subcontract arrangement to work efficiently there is a need for information technology that facilitates constant liason between the company and the contractor. Such technology is progressing rapidly, as witnessed by the recent announcement of new satellite tracking systems for fleet vehicles that will allow transport managers to separately plot the exact location of the container section of a lorry separately from the location of the cab unit.

In reality, most companies are wary of subcontracting out all of the distribution, and contracting will be used selectively, as is the case with J.Sainsbury, the UK food retailer, which now contracts out over half of its distribution, but, interestingly, not all of it.

In relation to all of the elements of the production and distribution process, it becomes clear that co-ordination demands the existence of good information and control systems. Going back to the basic functions of the operations manager in determining what, where and how goods are to be produced, then the information support systems need to be able to provide up-to-date statistics on what items are where in the supply-chain cycle, and in what condition. In other words an information infrastructure is a vital element in good operations management.

Moving beyond the more general problems of configuration and co-ordination, we can now look at how the way in which a company enters a foreign marketplace can have specific operational implications.

EXPORTING AND OPERATIONS MANAGEMENT

As you already know, companies engage in exporting operations for a range of reasons. From an operational perspective, when a company enters an export market, the problems related to quality, delivery and cost control are frequently magnified when compared with the domestic market.

Problems specifically created by the expansion of sales overseas can be classified under the headings of quality management and control, regulations, delivery, profitability and transportation logistics. We can look at each of these in turn.

Quality Management and Control

Overseas countries frequently have different specifications from those in domestic markets and also work to different national standards. These differences in quality regulations may require the use of additional operations or inspection procedures, or the establishment of a separate factory section to prevent production overlap between those products intended for domestic and overseas consumption.

Regulations

Technical regulations

The quality problem is compounded by the need to comply with technical regulations. These are often harmonised on a regional or international basis, but each country may insert their own subclauses. For example, a customer may specify that certain types of steel storage vessels delivered to that country should be made from steel sourced in that same country, even though the steel concerned could be sourced elsewhere to the same European or international standard.

It is sometimes the case that customers will quote international standards or detailed specifications for the main parameters of a product, but may then refer to a domestic standard for all unspecified or 'open' tolerances.

It should be the task of the marketing or sales department to resolve these technical problems before the order is accepted and manufacture is commenced, but these problems are frequently overlooked in the interests of gaining the sale, or because the sales force is not sufficiently well trained, from a technical viewpoint. In some cases, however, even the most highly trained salesperson could not have predicted the problem and many such problems may only become apparent when the customers' inspectors visit the manufacturing plant.

Export control regulations

These are specifications or regulations laid down by the exporting company's domestic government in addition to the standards and specifications laid down by the importing company's host government. Export-based regulations usually relate to armaments and defence products, although some items such as materials, electronic components and computers may have a 'dual use' (i.e. predominantly civilian in application but with some potential military uses).

The company may not be able to export products containing these components to certain locations. This, in turn, may create problems in supply or manufacture, as the replacement item may be purchased from a new supplier, or may lead to production problems due to unfamiliarity with the item in question.

Delivery Dates

Exports deals are frequently subject to the need to comply with exact delivery dates for shipment from a particular port. If that shipment is missed, delivery penalties may be particularly severe.

Profitability

The profitability of exports may be difficult to predict because of movements in currency exchange rates, which can also affect costs where imported materials are used. As a consequence, the operations management of the company may be called upon to economise in the use of a particular material, or to use a cheaper substitute, which in turn may lead to subsequent problems of quality and processing cost.

Transport and Logistics for Exporters

Road, rail and air transport development, combined with changes in storage and processing technologies (e.g. food processing and food storage), have radically altered the speed with which products can be moved to export markets. In addition, changes in materials handling and processing technologies have shortened the transport and distribution cycle. Back-up of the new distribution systems requires large-scale investment in logistical support, warehousing systems, and computer-based recording systems.

A company's willingness to invest so much in the distribution process may be contingent upon the channels of distribution used for export markets. Exports sold on a 'make-to-order' basis require low stock holdings in the relevant export markets, although speed of delivery of spares may require some attention. Agent-managed sales require sufficient levels of stock to enable competitive deliveries and an acceptable level of after-sales service. Similar levels of inventory support are also required if a wholly-owned sales and service subsidiary are selected.

The costs of transporting by sea and land still remain higher than those incurred when transporting by land alone, as a consequence of the additional costs of loading and unloading at ports of entry and exit. This means that UK companies face additional transport and logistics costs when competing on the large Continental mainland of the Single European Market. The completion of the Channel Tunnel may reduce these sea transport costs, but the volume of goods that can be economically transported by this tunnel has still to be established in practice. It is apparent, therefore, that UK industry can only compete in that larger market by providing competitive advantage in technical innovation, quality, price or delivery.

Nevertheless, a UK location is attractive to many subsidiaries of US and Japanese transnational corporations because of:

■ attractive inward incentives
■ a large host market near to the large European Union

- a trained and educated workforce incurring lower labour costs than in France, Germany, Sweden, USA and Japan
- a common language and culture with US companies, and the major second language for Japanese companies.

The cross-Channel shipping costs into Europe from British subsidiaries can be profitably absorbed via premium pricing of technologically advanced designs, or low costs resulting from production efficiencies. There are also significant economies of scale which can be earned in transportation.

LICENSING

As explained in Chapter 8, licensing may provide a useful way in to markets which are otherwise precluded because of tariff barriers or currency controls, but it can also cause an operations management problem because of its association with technology. A licensing agreement usually implies a transfer of technology, involving the delivery of technical documentation related to products and processes. It is consequently important to ensure that this technical data is correct, up-to-date and unambiguous.

In addition, the licensor will need to ensure that the licensee is conforming to the requirements of the design and process planning documentation, and is also taking sufficient care with inspection. As seen in the marketing context, this is particularly important to protect the reputation of the licensor in the overseas market, or where the licensee is being used as a source of supply to serve other markets.

JOINT VENTURES

Joint ventures are set up with the aim of sharing development and production costs, especially for expensive items. From an operational standpoint, such agreements can create problems in the co-ordination of inputs from several different suppliers and locations. This can be a particular problem for highly technical products with low specification tolerances. Such problems are clearly illustrated in the Airbus example which follows.

Mini Case Study

Airbus Industrie was established to design and manufacture the A300, A310 and A320 family of high-capacity short-range aircraft. Airbus Industrie was incorporated in France in 1969 and the joint venture was arranged to pool the resources of the partners and to sell the finished product. The partners of the joint venture included Deutsche Airbus (which subsequently became a 100 per cent subsidiary of Messerschmitt – Bolkow – Bloom MBB), Sud-Aviation (subsequently becoming Aerospatiale) and Hawker Siddeley (later nationalised as part of British Aerospace). CASA joined the programme as a full member in 1970, and Fokker also joined as an associate member.

Final assembly takes place at Aerospatiale's facilities in Toulouse, but 96 per cent of all the required work is completed before final assembly. Wing boxes are produced at British Aerospace and then delivered to Hamburg for connection to the central and rear fuselage. The fuselage is then delivered for final assembly at Toulouse.

The partners to the agreement have each gained advantages from participating in the joint venture. For the smaller participants, it became possible to secure business and design and production expertise in a larger project than would have been the case previously, whilst the larger participants could continue their business in large-scale projects with a lower outlay of research and development expenditures. This factor is critical in aeronautical development, as the pace of technical change has demanded escalating pre-production costs in order to remain in the marketplace. Furthermore, the prestige of the project has attracted support from each of the governments represented by the participants, usually through the provision of low interest rate loans. Major production problems were expected when interfacing the different assemblies made in different geographical locations, but these were partly resolved by the major participants being responsible for the prefabrication of a complete assembly. Teams from each participant were encouraged to tighten up their relationships with subcontractors and suppliers to maintain consistent quality levels. Furthermore, the extended use of computers in design and production enabled precision of manufacture to be increased to reduce the problems of interfacing. A modified just-in-time system was used for final assembly, with all subassemblies being available some twelve days prior to final assembly, and large transporter aeroplanes are used to move the subassemblies between the participants.

Some problems have occurred in co-ordination of production between the various locations as a committee structure arranged to facilitate this has sometimes been found to be cumbersome. Furthermore, some problems were encountered in the provision of infrastructure facilities such as education, following a high influx of expatriates into Toulouse.

OPERATIONS MANAGEMENT AND FOREIGN DIRECT INVESTMENT

As already suggested earlier in this chapter, and also in chapters 2 and 4, foreign direct investment is concerned with gaining access to particular benefits associated with foreign locations. The benefits will be specific to the location, and foreign direct investment is seen as a way of adding value to the business.

On the one hand there may, in theory, be expected to be little operational difference between directly investing overseas and using foreign companies as part of the production chain, but in practice this is not always the case, because of what Dunning[15] terms 'owner specific' advantages. The ownership-specific aspects of the location of operations relate to those factors that cause a company to locate in a particular overseas location because the company itself has specific advantages compared with indigenous companies in the host country, such as technological knowledge or capital. A company may also have an advantage in a market because of a new product innovation. One consequence of recognising the role of owner-specific advantages is that the choice of location for foreign direct investments can have operational implications. The effects relate to each of:

- External economies arising out of local synergies
- The operational requirements for skilled production staff, particularly with production technology expertise
- The suitability of alternative production technologies.

Synergies

Firms that are involved in manufacturing similar products or using similar materials often cluster in certain locations; Silicon Valley in California is an example of this type of trend, and within these location clusters advantages of synergy will arise.

Mini Case Study

Silicon Valley is the term commonly used to describe the region on the San Francisco Bay peninsula which houses some of the world's largest high-tech companies. The area started out in the 1950s as Stanford Industrial Park, established on land owned by the nearby Stanford University. In order to raise money to fund its expansion, the university decided to grant 99-year leases on some of their land to high-tech companies. Early entrants to the industrial park included GE, Lockheed and Hewlett Packard. In 1971, the term Silicon Valley was used for the first time to describe the area, when Intel developed the first microprocessor 4004 chip. Today, many of the original companies remain, and the region is a valuable centre of expertise in electronics and telecommunications technologies. Hewlett Packard, one of the first companies in the area, was ranked the second largest computer company in the USA in 1998 in terms of sales, which reached just over $47,000 million. Today, Silicon Valley contains around 4,000 IT related companies, which together generate around $200 billion of revenues each year.

The type of synergies that arise in Silicon Valley are common to all such localised clusters of specialist businesses, including:

- Easy access to well-trained labour with specialist skills
- Access to experienced local supplier networks
- An organisational environment which understands the industry/sector, e.g. banks and venture capitalists.

In other words, the key resources for the efficient functioning of business. There is, however, a problem insofar as the synergies may deter relocation to new sites, even when there are changes in the locations of markets or increases in transport costs. For example, it is often found in practice that a well-established and highly skilled workforce may be able to compensate for variations in materials, incomplete specifications for component production and assembly, and even errors in design. As a result, a paradox of what Markusen[23] had termed 'sticky places within slippery space' has emerged. Markusen's argument is that companies find it difficult to move away from areas where they can exploit local synergies such as local supplier networks, because of the cost impact of losing such benefits. Consequently although theory suggests that technological changes and the reduction in trade barriers is making it easier to locate anywhere in the world, the practical realities may be different, and the location choice much 'stickier'. As already suggested, the way in which companies get locked in to particular locations cannot be clearly separated from the issue of access to skilled staff.

Skilled Staffing Requirements

As the manufacturing process moves towards ever increasing investment in advanced technologies, there is generated a requirement for a highly skilled core workforce and highly trained team of technologists to implement the technology, and resolve many of the problems that invariably occur in the implementation and operation of advanced manufacturing technology hardware. Problems commonly arise in the integration of processing machinery with materials handling equipment, the interfacing of mechanical assemblies with hydraulic and electronic units, and the integration of different control systems, and the solution of those problems requires technical and tacit skills of the highest order. In foreign locations, therefore, it is often necessary to have a team of expatriates to carry out key managerial and related tasks related to setting up in a new location, and it will be consequently necessary to ensure that social, welfare and educational structures are in place to meet the needs of these personnel.

Once systems have been installed, however, most advanced manufacturing systems are now computer-operated and controlled, and the process parameters may be programmed in almost any part of the world provided that there is access to the requisite computer system. In addition, plans for factory outputs can be compiled at a company's central office, and distributed to factories throughout the world by means of electronic data interchange. In many ways, therefore, the selection of sites for manufacturing facilities can be based on factors relating to costs for access to markets and supplies rather than labour, whilst locations for research, development and design centres may be based on their attractiveness to scientific and technical personnel, provided that the distance of separation is not too great to cause operational difficulties during the design stages for products.

If you look at the geographical structure of IKEA in the case study in Chapter 5, you will see that the company's headquarters, research and development facility and manufacturing processes are all in different countries. The research and development remains in Scandinavia, close to the company's origins where it is able to exploit high levels of local skill, whereas the manufacturing has moved towards Eastern Europe, where resources are cheaper but there is still easy market access.

Suitability of Production Technologies

The growth of American industry was driven by the development and assimilation of technology related to the high volume (or mass) production of identical or very similar products meeting consistent quality requirements.

The capital investment in such systems is usually high, and they have a number of disadvantages caused by their inflexibility in terms of product mix and volume. Even minor product modifications can be costly to implement, and mass production often requires high volumes to gain maximum efficiencies. For example, in the automobile industry the volume of output required to achieve minimum production costs is some 250,000 units for painting and final assembly, but between 1 and 2 units million for the pressing of various panels.

In response to these difficulties, recent technical developments have increased the flexibility of manufacturing systems. The development of flexible manufacturing for medium volume production conditions usually requires the integration of a wide range of technologies, and significant technological expertise is required to successfully implement these systems, and maintain their operating efficiency. Experience has shown that they require certain managerial conditions, such as a suitable quality management system and production planning and control procedures. The expertise required to select and implement these procedures is usually quite high, and care consequently needs to be exercised when selecting manufacturing locations to ensure that such expertise exists. It is usually the case that many of the key technologists and technicians are relocated from other divisions within the group, or from the company's head office. Attention consequently needs to be paid to the employment and locational conditions for these key personnel and their families, and also their capabilities to train local personnel.

In practice this means that location can affect the choice of production technologies, in respect of the alternatives of mass versus flexible systems. Because, however, the choice is also linked in to the question of access to skilled labour for certain types of technology, we find that the concept of synergies, and the complementary nature of labour, supplier and technology requirements become the key determinants of the location decision. In other words, there is accumulating evidence to support Dunning's[18] view that the main factor influencing operations management and the distribution of economic activity around the globe is access to strategic assets, particularly technology, rather than the traditional resources of materials and cheap labour.

SUMMARY

This chapter has focused on the importance of operations management to international company strategies and competitiveness, drawing attention to the particular features of the various channels of international business such as exporting, industrial cooperation, joint ventures and foreign direct investment. Each of these channels of international business presents its own particular problems to operations management, and these problems should be clearly understood in relation to the core operational problems of managing configuration and co-ordination of business activity.

The chapter has also highlighted the importance of technological considerations in relation to operational decisions. Certain core technologies have been identified, but alongside these it can be seen that the changing role of mass production compared to flexible manufacturing systems can influence a company's choice of location.

Success in international business is strongly influenced by locational decisions taking account of materials supply, labour and transportation costs, but in recent years the relative importance of different groups of assets has changed. The consensus view at the start of the twenty-first century is that strategic assets are more important influences on location than more basic factors; strategic assets include technical knowledge, and organisational competence. Such assets tend to be concentrated in the richer, more advanced industrial nations, and so much of the foreign investment in recent years has been within the richer regions of the Triad. Once locational synergies have developed, relocation becomes costly, and this raises the question of whether, from an operations management perspective, the Triad will continue to be the focus for investment and grow relatively more rich as a result. One hundred years from now we will know the answer to that question.

CONCLUSION

The efficient selection of locations for the supply, manufacture and assembly of goods is clearly a vital ingredient for ensuring the profitability of an international business. Both technological and marketing considerations work to influence location choice, and it is becoming increasingly important to access strategic rather than basic commodity-type assets.

The last functional area that requires consideration is human resource management, because no factory, marketing or distribution system can work effectively without good staff. HRM is the subject of the final chapter in this section of the book, and on its completion you will have a good understanding of the importance of clear strategic planning in all of the main functional areas.

References

1 Akkermans, A., Bogerd, P. and Vos, B. (1999) Virtuous and vicious cycles on the road towards international supply chain management, *International Journal of Operations and Production Management*, Vol 19, no.5/6, pp.565–581

2 Vos, G. and Akkermans, A. (1996) Capturing the dynamics of facility allocation, *International Journal of Operations and Production Management*, Vol.16, no.11, pp.57–70

3 Thomas, D. and Griffin, P. (1996) Co-ordinated supply chain management, *European Journal of Operational Research*, Vol.94, pp.1–15

4 Holmes, G. (1995) Supply chain management: Europe's new competitive battleground, *EIU Research Report*

5 Muhlemann, A., Oakland, J., Lockyer, K. (1992) *Production and Operations Management*, Pitman, London

6 Porter, M. (1990) *The Competitive Advantage of Nations*, Macmillan, London

7 Sweeney, M.T. (1991) Towards a Unified Theory of Strategic Manufacturing Management, *International Journal of Operations and Production Management*, Vol. 11, No.8, pp.6–22

8 Stalk, G. (1988) Time – the Next Source of Competitive Advantage, *Harvard Business Review*, July/August, pp.41–51

9 Sweeney, M.T. (1993) Strategic Manufacturing Management: Restructuring Wasteful Production to World Class, *Journal of General Management*, Vol,18, No.3, Spring, pp.57–76.

10 Sweeney, M.T. (1993) The Strategic Management of International Manufacturing and Sourcing, in Pawar, K., *Proceedings of International Symposium on Logistics*, University of Nottingham, pp.57–84

11 Spanner, G.E., Nuno, J.P. and Chandra, C. (1993) Time-Based Strategies – Theory and Practice, *Long Range Planning*, Vol.26, No.4, pp.90–101

12 Bower, J.L. and Hout, T.M. (1988) Fast-cycle Capability for Competitive Power, *Harvard Business Review*, November-December, pp.110–118

13 Tunc, E.A. and Gupta, J.N.D. (1993) Is Time a Competitive Weapon among Manufacturing Firms, *International Journal of Operations and Production Management*, Vol.13, No.3, pp.4–12

14 Dicken, P. (1998) *Global shift: transforming the world economy*, Paul Chapman, London

15 Dunning, J. (1980) Towards an eclectic theory of international production: some empirical tests, *Journal of International Business Studies*, 11, pp.9–31

16 McGrath, M. and Bequillard, R. (1989) International manufacturing strategies and infrastructural considerations in the electronics industry, in Ferdows, K. (ed.) *Managing international manufacturing*, Elsevier, London, pp.23–40

17 Ohmae, K. (1985) *Triad Power: The Coming Shape of Global Competition*, Free Press, New York

18 Dunning, J. (1998) Location and the multinational enterprise: A neglected factor? *Journal of International Business Studies*, 29, 1, pp.45–66

19 Armistead, C.G. (1990) *Avis Europe plc.: Rent a car operations*, Case No. 693–008–1, European Case Clearing House

20 Ferdows, K. (1997) Making the most of your foreign factories, *Harvard Business Review*, March, pp.73–88

21 Scully, J. and Fawcett, S. (1993) Comparative logistics and production costs for global manufacturing strategy, *International journal of Operations and Productions Management*, Vol.13, No.12, pp.62–78

22 *Financial Times Special Survey* (1994) Logistics, September

23 Markusen, A. (1996) Sticky places in slippery space: A typology of industrial districts, *Economic Geography*, 72(3) 293–313

24 Levy,D. (1995) International sourcing and supply chain stability, *Journal of International Business Studies*, 2nd quarter, pp.343–61

25 Dyer, J., Cho, D. and Chu, W. (1998) Strategic supplier segmentation: the next best practice in supply chain management, *California Management Review*, Vol.40, No.2, pp.57–77

26 Carbone, J. (2000) Internet is key to Cisco outsourcing model, *Purchasing*, Vol.128, no.8, pp.103–104

Further Reading

For some additional detail and commentary on the operational management function you may find it helpful to look at:

Hill, T. (2000) *Operations Management*, Macmillan or
Cooper, J., Browne, M. and Peters, M. (1994) *European Logistics: Markets, Management and Strategy*, Blackwell, Oxford.

TUTORIAL EXERCISE

Taking information on a company with which you are familiar, look at the geographic spread of their supply, manufacturing and distribution units. Outline the operational difficulties that the pattern suggests to you, and draw up a list of 'Beware' points which you might give to the company's new operations manager.

ESSAY QUESTIONS

1   Specify the problems created by internationalisation of a company under the headings of the 'five Ps' of operations management.

2   Do you think that service companies face fewer operational management problems in becoming international, than do manufacturing companies, and if so, why?

3   Present the case in favour of the use of regional distribution centres, based around continent-wide markets. Is such a system equally easy to manage regardless of the continent concerned?

4   As manufacturing industry becomes increasingly mobile in terms of its choice of location, should politics play any role controlling the world-wide distribution of industry, or should it be left to free market forces?

5   What are the non-financial factors influencing the choice of location for a plant?

Case Study: NEC, BMW, Nissan Motor Company, and Philips

This case study looks at the factors influencing foreign direct investment in each of these companies.

This sample includes two European and two Japanese companies, with one from each national grouping in the electronics and automobile industries.

Electronics Industry

To consider NEC first, the electronics industry is a sector which has become dominated by Japanese companies accounting for 43 per cent of the world market share of semi-conductors, integrated circuits and micro-processors, compared with 26 per cent for American companies and 12 per cent for European firms. In the case of dynamic random access memory (DRAM) devices, the Japanese share of world production has been even higher at 88%. NEC is the world's largest manufacturer of semi-conductors, ranking fourth for information systems and personal computers, and fifth for telecommunications equipment. The bulk of the company's sales in 1992 were to Japan (79%), followed by North America (9%), Europe (5.5%) and other Asian countries (4.5%). The bulk of its product range is accounted for by computers and electronic systems (52%), followed by communications systems and equipment (27%) and electronic devices (16%) (Griffiths and Nakakita, 1993).

Although the majority of the company's sales are to the Japanese market, the proportion of overseas to domestic sales has been gradually increasing since the mid 1960s, and the company has established overseas manufacturing facilities since 1968. In many ways, these decisions were similar to those previously taken by the major US electronic companies who dominated the market in the mid 1960s, and began to change the electronics industry from a national to a global scale. By 1991, NEC had established 69 overseas subsidiaries, employing some 24,500 people out of a total of some 117,000.

At first sight, therefore, the proportion of total employees in overseas subsidiaries is equivalent to the proportion of overseas sales to the company's total turnover, but the distribution of these employees appears to vary between different regions. One third of the company's overseas subsidiaries are based in Asia which accounts for some 21% of total overseas sales. These Asian subsidiaries include 40% of the company's total of 27 overseas manufacturing subsidiaries, but only some 26% of the company's overseas marketing, service and research organisations. North America and Europe, on the other hand, together contain more than 60% of the company's overseas marketing, service and research subsidiaries serving some 65% of its total overseas market, but only some 25% of the company's manufacturing subsidiaries (Griffiths and Nakakita, 1993).

In addition, a significant proportion of the company's output consists of semi-conductors, which are basic components for a wide range of industrial and consumer products. The bulk of the basic production of the less sophisticated semi-conductors takes place in the Asian newly industrialised countries, and a significant proportion of assembly of the finished electronics products such as personal computers also takes place in those countries because of their highly competitive labour costs. The manufacture of the more sophisticated semi-conductors, however, and the more advanced dynamic random access memories has been retained in Japan because of the close links required between development and production, or carried out in the United States because of the high degree of technological expertise in that country (Griffiths and Nakakita, 1993).

The Philips company, however, has had to rethink its product and organisational strategies, because of severe competition from Japanese companies (including NEC) now operating in the electronics sector. Markets for electronics products have demanded an ever increased pace of innovation as evidenced by reduced product life cycles, higher levels of research and development expenditure to support that innovation, and severe price competition. These pressures in the late 1980s forced Philips to reduce their investments in cables, defence products, fibre optics and office systems but to commence production of high definition video and personal information products, such as mobile telephones. The company also attempted to use its resources in a more competitive manner by joint ventures and collaborative research through strategic alliances, as the funds available from divestment of non-core activities such as fibre optics did not necessarily create sufficient funds for increased research and development. Joint ventures have been established for the production of VCR equipment with Grundig and JVC Malaysia, and a joint research and development project with Siemens and the Dutch and German governments (Hewins, 1993).

These changes in product strategy can be linked to changing locational strategies for manufacturing. The company was previously 'multinational' consisting of affiliates in all of the West European countries, North America, Mexico, Brazil, Japan and Taiwan, which predominantly served their own defined markets. The company was organised on a federal basis, with the management in each country having quite extensive control over product range and materials sourcing. This frequently led to product duplication in various countries preventing economies of scale from being fully realised, and a lack of development of competitive pricing for components. In recent years, the company has moved towards a 'global' organisational structure rather than the previous 'federation', enabling more efficient global production to be achieved of the rationalised product range and their associated components.

Motor Industry

Nissan Motor Company Limited ranks amongst the world's four largest car manufacturers, and is the second largest in Japan. The company sold almost 3 million cars and commercial vehicles in 1991, with almost 50% of these sales in Japan, some 20% in North America, some 17% in Europe and some 6% in Latin America (Nissan, 1991). Nissan's decision to locate in Europe in the mid 1980s was apparently based on the advantages to be gained from a production location within the European Community as sales in that region gradually increased, and break-even points could be reached where manufacturing in Europe itself could be cheaper than manufacturing in Japan with associated transport costs. The attractiveness of a European location was also increased with the growing strength of the yen, and the potential for reductions in tariff costs encountered by products imported from outside the European Community.

In other words, the problems of currency movement and market tariffs could be internalised by investment in Europe and the establishment of a series of European suppliers. The United Kingdom was an attractive location in the West European market in view of the various financial incentives available for location in the North-East of England, and the opportunity to expand existing European production capacity.

Nissan's investment in Sunderland is expected to reach almost £900 million by the end of 1993, achieving an output of some 175,000 cars in 1992, some six years after commencement of original production. This total output included some 130,000 units of the 'Micra' model. The factory originally produced the 'Primera' which was a 'global' model of car with sales throughout the world, and accounting for 125,000 of Nissan UK's manufacturing in 1991, and 175,000 in 1992. As a result of successes in production output and quality consistency in the UK, the company decided to design a particular model of car for the European market (the Micra), and to invest some £35 million in two technology and design centres located in the UK (Allison, 1993). The existence of manufacturing facilities in the UK has assisted Nissan in reducing some of the major problems caused by a strengthening yen, and the capability to produce the smaller Micra model has helped to compensate for reduced demand for the Primera during the current European recession (*Guardian*, 1 June 1994, p.13).

BMW, in contrast, chose to locate one of its new manufacturing facilities in USA rather than Europe, when the production demands on its existing facilities in Germany continued to increase to levels beyond its capacity. The choice of location in the USA was driven by market requirements, as the US market accounted for some 96,000 cars in 1986, although this declined to some 53,000 cars in 1991 out of a total world-wide sales figure of 552,600. Forty-three per cent of these total sales were to the German home market, and some 57 per cent were sold abroad. The American assembly plant is expected to have a production capacity of some 70,000 cars per year, providing some facility for transferring production between the American and German plants, dependent upon currency exchange rate and demand levels in different locations.

In February 1994, however, BMW extended their European operations through the purchase of an 80% share in the UK-based Rover motor manufacturing company. The Rover group was owned by British Aerospace plc. who had previously bought the motor manufacturer when it was first privatised in 1988, and subsequently wished to realise some of its assets to finance its aerospace operations. The Japanese partner was only prepared to purchase up to 47.5 per cent of the operations with the remaining capital being obtained by stock market flotation as Honda's preferred policy was to hold less than a majority share in its overseas joint ventures (*Guardian*, 8 February 1994; *Daily Telegraph*, 8 February, 1994).

Rover has extensive experience in the manufacture of small cars, executive range cars, and four-wheel-drive vehicles, which have been sold successfully in British markets under the Metro and Rover and Land Rover badges, with significant shares in the international market for four-wheel-drive 'Land Rover' vehicles.

In addition, Rover has assimilated a wide range of Japanese manufacturing techniques through its association with Honda of Japan, which had culminated in a 20% shareholding in Rover by the Japanese company, and a 20% shareholding by Rover in Honda's British manufacturing operation in Swindon. Furthermore, supply arrangements also existed between Rover and Honda, with Honda engines being supplied to Rover for its executive car range, and body panels being supplied by Rover to Honda. The two companies were also engaged in shared technological development programmes, related to the design of cars for the British market.

BMW was consequently able to purchase viable manufacturing and design abilities, and channels of distribution which could complement and extend its own product range. The main disadvantage to this arrangement, however, may prove to be the possible withdrawal of Honda from the partnership because BMW is viewed as a strong competitor. The withdrawal of Honda may lead to a slow-down in technological development, particularly in engines for new products, and subsequent changes in mutual supply arrangements.

Case Study References

Griffiths, A. and Nakakita, T. (1993) Structure and strategy in a global environment: the case of the NEC Corporation, in Preston, J. (ed) (1993), pp.241–256.

Hewins, M. (1993) Philips: a Dutch electronics giant, a multinational or a global, in Preston, J. (ed) (1993), pp.257–272.

Nissan Motor Co. Ltd. (1991) *Annual Report 1991*, Tokyo.

CASE STUDY QUESTIONS

1 Discuss how the increased competition that is a result of greater globalisation of business has affected each of the four companies in the case study.

2 Explain why the location of the overseas subsidiaries differs between the two industries.

3 With the withdrawal of Honda and BMW from involvement with Rover in the period since the case was first written, what do you see as the best operational organisation for Rover and why?

CHAPTER TEN

International Human Resource Management

INTRODUCTION

The first section of this book dealt with the scenario of international business in the twenty-first century. In Chapter 5 the focus of interest moved to the individual company, and the ways in which strategies might be developed to enter the international marketplace and successfully grow as an international organisation. Following on from this we looked at various elements of the functional management of the organisation, and this chapter concludes the functional discussion by looking at the issues that need to be taken into account when managing HRM in a company that has operating units/divisions and alliances in several different countries.

The first part of the chapter deals with the international context of HRM, and takes a contingency theory approach to identify the factors that might influence the development of HRM strategy in a multinational company. This leads into discussion of how to balance global and local cultures and the question of centralised versus decentralised management of HRM. The central section of the chapter deals with the core areas of difference in employment conditions and practice around the world, and their implications for recruitment, training and remuneration of staff. In conclusion, the role of 'global' managers is discussed – what is meant by the term, and how companies can recruit and train managers to work and think internationally.

In the same way that all people are different, so too are companies, and it is important to acknowledge that it is not possible to prescribe a 'best practice' approach to HRM which is universally applicable. Management styles vary across corporate cultures as well as across national cultures and so whilst it may be helpful to learn from what other companies are doing to improve their international HRM it is dangerous to assume that directly copying those ideas into one's own organisation will be beneficial. This chapter does not therefore seek to present an ideal HRM system, but instead to point out the factors that affect international HRM strategies, and describe a variety of different approaches.

As Porter[1] points out, HRM can be a potential source of competitive advantage, because staff are corporate assets and using them effectively can add value to the business. Most particularly, staff are *the* most precious asset insofar as they are essential to the exploitation of potential in all of the other company assets. On this basis, then, it can be argued that a company that wishes to be successful in its international business operations needs to pay close attention to how it manages its staff across the world.

FACTORS AFFECTING INTERNATIONAL HRM STRATEGY

International HRM involves the recruitment, training and remuneration of staff in an organisation that operates in more than one country. The work will therefore involve the management of staff in a variety of different cultural settings, decisions on the ideal mix of local:expatriate staff and the pay and remuneration of those working in a foreign location. The HRM department will also need to take responsibility for ensuring that international business managers have a clear understanding of the language and cultures of the staff for whom they are responsible. The last task of the HRM manager is to recognise that the workforce, training and remuneration requirements are likely to change and evolve over the life of the business, and be prepared to amend HRM policies accordingly.

Chapter 4 included discussion of the ways in which external and internal influences work to affect the process of internationalisation of a company, and in a similar way the HRM manager needs to be aware of a mix of cultures, nations, regulations and a whole host of other factors which may be important to decisions on how to manage staff. An approach to HRM which recognises that policy choices are dependent upon a number of external and internal influences may be described as a contingency theory, and this section of the chapter outlines one such approach to international HRM.

The idea of a model of HRM strategy which interacts with the external environment was first put forward by Brewster[2] in 1994, who recognised that US approaches to HRM did not work very well when put into a European context. Brewster suggested that rather than spend time criticising either the American or European styles of HRM, it would be preferable to look at the various forms and styles that have developed over time and try and identify the determinants of a successful HRM strategy. This is very important for the individual company because of the link between HRM and competitive advantage, as already mentioned. Armstrong[3] supports Porter's view that good HRM can grant a competitive advantage, and so if a manager understands what factors to take into account when establishing an HRM strategy, he/she is well placed to minimise the risk of policy mistakes.

The question therefore arises as to what might affect HRM policies in a company that owns a number of sites around the world? The answer lies in the external and internal environment of each location. Brewster developed a simple model of international HRM which showed how a number of external factors serve to influence business strategy, HRM strategy and HRM practice in respect of recruitment, training and remuneration policies, but his approach can usefully be broadened by incorporating some of the material already covered in Chapter 5.

If you look back at Table 5.2 you will see that the table summarises the internal and external factors that help to determine business strategy in relation to internationalisation. The external influences range from aspects of global trade liberalisation through to industry level issues such as the level of competition in the business. Internally, the extent to which the company is operating at or close to capacity, its current financial performance and the attitudes of management will all influence the pace and extent of international involvement. In other words, before the business ever reaches a stage of trying to establish an international HRM strategy, its business strategy has been subject to a significant number of influences.

Cascading the business strategy down into the functions brings into play yet more factors, again both internal and external in source. Based on the Brewster model, the external influences on HRM strategy can be summarised as:

- Regional/local culture
- The relative importance of private business as opposed to state intervention in the economy
- National and international regulations and legislative framework
- The role of trade unions and methods of employee representation and involvement
- Labour markets
- The local education system.

We will return to each of these in more detail shortly.

Having responded to these external influences, the next stage in the process is to take into account the internal context. If, for example, an HRM manager is setting policies for an overseas subsidiary, (s)he needs to think about the nature of the relationship between the subsidiary and the home base/headquarters as well as the subsidiary and all the other companies in the group. The internal influences on HRM strategy can be summarised as:

- The geographic distance between the overseas 'unit' and the parent
- The extent of international integration of production
- The level of dependence of the unit on the parent for resources
- The history of development of the overseas unit – organic growth versus growth by acquisition.

In combination the external plus internal factors serve to affect the way in which business strategy is converted into HRM strategy and practice, as illustrated in Figure 10.1. The model also recognises that the process is not static, because as the environment and the company itself change and evolve, there is a need to review the suitability of certain practices and change accordingly. A control loop therefore links practice back to the business strategy.

Figure 10.1   *Determinants of International HRM Strategy*

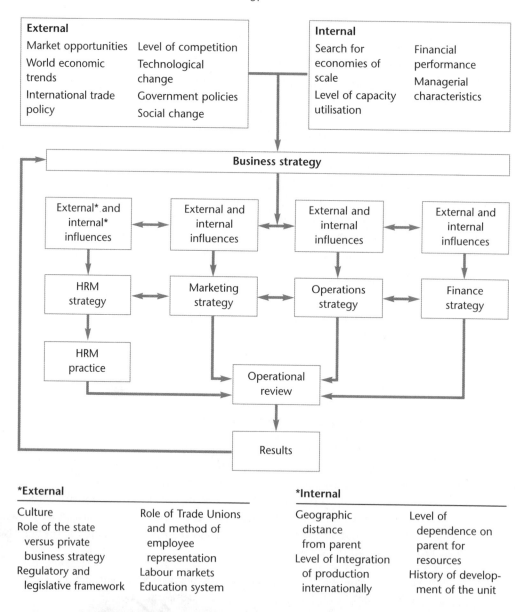

Note: The external and internal influences listed as affecting HRM strategy will not be the same as those affecting marketing operations or finance. The determinants of each function must be viewed separately.

The model illustrated in Figure 10.1. is useful in highlighting two key points:

■ The dependence of HRM (or any other functional strategy) upon business strategy

■ The interdependence of the functional strategies which together create an internal environment that constrains how HRM practice might be developed.

Looking in more detail at the factors indicated as affecting the process of converting a business strategy into an HRM strategy, the external factors will be considered first.

Regional and Local Culture

The idea that an HRM manager in a multinational company could cast off the culture of their home nation and manage their staff in a culture free manner is pure idealism. As Vernon-Wortzel[4] has observed, 'the most critical and the most trivial aspects of management are influenced by cultural traditions and patterns.' The evidence presented in Chapter 4 supports this view in relation to general management practice, and in relation to HRM in particular Gaugler[5] argues that 'an international comparison of HRM practices indicates that the basic functions of HRM are given different weight in different countries and that they are carried out differently.'

In fact it is not just the culture of the HRM manager's home nation that is relevant here, but also that of the country of operation and the geographic region of which it is a part. Three levels of culture therefore interact to affect the way in which HRM is practised in any particular location.

Culture may influence HRM practice both directly and indirectly. Some examples of the way in which practice might vary across cultures include:

Working hours: in Southern Europe, for example, it is still common to start work early and stop for an afternoon siesta before recommencing work until around 8pm. This break in the working day is specific to a particular region and culture in response to the climate, but it is a practice which may not readily be accepted by foreign companies investing in the region.

A similar cultural factor affecting working hours is the Muslim tradition of regular daily prayer. Time and space may need to be set aside in the workplace to accommodate such needs, and work schedules designed to accommodate the interruptions.

Working methods and remuneration systems: Japanese and other South East Asian cultures encourage multi-skilling amongst the workforce, so that people are able to perform a variety of work tasks and teamwork is widely encouraged. In the individualist culture of the USA (and to a lesser extent the UK)* teamwork is disliked because it does not encourage personal advancement. These cultural differences are further emphasised in work by Nevis[6] that shows that when comparing American and Chinese managers in the People's Republic of China it was found that unlike their American counterparts, the Chinese wanted rewards for good

* See the references to Trompenaars and Hofstede in Chapter 4.

performance to be shared equally, rather than to highlight and reward individual workers who were very productive.

Employee participation in management: Studies of Chinese and South Korean managers and employees show that they follow traditional Confucian values such as loyalty and obedience to authority, and such cultural values make it difficult for them to accept the Western approach of employee representation on works councils or management committees, and thus share management responsibilities.

The examples illustrate just some of the ways in which cultural attitudes can lead to differences of opinion about employment practices, and many more examples are scattered throughout this chapter, but the examples demonstrate that care needs to be taken to ensure that HRM policies are sensitive to local cultural requirements.

The Role of the State versus Private Business in the Economy

One of the characteristic features of HRM in the USA is the way in which the country's political and economic model of individual freedom and self-reliance is reflected in the absence of state interference in the area of HRM and labour policy. The orientation towards self-fulfilment and personal achievement has led to writers such as Pieper[7] observing that the major difference between HRM in the USA and Western Europe is the extent of state influence.

The 'balance of power' between private business and the state can have a significant influence upon HRM strategy, because the influence of the state is felt in the form of legislation and regulation of employment practice. Consequently it is difficult to separate the twin influences of balance of power and regulatory framework. The role of the state in business is largely a consequence of a country's political history and cultural inheritance and some specific examples of how state regulation of HRM issues vary include:

- The UK, in common with most of Western Europe has legislation governing the length of notice which must be given, and redundancy payments made, when a factory is closed down. In the USA and Canada employers are rarely required to give more than one week's notice of closure. The difference between Europe and North America reflects the political views of whether the state should intervene to protect workers' rights.

- The Scandinavian nations grant fathers paid paternity leave, plus the option to take extended unpaid leave in the early years of their children's lives. The UK currently has no laws on paternity leave.

- The scale of social security provision for people out of work varies widely across the world, ranging from zero in most of the poorer nations, through minimal provision in the USA, to extended benefit periods in much of Western Europe.

■ Health and safety rules may vary, with some states employing inspectors to ensure compliance, and others leaving standard-setting and compliance in the hands of the company directors.

The Role of Trade Unions and Employee Involvement

As already suggested in discussing the influence of culture on working practice, not all nations are familiar with and accepting of the trade union movement and its role in representing staff in negotiations with employers. Statistics from the OECD, quoted by Brewster[2], suggest that continental Europe is heavily unionised, although the level of union membership has fallen in recent years, particularly in the UK and France. At the same time the relationship between unions and management in Europe is generally more cooperative than antagonistic. In contrast, in the USA the relationship between management and unions can generally be described as adversarial. A recent article in the *New Yorker* by Hendrick Hertzberg[8] condemns 'the utter disregard of American employers for labour rights', which mean that pursuing a case for breach of rights is such a lengthy process that employers 'feel free to hire and fire at will.' He describes the unions as toothless.

Where the union movement is historically strong, the requirement for companies to recognise the union as an official representative of the workforce may be enshrined in legislation. For example, in the United Kingdom such legislation has recently been introduced to encompass even small businesses which were previously exempt, but the existence and scope of such regulations will vary from country to country.

In relation to worker representation on management boards, European Union law now requires that multinational companies of over 1,000 employees establish works councils which are composed of representatives of both management and employees. UK employers have opposed the EU legislation, and in countries such as the USA such an arrangement is almost unknown.

As with cultural differences, the HRM manager needs to be aware of local custom and practice regarding employee representation and managerial involvement when employment policies are being determined.

Labour Markets

When taking on staff for senior positions, managers may choose to recruit from either inside or outside the company. Recruiting from inside – using an internal labour market – is common in Europe where just one third of organisations recruit more than 30 per cent of senior managers externally. The Japanese employment system is also heavily dependent on internal labour markets. The use of an internal market offers the advantage of being able to recruit externally into the lower staff grades and then train staff in-house over a long time scale, so that by the time they are ready for a senior management post, staff are very well integrated into the company and fully understand the corporate culture and working methods.

In contrast, the US labour market has a tradition of job switching, so that a very high proportion of senior managers are recruited from external sources, often direct competitors. Linking back to the influence of the state on HRM practices, such recruitment methods are acceptable in the USA because the government does not impose restrictions on advertising and recruitment for jobs, unlike some European countries. In Sweden, for example, private recruitment agencies for clerical and manual staff are illegal.

The relative use of internal versus external labour markets has implications for training policies. Where the internal labour market is dominant, the HRM manager will need to take on greater responsibility for in-house training programmes to ensure that future managers gain the necessary experience. For staff recruited externally, provision needs to be made for induction programmes to familiarise new employees with the company and its culture. In other words, the type of labour market will affect the scale and type of training programmes managed by the HRM department.

Education System

Educational systems vary across the world in the extent to which they are academic versus vocational in their focus. Where education is vocational in nature, it equips young recruits well for the world of work, and this in turn reduces the risks for employers looking to use external labour markets to fill lower level vacancies. In effect, the state has already taken some responsibility (including the cost) for some of the employment training within the educational system. Germany is an example of a country where state-sponsored vocational training is very important. In contrast, in economies such as Japan the education system produces very literate and numerate 18–20-year-olds who lack any form of vocational training; consequently employers must bear the responsibility for on the job training of such recruits.

There are also differences between countries in the specific educational background of senior management. In France the *grandes écoles* remain the route into a senior position in business, similar to Oxford and Cambridge universities in the UK. In the USA the entry route is based on ability to do the job rather than who you know or where you have studied. In recruiting management trainees, HRM departments should be aware of these differences of approach.

On a much broader level, the general quality of the education system will determine whether or not a company can recruit staff with the basic knowledge and skills to work as lower, middle or senior level managers in any particular location. For example, basic numeracy skills may be essential even for relatively low levels of management and if suitably skilled recruits are not available this will affect the balance of local : expatriate staff employed by multinationals. This is perhaps why some of the Tiger economies of South East Asia are placing such a strong emphasis on the importance of higher education, in the hope that local managers can take over jobs formerly held by expatriates. Singapore is the most obvious example of this, where government policies are promoting moves to maximise the number of university graduates and increase the average educational level of the population.

Internal Influences

Overall, then, a wide variety of external influences play a part in restricting the ways in which HRM can be practised in any particular country, and they set the scene for choices of policy which are further constrained by the internal environment of the business. As Figure 10.1 illustrates, HRM strategy and practice is determined, in part, by structures and issues which are internal to the company because such structures create a mind-set and organisational framework which determines how functions can be organised. Figure 10.1 identifies four factors being of importance here – geography, the level of integration of production, the dependence of the subsidiary on the parent company and the history of the overseas unit. All four factors help to determine the degree of centralisation of HRM management in a company, and the extent to which practice is modified to take account of local cultural/political needs.

Geography matters because as the distance between parent and subsidiary increases, the problems of retaining control increase, even in the current technological environment where e-mail and fax systems allow for the instant interchange of information. At the same time, if international production is integrated, units need to liaise more closely and central management is desirable to ensure effective co-ordination across the world. When a parent organisation is responsible for providing a high level of resources for a foreign subsidiary, it is likely that central control will be increased to ensure effective use of those resources. Lastly, if an overseas unit has developed internally, it may be easier to control from the centre than if it was acquired through a take-over or merger.

Within an individual company, recognising the strength of the pressures for centralisation is helpful, but they need to be viewed in the context of the company's overall vision. The centralisation of decision making allows the company to adopt a common way of doing things at all locations world-wide, and this can be a useful way of welding units together to create a global company, but it can also create difficulties when there are cultural clashes – going global may not work. The opposite approach of decentralisation, granting autonomy to local managers, puts the company's culture and modus operandi into second place behind local needs, and for certain companies and spread of locations this may be a more effective style of management. The question of whether to think and act globally or locally, or how to balance the two opposing pressures is usually resolved at the business level, as discussed in Chapter 5. In other words, when it comes to establishing HRM policies, the manager is likely to find that internal opinion is already biased towards an emphasis on either local or central needs.

This idea that the style of HRM management is actually predetermined and not a matter for choice is illustrated by the fact that for a long time academics have accepted Perlmutter's[9] model for staffing in multinational companies which identifies three possible perspectives on the extent of central control of HRM. The three approaches are as follows:

- ethnocentric
- polycentric
- geocentric.

The ethnocentric view is that local considerations are of secondary importance because the standards, procedures and managers from the home country are superior, and so control is centralised. The polycentric approach is one which is closely oriented towards the host country, to the extent that local managers are able to run the subsidiary virtually independently of the central headquarters and hence HRM is decentralised. In the geocentrically structured company the outlook is global and in HRM terms this means that managers are selected on the basis of their ability to do the job, without reference to nationality or culture. Neither a home nor a host country bias affects the staffing, but organisationally speaking HRM is largely, but not wholly, centralised.

The Perlmutter classification system suggests that staffing policies merely reflect the company's overall strategic outlook, and that HRM policies are just a further reflection of this. The idea that human resource practice is strongly anchored in the overall market and strategic positioning of a company is well covered in the HRM literature by writers such as Schuler[10]. At the same time it is widely accepted that in practice companies cannot easily be classified as ethno, poly or geocentric because each company tends to work out its own version of the model, and so no 'pure' examples exist in reality.

Looking at the issue on a more general level, and trying to see whether the trend is moving for or against centralisation, the growing evidence that the structure of international companies is changing towards networks of organisations rather than hierarchies is important. Belanger[11] argues that the increased use of networks has resulted in the decentralisation of human resource management. Gunnigle et al.[12] cites examples of this amongst multinational companies located in Ireland where he observes a trend towards more proactive and individualist approaches to employee relations management amongst foreign owned companies. The reason why networks encourage decentralisation is quite straightforward – the subsidiary's involvement in a series of networks grants it some powers of control that directly offset the hierarchical power of headquarters. Suppose that a French-based toy company uses a wholly owned manufacturing plant in China to produce some of its product range and the managers in China have a network of subcontractors whom they use to supply various toy components and package the products. The numbers and type of staff required at the Chinese plant will be dependent upon the work required to assemble the components coming in from the subcontractors, and so many of the recruitment and training decisions need to be made locally rather than centrally. In other words, networking grants greater autonomy to local managers.

There is some concrete evidence of the link between the growth of network type organisations and the decentralisation of HRM. There have been a number of studies of the relationship between parent and foreign subsidiary's HRM departments which suggest that the amount of contact between the two seems to be quite limited, and policy making is being put in the hands of local managers. In a study of nine MNCs operating in Ireland, covering a range of sizes, industries and nationalities, Monks[13] found that all of the Irish personnel managers reported limited contact, mainly via reports, with headquarters. In all but one finance company the personnel policies were devised in Ireland rather than the parent country and as a result, local control over personnel issues was perceived as total. The main exception to the view that control was localised was in a Japanese-owned company, where the personnel manager found himself constrained by the central hierarchy. Monks quotes him as saying 'everything runs from a central figure with total power and control. Subservience is guaranteed and never challenged.' This evidence fits with other reports of Japanese HRM practice in overseas subsidiaries, where policies are dictated by the parent company and not by host country managers. It takes us back to the idea that styles of management cannot be viewed separately from the culture of the managers themselves. American and European MNCs tend to be structured something like a decentralised federation, whereas Japanese companies retain much more of a domestic focus and these attitudes are directly reflected in the management of human resources.

If the trend in international HRM is towards increased adaptation to local needs within the framework of overall company strategy the HRM staff should think about the detail of how practice may vary between countries. As suggested earlier, the range of factors affecting how people work and interact in the workplace are many and varied, and these differences can be translated into observable differences in the day to day practice of HRM.

COMPARISONS OF LOCAL PRACTICE IN HRM ACROSS THE TRIAD

In this section of the chapter, the practice of HRM in the three legs of the Triad is compared: the USA, versus Europe versus Asia, particularly Japan. The comparison focuses on some of the core aspects of HRM practice including planning, staffing, training, performance appraisal and remuneration, and management of industrial relations.

Planning

HRM planning involves making decisions about the level and type of skills required in a business in the foreseeable future. Clearly such plans will be very closely tied in to operating and marketing plans because *what* is being made, *where* and *how* it will be marketed will all serve to affect staffing requirements. In the immediate future, planning is concerned with recruitment at the appropriate level and over the longer term the concerns may focus more on training of staff to meet future requirements.

USA

US dependence upon external labour markets means that staff are highly mobile between companies and this makes long-term planning very difficult. If staff may only be around for a few years, it is almost impossible to plot a career path for the high fliers who might be the next CEO. Not surprisingly then, Humes[14] observes that most American multinationals have no, or severely limited, corporate-wide schemes for identifying future managers.

Europe

It is difficult to generalise about approaches to staff planning in Europe because attitudes vary quite widely between countries. For example, Derr[15] noted that in identifying individuals with strong management potential the attitude of the French differed greatly from that of the English. English companies preferred people who might be described as generalists with a strong psychology/human relations orientation. In contrast the French sought out individuals with high levels of engineering and technical expertise. Regardless of such differences in requirements, however, there is a suggestion that planning is more formalised in Europe than in the USA.

One problem in planning for senior management roles is the fact that attitudes towards promotion and geographic mobility vary across Europe. Swedish people hold a very egalitarian view of the world and this works to make them geographically immobile because the need to protect the wife's career is deemed as important as individual promotion. At the same time the Swedish tax system makes salary increases less desirable than in a low tax society. Nonetheless, Tung[16] did find that Europeans were more internationally oriented than their American counterparts and so planning for a series of international assignments in a career path for a senior European manager might be easier than for his equivalent in an American company.

Japan

The Japanese approach to staff planning is dominated by its focus on the long term. There is a two-tier employment system in Japan, composed of lifetime employees and temporary workers, which is reinforced by what has been described as 'industrial dualism' or yasuda. The dualism refers to the way in which the major companies are able to recruit the best students from the best universities and offer them a lifelong career path within the same organisation. Consequently, senior management tends to be company specific – Mitsui, Sony, Hitachi – indoctrinated in company systems and extremely loyal. Under such circumstances, long-term planning is made much easier because promotion is almost entirely from within, in direct contrast to American multinational companies.

Staffing Policies

The term 'staffing policy' is used here to refer to the extent to which MNCs from different parts of the world rely on the use of local managers. In theory, the level of employment of local managers is viewed as being dependent upon:

■ The corporate image to be projected – global versus local.

■ The maturity of the overseas site. As maturity increases so too does the pool of skilled local staff that can be promoted into management posts.

■ The degree of common 'mind-set' between home and host nations. Large differences in mind-set (culture) tend to work to increase the need to use local managers.

It might be expected that such a theory could be equally well applied to the USA, Europe and Japan and observations of practice suggest that this is generally the case.

Europe and USA

European and US multinationals have a long history of development, and being well established in the two continents they tend to have a well trained supply of local managers, so that the general policy is to employ host country managers wherever possible. IBM is just one example of a company that has a policy of using host country nationals who are promoted from within. When looking at the operations of US and European MNCs in Asia, South America and Africa, however, there is a much greater emphasis on the use of parent country employees as managers. The exact reasons for the difference of approach are not revealed, but cultural diversity and lack of availability of locally trained staff would both seem reasonable explanations.

The approach to staffing that is used by US and European multinationals is therefore a blend of the polycentric and ethnocentric models described by Perlmutter[9].

Japan

Japanese multinationals make very limited use of local managers – the majority of senior positions at country and regional level are filled by Japanese nationals. Senior international managers have often received training through a wide range of job assignments straddling all of the key functions, and most will have spent some time at corporate headquarters. The Japanese system of pay-based upon rank and seniority has meant that the dependence on Japanese nationals as managers has been perpetuated. It is very difficult to bring in staff from outside if they first have to serve a 10–20 year 'apprenticeship'. This means that the staffing approach used by Japanese MNCs can be described as ethnocentric.

Training

The importance of management training is well recognised by MNCs-based in all of the major world markets. Handy *et al.*[17] note that as a general rule MNCs from all such markets devote a minimum of five days per year to such training, but the overall style of training and the balance of on-the-job:off-the-job still varies between continents.

USA

Most if not all of the big US-based MNCs operate large in-house training departments. General Motors, for example, attaches great importance to developing individual careers through on the job training but in contrast to the Japanese companies the training tends to keep employees within their own division of the company; divisional rotation is rare. This reflects a US tendency to train people in specific skills. Other US companies such as General Electric (GE) have begun to use team-based international training as a way of broadening the focus of their managers, but the change is still quite slow.

IBM runs training centres in the USA, Europe and Asia which are used for continuing employee education. The company's annual report highlights the importance of training, with European employees spending an average of almost twelve days per year of formal education programmes. As such, much of the training is classroom-based and off the job in contrast to the experience of employees of Asian multinationals.

Europe

In common with fellow MNCs from other parts of the world most European companies place management training high on their list of priorities. Some of this emphasis on training arises out of legislation as, for example, is the case with French companies. French law requires all companies with over ten employees to spend 1.6 per cent of their wage bill on training. In Germany, the education system encourages extended pre-employment training so that many Germans do not embark on their career until their late twenties, but it is then assumed that their training needs have been fully met. In the UK, the education system has recently moved back to an increased emphasis on vocational training, particularly for 16–20-year-olds through National Vocational Qualifications (NVQs). These link study in college with work experience and so provide training that is both on and off the job in nature.

The overall picture of how training is organised in European MNCs is very diverse. Some companies have responded to the shift towards network structures by revising training programmes to provide broader, corporate-wide education for future managers. Fiat's system is an example of how such broad-based training can be organised. There is a strong family culture in Fiat, built around the Agnelli family, but the company runs intensive education and training courses intended to promote a global vision amongst its managers. Each time a manager is promoted or given a new international assignment further training is given. The training is aimed at drawing managers away from the traditional specialisation on functions/products and towards a vision of a global organisation. In contrast, Philips, the electronics firm, is organised around a number of product divisions and its training system reflects this. Humes[14] estimates that more than 70 per cent of Philips' middle or higher managers spend their entire career within a single product division of Philips. As with US companies, the emphasis here is on nurturing specialist skills.

The wide variation in practice means that it is not possible to construct a universal model of how training is organised within European multinationals.

Japan

As already suggested in discussing planning and staffing in Japanese MNCs the emphasis in the companies is on in-house training which extends throughout the manager's career. In keeping with the lifelong employment principles, trainees will spend their first 3–8 months in a company 'indoctrination' programme, which is then supplemented by regular 'spiritual renewal' sessions. The greatest training effort is devoted to corporate HQ staff who are routed through a series of different departments to develop their general management skills. In summary, then, the Japanese believe very strongly in on the job training, and the whole employment system that governs recruitment, remuneration and promotion is linked to this idea.

Performance Appraisal and Remuneration

Performance appraisal systems assume that it is possible to measure what has been achieved and that people should be rewarded for their performance, but such thinking is generally associated with Western management and it does not fit readily into Eastern cultures. As a result, the remuneration systems used in American and European companies tend to differ substantively from those used in Japanese MNCs.

USA

Within North America, the individualist culture has led to the widespread use of performance related pay, which in turn results in big differences between the lowest and highest paid workers doing the same job. Basic pay is determined by the rank of job, as defined by the level of responsibility held, and performance linked bonus payments then supplement the basic rate. Remuneration via receipt of fringe benefits such as health insurance is also common.

Europe

Perhaps not surprisingly, the acceptability of performance related pay systems is not uniform across Europe. In common with the USA, pay levels in Europe are linked to job responsibilities, but whilst the market-focused individualist UK culture is supportive of pay linked to performance, other nations are less so. In the Nordic states the egalitarian culture supports uniformity of pay levels, and there is evidence that staff are better motivated by the offer of benefits that improve the quality of life rather than those that increase income levels. In France there is a certain ambivalence about the idea, but in Germany the formalisation of links between performance measurement and rewards is appreciated.

Japan

As already indicated, the Japanese system of pay and remuneration is based upon seniority which is determined by length of service rather than job performance. For example, in Mitsubishi managers must spend a minimum number of years in each job grade, and after a set length of time promotion occurs automatically, even if one's job is unchanged. The career process is thus one of initially low pay and slow steady promotion. Basic pay is often supplemented by other benefits, particularly through the provision of housing, and such a system works to further increase the long-term commitment of employees to a single company.

The complete avoidance of any link between rewards and performance is a consequence of the concern with the individual's integrity and corporate loyalty rather than their contribution to the organisation's financial performance. It also fits well with the long planning horizon of Asian cultures because progress towards a long-term target may be difficult to assess objectively, and so short-term performance awards are inappropriate. At the same time, many Eastern cultures consider it tactless to openly criticise an employee for their failures, and so performance feedback would require the use of a third party to mediate between employer and employee. Such a view of how levels of pay should be established and performance monitored is a great contrast to the direct and open style of North American culture.

Industrial Relations Management

You may recall that earlier in this chapter you saw that the level of unionisation and the relationship between unions and management differed between the USA and Europe. Within Europe the picture is one of positive cooperation between unions and employers, rather than the antagonistic relationship which characterises the US labour market. In Asia, the story is different again. Employees belong to enterprise-based unions rather than national unions that straddle many companies, and the emphasis tends to be on cooperation rather than conflict with management.

USA

Unions are nationally organised around particular classes of workers such as airline pilots, flight attendants, shop workers, etc., but bargaining on employment terms tends to be done on a company by company basis. In any single company there may be five or six different unions each representing their own group of workers and so negotiations with one or other union may be ongoing throughout the year. Workers' rights are governed by legislation but obtaining legal redress for breaches of rights can be very time consuming, and so the balance of power rests firmly on the side of the employers.

Europe

Although the level of union membership across Europe is high, the method of union organisation differs from country to country. In Germany unions are industry-based with one trade union per industry; in the UK they have historically been skill-based, e.g. NUSAWT, the schoolteachers' union, but a number of broad-based cross-industry unions also exist. In Sweden, industrial bargaining with trade unions is conducted via trade federations that deal with several unions simultaneously on behalf of large numbers of different employers.

The widespread use of works councils in many European countries supplements the role of the trade unions in representing workers' interests because such councils have strong powers to influence employers' policies. This helps to ensure that the labour : management relationship is amicable in nature and strikes are much less frequent than in the past. Some writers argue that the role of the state in the economy as a protector of workers' interests is one reason for the reduced level of activism amongst trade unions.

Japan

Trade unions in Japan are organised on a plant-wide basis and the relationship with management is usually harmonious. The lack of militancy is partly a reflection of the cultural emphasis on loyalty, combined with the fact that unions are company centred – hence a strike would imply disloyalty to one's employer. Wages and working conditions are usually the subject of separate negotiations, and unions see their role as representing the group rather than the individual. In contrast to Europe therefore, it is uncommon for unions to take up a dispute on behalf of a single individual who feels that their rights have been breached.

Recognising that HRM customs and practice differ in the three legs of the Triad is the first step towards successful management of an international staff. The issues discussed in this section have dealt primarily with management at the level of the local overseas unit, but for the multinational company there is also the question of how it recruits, trains and remunerates the international managers who will be responsible for products of functions over a broad geographic area. This is the subject of the concluding section of this chapter.

DEVELOPING INTERNATIONAL MANAGERS

As the earlier chapters of this book have clearly demonstrated, companies and business in general are becoming increasingly international, and so they need managers who are capable of working across cultural boundaries. Research published by Barham and Antal[18] in the early 1990s found that the recruitment and development of international managers was one of the highest priorities on the agenda of European-based MNCs. It is therefore useful to think about what exactly is meant by the term international manager, how they may be recruited and trained and how the current shortage of such managers can be eradicated.

Bartlett and Ghoshal[19] acknowledge that 'there is no such thing as a universal global manager.' More precisely they suggest that there are four types of international managers that are required in transnational companies, namely product, country, and functional specialists, plus senior level executives-based at corporate HQ. The difficulty with the Bartlett and Ghoshal approach is that is assumes that an organisation is already global in scope, whereas the reality is that many smaller organisations will also require managers who can work across different cultures, and such companies may only be in the early stages of becoming international.

What this means is that when trying to define the role of an international manager it is important to take into account the current position of the individual company, as the range of skills required will be, at least in part, dependent upon existing strategy. Adler and Ghadar[20] identified four different types of international manager, linked to the stage of internationalisation of a company:

Type 1 – works in a company which has a primarily domestic focus, where few managers are sent abroad on rare occasions.

Type 2 – describes functional specialists sent abroad by companies in the early stages of internationalisation. Such managers frequently report back to an international division at corporate headquarters.

Type 3 – when a company moves from being a collection of separate overseas units to a multinational company where all units are becoming linked, the international manager becomes much more involved in extensive cross-cultural interaction. The number of international managers is also substantially increased.

Type 4 – at the final stage of international evolution – equivalent to Bartlett and Ghoshal's transnational company – people from all over the world are in constant communication with each other and work together to the extent that the traditional distinction between local and expatriate staff becomes obsolete.

The idea that the need for international managers changes as a company develops leads on to the need to accept that the type of skills required of such staff will also vary. This was confirmed by work in the Fiat company reported by Auterio and Tesio[21], in which Fiat found that more than 40 per cent of jobs in the company required staff to deal with international matters. The level of involvement varied from managers in a single country working closely with/reporting to elements outside their country, e.g. a purchasing manager sourcing components from a foreign supplier, through to transnational managers whose responsibilities straddled all areas of the global business, e.g. marketing director. Obviously the skills required by these different levels of manager will not be the same.

Trying to specify a list of competences for international managers is therefore difficult, but it is nonetheless important if human resource managers are to be able to effectively recruit and train the next generation of senior executives in MNCs. The way forward is thus to try and establish an 'ideal' list of the qualities desirable for the highest level of management.

In a survey of managers of MNCs Barham and Wills[22] were able to classify the type of skills desired in international managers under the headings of 'doing' skills and 'being' skills. 'Doing' skills describe the tasks that are essential to effective cross-cultural management, namely:

- Championing international strategy

- Acting as a coach and mentor across borders

- Working as a mediator to resolve cross-border/functional/business conflicts.

'Being' skills are more concerned with the personality of the manager, and defined as:

- Ability to view problems from a variety of perspectives. Humility and fluency in at least one other language were thought to increase this ability

- Emotional energy – to cope with the stress of such work

- Psychological maturity, defined as having a curiosity to learn, to live 'here and now' and not in the past, and a strong sense of personal morality.

Looking more closely at the competences listed above it becomes clear that good international management at a senior level is perhaps as much about individual personality as it is about skills that can be taught either on the job or in the classroom. There is some debate in the HRM literature about this point, but it suggests that companies may be better to spend time and effort in careful recruitment of the 'right' people, rather than in training the 'wrong' ones.

In trying to recruit trainees and develop a cadre of future executives, companies have the choice of staffing foreign management posts with parent company nationals, host country nationals or third country nationals. Surveys suggest that despite the growth of more global corporations, there is still very extensive use of parent country nationals, i.e. expatriates, for these roles and this is causing some problems for MNCs. The continued use of expatriate staff is explained in terms of inadequate pools of local talent, foreign expectations that global branding implies the use of expatriate managers, and the fact that expatriates grant the parent company greater control of foreign operations. Unfortunately, however, the inability of some staff to work well and fit in to foreign postings, and problems with the repatriation of staff who have completed their foreign contracts combine to create substantial headaches for some MNCs. Difficulties in adjusting to life abroad include finding a role for spouses in dual-career families, a failure to understand and fit in with the local culture, and possible language problems. On repatriation people often dislike the resulting loss of status when a suitable equivalent job is not always immediately available, and they suffer from the loss of autonomy at work. Successful management of people in overseas posts is therefore very difficult in practice.

MNCs also face potential difficulties in finding sufficient international managers because of the increasing pace of internationalisation combined with recruitment problems for international posts. The recruitment problems are thought to stem from the growth of dual-career households, and a growing concern amongst staff of the need to preserve quality of life. International postings shift families into an alien foreign environment and may involve managers in extensive foreign travel and time away from home.

Scullion[23] suggests a number of solutions to the problem of shortage of international managers, including greater emphasis on recruiting graduates from a wide range of countries and not just the parent nation, combined with good language training and increased external recruitment of senior level managers. Running a common training programme for graduates from across the whole of Europe, for example, gives them exposure to cross-cultural issues early on in their career and also helps to instil a global team outlook. Barham and Antal[18] clearly think this is the way forward, as they believe that the international management problem needs to be seen as a long-term issue in which 'instead of seeking the elusive "superman" composite of desirable competences for international management, it is advisable to compose and develop teams whose strengths can be pooled and weaknesses balanced.' This represents an ideal scenario which is likely to take time to develop and it is also one which better suits Eastern rather than Western cultural thinking. In the meantime, the question of how to ensure the necessary supply of future international managers will remain a problem for human resource departments.

SUMMARY

It is impossible to define a framework for the best practice of HRM in an international company, because all companies are different. Nonetheless, the staff of a company can be viewed as assets that can create a competitive advantage for the business, and so maximising the quality of HRM is vital to business success. External influences such as culture and the role of the state in employment and education act as important influences on company strategies in respect of HRM, as does the basic issue of geography. Companies may choose differing levels of centralisation of HRM operations, and the choices range from ethnocentric to geocentric respectively. Local practices in HRM vary across the world, and the chapter high-lighted differences amongst the member nations of the Triad group. As a way of dealing with the growing internationalisation of business, companies are seeking to develop 'international managers', but the literature suggests that this is a difficult concept to define. Perhaps the best form of definition works by specifying the desirable skills of such managers. As things stand, there would appear to be a shortage of individuals with the necessary skills, which will lead to a recruitment problem amongst multinational companies.

CONCLUSION

HRM is a vital part of the value chain of a business, serving as a support function to ensure that the core functions are adequately staffed with people with the requisite skills. International HRM poses particular problems for management because of cultural differences that strongly affect the way that people behave. The successful management of HRM is thus a vital element in ensuring that a company's overall internationalisation strategy is successful.

At this point in the book we have concluded our analysis of both the external and the functional issues facing international business today. The only issue left to address is that of how international business affects the world – what impact do multinational companies have on the home and host countries? This is the subject of the final chapter.

References

1   Porter, M. (1986) *Competition in Global Business*, Harvard University Press, Boston
2   Brewster, C. (1994) European HRM: reflection of, or challenge to, the American concept? in Kirkbride, P. (ed.) *Human Resource Management in Europe*, Routledge, London
3   Armstrong, M. (1992) *Human resource Management: Strategy and Action*, Kogan Page, London
4   Vernon-Wortzel, H. and Wortzel, L. (1990) *Global Strategic Management: the essentials* 2nd Edition, Wiley, New York
5   Gaugler, E. (1988) HR Management : an international comparison, *Personnel* 65 (8): 24–30
6   Nevis, E. (1983) Cultural assumptions and productivity: the USA and China, *Sloan Management Review*, 24(3)

7 Pieper, R. (ed.) (1990) *HRM: An international comparison*, Walter de Gruyter, Berlin

8 Hertzberg, H. (2000) It's time the unions stood up for the workers, *New Yorker*, quoted in *The Week*, June, London

9 Perlmutter, H. (1969) The tortuous evolution of the multinational corporation, *Columbia Journal of World Business*

10 Schuler, R. (1987) Human resource management practice choices, in Schuler and Young-blood (eds) *Reading in personnel and human resource management*, 3rd edn, West, St Paul, Minn

11 Belanger, J. (1999) Best HR practice and the multinational company, *Human Resource Management Journal*, Vol.9, no.3

12 Gunnigle, P., Brewster, C. and Morley, M. (1994) Evaluating change in industrial relations: evidence from the Price Waterhouse Cranfield project, *Journal of the European Foundation for the Improvement of living and working conditions*

13 Monks, K. (1996) Global or local? HRM in the multinational company: the Irish experience, *The International Journal of Human Resource Management*, 7:3

14 Humes, S. (1993) *Managing the multinational, confronting the global-local dilemma*, Prentice-Hall, London

15 Derr, C. (1987) Managing high potentials in Europe, *European Management Journal*, Vol.5, No.2

16 Tung, R. (1987) *Expatriate assignments: enhancing success and minimising failure*, Academy of Management Executive

17 Handy, C., Gow, I., Gordon, C., Randlesome, C. and Maloney, M. (1987) *Making a manager: A report*, National Economic Development Office, London

18 Barham, K. and Berthoin Antal, A. (1992) *The quest for the international manager: A survey of global human resource strategies*, Special Report No.2098, Ashridge Research Group/Economic Intelligence Unit, Berkhamsted/London

19 Bartlett, C. and Ghoshal, S. (1989) What is a global manager?, *Harvard Business review*, Sep-Oct

20 Adler, N. and Ghadar, F. (1990) Strategic human resource management: a global perspective, in Pieper, R. (ed.) *Human resource management: an international comparison*, de Gruyter, Berlin

21 Auterio, E. and Tesio, V. (1990) The internationalisation of management in Fiat, *Journal of Management Development*, Vol.9 (6)

22 Barham, K. and Wills, S. (1992) *Management Across Frontiers*, Ashridge Management Research Group and Foundation for Management Education, Berkhamsted

23 Scullion, H. (1992) Strategic recruitment and development of the international manager, *Human Resource Management Journal*, Winter

Further Reading

There are a number of useful books on International HRM as well as some good journals covering this field of study, and some of these are listed below:

Kirkbride, P. (ed.) (1994) *Human Resource Management in Europe*, Routledge, London
Armstrong, M. (1992) *Human Resource Management: strategy and action*, Kogan Page, London
International Journal of Human Resource Management
Human Resource Management Journal
Human Resource Management Review
Columbia Journal of World Business

TUTORIAL EXERCISE

Find a diagram of the organisational structure of a major multinational company, perhaps using the company website or the annual report, and discuss how it might best approach organising its human resource management – should it work on a regional, local or global basis and why?

ESSAY QUESTIONS

1 Does centralisation of the HRM function mean that local culture and needs are ignored?

2 If US companies are faced with highly mobile labour forces, does this mean that they are 'wasting' their money on training?

3 From the point of view of your own native culture, what would be the pros and cons of working for a Japanese multinational and adopting their system of lifetime employment?

Case Study: Measuring the performance of the HRM function in GTE Corporation

The American-based GTE company is one of the world's largest telecommunications companies, with 1999 sales in excess of US$25 billion. Through a mix of licence agreements, joint ventures and wholly owned subsidiaries the company provides a range of telecommunications services to a large number of countries, primarily in South America and Asia. Managing staff across this range of continents is a difficult challenge, but it is also difficult for the senior management at GTE to measure the contribution of good HRM to overall business performance. The strategic HRM literature highlights the importance of integrating HRM into corporate strategy, but there is little evidence to date on how companies seek to achieve this aim in practice. There is even less on how the effectiveness of HRM is assessed, and so the decision to try and do this at GTE was to prove particularly challenging.

In 1998 HRM managers at GTE were looking for a measure by which they could *quantify* the impact of their department on the achievement of strategic objectives, with the aim of assessing the effectiveness of HRM practice. The method chosen was based on the Balanced Scorecard approach of Kaplan and Norton* which combines financial and non-financial measures of performance. The idea of measuring performance in a support function was viewed as innovative, but important to helping GTE secure its market position in a rapidly changing and highly competitive industry sector. The challenge for the human resource department was to define a set of criteria against which its performance could be measured *and* used as a basis for performance related pay for the HRM staff.

The Scorecard in Practice

The first stage in devising the scorecard involved defining the strategic aims of the HRM department. These were classified under five core headings:

- Nurturing talent
- Developing world-class leadership
- Customer service and support
- Creation of an integrated organisation
- Enhancement of GTE's HR capability.

Divisional managers in GTE are told in detail about these aims for HRM, and they are then asked to make judgements about the extent to which HRM staff have achieved the aims in respect of their individual division. In order to help the managers to make their judgements more easily, each aim is subdivided into more explicit objectives as explained below.

Nurturing talent is measured in terms of the extent to which HRM:

1 increases the pool of talent
2 invests in people, via training
3 creates opportunities for people to develop and grow, by offering remuneration packages that ensure the retention of talent.

Developing world-class leadership requires that the HRM department takes responsibility for:

1 defining leadership competences
2 rewarding leadership behaviour.

Customer service and support is measured in terms of building up GTE's service capability.

* Kaplan R. and Norton D. (1992) The Balanced Scorecard – Measures that drive performance, *Harvard Business Review* Jan–Feb p.72

Creating an integrated organisation involves the establishment of systems to:

1 link rewards to integration
2 invest in staff training to facilitate exploitation of technological advances to aid integration.

Each divisional manager is asked to complete a regular questionnaire and complete a database relating to each of these objectives. If, for example, a manager was unable to retain a graduate recruit with excellent management potential because he could not pay him enough, this information would be recorded in the completed questionnaire. The returns from the managers are then used to generate a 'score' against each objective, and the results are posted quarterly on the company's intranet site. In this way the HRM function is made accountable to the rest of the company because the scorecard directly measures its contribution to business success.

The level of achievement of the objectives is also measured against established targets for the number of talented staff and the desirable skill/pay profile of the company. Most importantly, the department's success is assessed by the divisional managers who use their service; the emphasis is on meeting corporate needs.

Sources: www.gte.com/About GTE/News Center/ Fact Sheets and 'Putting HR on the score card', Solomon, C., *Workforce* Vol.79 Issue 3

CASE STUDY QUESTIONS

1 In what respects does this way of looking at the effectiveness of the HRM function reflect US culture?

2 How might some of the performance targets be affected by factors outside the control of performance managers?

3 Does it make sense to try and quantify the contribution of a function such as HRM?

4 How might an Asian divisional manager respond to a request to answer questions relating to the performance of an HRM department-based at US headquarters?

5 Can you suggest any other HRM objectives that might be added to the list, and can be said to influence a company's competitive position?

Impact on the Broader Environment

CHAPTER ELEVEN

The Impact of Multinational Corporations

LEARNING OUTCOMES

When you have completed this chapter you should feel competent to:

- Summarise the main trends in MNC growth and the volume and pattern of foreign direct investment
- Identify and critically comment upon the ways in which multinational companies (MNCs) may affect their home and host nations, both economically and socially
- Discuss the special issues which need to be considered when measuring the effect of foreign direct investment in less developed countries
- Explain and comment upon elements of the current political debate about the need to control the global economic power of multinational corporations

---

INTRODUCTION

Throughout most of this book the focus of attention has been with the individual company and how it establishes a strategy, manages all of the business functions, and measures its performance in the international arena. The overall picture that has emerged is one of a complex world in which decisions about marketing, managing staff and overall strategy are very dependent upon what is happening in the external environment as well as within the company itself. It is now time to stand back and look at the picture from a different angle, by considering the effect that the company might have on the environment. The scale of impact is likely to be closely linked to company size, and as John Dunning observed in a memorable turn of phrase, multinational companies can be likened to animals in a zoo which 'come in various shapes and sizes and make their individual impacts on the environment.' The networks which are established by multinational companies straddle the world, and the aim of this chapter is to try and identify the effect of such networks on both home and host nations. In addition, the broader question of the global political debate about the role and power of multinationals will be discussed, particularly in relation to the problem of control of their economic power.

MAIN TRENDS IN MNC GROWTH AND INVESTMENT

This discussion draws heavily on the material covered in the middle section of Chapter 2 on international trade and investment flows. You may, therefore, find it useful to go back to those pages and refresh your memory on the general areas of concern.

One of the most important observations that emerges from looking at trade and investment flows post World War Two is that the distribution of production and wealth across the globe has changed over time. Simultaneously, the value of FDI has grown at a rate faster than international trade, partly because investment is moving to the new centres of world production. The growth of FDI has been accompanied by a massive expansion in the numbers and size of multinational and transnational corporations, as was illustrated in Table 2.4*. The transnational corporation is defined as comprising parent enterprises and their foreign affiliates where a parent controls the assets of foreign entities usually through the ownership of an equity stake. The Table shows that the economic activity of MNCs is concentrated in a limited range of business sectors and that company ownership is predominantly in the developed world, as illustrated below.

Table 11.1   *The Activity and Ownership of Transnational Corporations*

Sector of Activity	Key Home Nations	Key Host Nations
Electronics and electrical components e.g. General Electric	USA	EU – UK – Germany –France
Automotive, e.g. Toyota	UK	USA
Petroleum, e.g. Royal Dutch Shell	Japan	Japan
Chemicals, e.g. Hoechst AG	Germany	China
Pharmaceuticals, e.g. Glaxo Wellcome	France	Thailand
Food, e.g. Nestlé		Korea

Developed countries are important to multinational companies in the role of both home and host and so for the five main countries of Germany, France, the United Kingdom, USA and Japan, understanding the impact of such companies on the domestic economy is very important.

The biggest issue for the home nations in recent years has been the employment consequences arising out of companies relocating their production to developing or newly industrialising nations. When, for example, the NAFTA trade agreement was signed, US labour unions were concerned that the agreement would lead to a widespread shift in production out of the USA and into Mexico, where labour costs are

---

* Multinational corporation and transnational corporation do not differ in definition but perhaps in size. For the rest of this chapter it is therefore assumed that the two terms are interchangeable.

lower. Similarly, in the United Kingdom there has been concern over potential job losses in the automotive trade because of decisions by foreign investors such as Ford and BMW to cut production in the UK and either sell up or move facilities elsewhere. The individual employee will obviously suffer hardship if they lose their job as a result of a company's decision to invest overseas, but from the perspective of the overall home economy, the net effects may still be beneficial. If the profits from overseas operations are repatriated, and those operations use inputs which are exported from the home country, the overall impact on the balance of payments may be positive. At governmental level, then, it is important to look at the overall picture rather than fall into a trap of seeking to pacify labour groups who might be protesting at job losses. The problem with doing this is of course that the possible price to be paid for ignoring the protestors is loss of votes in the next election, and potential loss of power. Thinking about how to determine the net gains or losses at national level is thus a very important issue.

In particular, understanding whether host nations receive net economic gains/losses can be helpful in determining national policy towards inward foreign investment. Many governments offer incentives such as temporary tax free status to foreign companies in order to entice them into investing in their country, but this assumes that the nation will benefit from the investment, and this may not be the case in reality. Governments also recognise that foreign investment can have social effects in terms of changing cultural attitudes and taste, changing life styles (urban versus rural) and influencing the distribution of income. These various effects require more detailed discussion, but as you will see, quantifying the costs and benefits is no easy task, not least because political bias can get in the way of objective assessment. On the one hand there are those who view multinational companies as destructive, whilst at the other end of the political spectrum there are those who believe that such companies can offer positive benefits. The truth probably lies somewhere in the middle, but we can begin analysing the reality by looking at how transnationals impact on host economies.

MNC IMPACT ON HOST ECONOMIES

The impact of any single company or investment by a multinational concern is dependent upon a number of factors including:

WHY? – what is the purpose of the investment: (a) to seek raw materials, (b) production facilities, or (c) local or export markets?

WHAT? – is the nature of the investment – the level and type of technology used, the industry involved. Is capital raised in local markets or brought in from the home nation, and what is the balance of local : international sources for key resources?

HOW? – is the foreign investment made – through a joint venture, merger, acquisition or wholly owned new investment site.

Why, what and how the investment is made will directly determine its impact on the host nation. We can look at each of these factors in turn.

WHY?

In Chapter 2 we identified two main reasons why companies invest abroad:

– To gain access to new markets. These may be within the host country itself perhaps because FDI offers a way of circumventing import regulations or elsewhere in the region, with the host serving as an export producer.

– To gain access to new supply facilities in the form of raw material or production facilities.

WHAT?

The industry sector which is the subject of the investment is likely to affect both the sum of money invested and the technology used, and depending on the size and sophistication of local capital markets this may in turn influence the proportion of funds which are raised locally. At the same time, the skill levels required of staff and the number to be employed will be partially dependent on the industry type. All of these variations alter the potential impact of the MNC on the economy.

HOW?

The choice between a joint venture, greenfield investment or acquisition will potentially alter the impact of the investment upon the host nation's balance of payments, through changes in the absolute value of capital transfers from the home nation. In a similar way, it is fair to assume that in the case of an acquisition, the net addition to local employment opportunities will be much less than if the investment relates to an entirely new venture. In other words, the economic impact of the MNC will be sensitive to the chosen mode of entry into the foreign location.

The link between the what, why and how of investments and the economic and social impact of multinational companies can be illustrated by reference to two contrasting examples:

Case 1

A French supermarket chain purchases a Kenyan company which owns pineapple plantations and a cannery for processing the lower quality fruit. Top quality fresh fruit is exported by air freight direct to the European markets.

Case 2

A Japanese automotive company purchases a greenfield site in the United Kingdom and builds an assembly plant for cars which are then sold across mainland Europe as well as in the UK. The vehicle components are sourced from a number of company owned plants around Europe, and just 10% (by value) of these originate in the UK.

In Case 1, the Kenyan Balance of Payments will benefit from a capital inflow equal to the price paid for the local producer in the take-over. The basic operations and practice of the plantations and the cannery are likely to remain largely unchanged, and so the effect on the numbers employed is likely to be limited. It is, however, possible that working conditions, training and pay levels will be upgraded to meet international standards. The biggest economic effect is likely to occur through the fact that the profits from the sale of the fresh and canned fruit will now accrue to the French owners instead of the Kenyans. These profits may either be re-invested in the country or repatriated (minus any local tax/dividends payable) back to the company's home country. Overall, the economic and social effects on the host country might be expected to be limited in scope because the operation is relatively small, the industry is a low technology one, and the mode of entry was via an acquisition.

In Case 2, the economic effects will be more exaggerated but also more difficult to calculate. Investing in a developed country, it is likely that the capital required would come either from the profits of the company's operations in Europe or from European financial markets, for example through the issue of a Eurobond. Consequently there may be limited capital inflows to benefit the UK Balance of Payments. On the other hand, the Balance of Payments will gain a regular boost from the export sales of the plant, although these will be partially offset by imports. If the assembly plant is servicing the whole European market, then the investment in technology will be substantial, to ensure high volume and flexible working methods, and as an assembly plant the value added will be high compared to that associated with component production. In aggregate, the plant may have quite a big effect on the economy, particularly at the very local level, via job creation, increased local consumption, training in new skills and the positive or negative Balance of Payment flows. The complexity of the links between the company both domestically and internationally, however, make the calculation of the net impact of the MNC very difficult to quantify. Figure 11.1 portrays the typical pattern of impact of the MNC on the host economy, which serves as a starting point for calculating the economic value of the inflows and outflows associated with inward investment by a multinational. The direction and nature of the links is reasonably clear, the problem lies in trying to convert them into monetary values.

The two simple examples described above demonstrate the variety of type and scale of interaction between a multinational and the host country, and Figure 11.1 shows that the gravity of the impact is dependent upon a whole number of inter-related issues. It is therefore useful to elaborate on the most important ways in which MNCs can exert an influence on host nations. The effects may be economic or social in nature, and we will look at each one, working through Figure 11.1 from left to right.

Trade Effects

The first major area of the economy to be affected by multinational companies is the Balance of Payments*, through both the trade and/or capital accounts. The trade account is the section of the Balance of Payments concerned with the import and export of goods and services. If the value of exports exceeds that of imports, the Balance of

---

* The Balance of Payments position influences the exchange rate, as economies that are in deficit will generally have a weaker currency than those that are in surplus.

Figure 11.1 *Foreign Direct Investment*

Impact on the home nation is a function of **what**, **why** and **how** the investment is made.

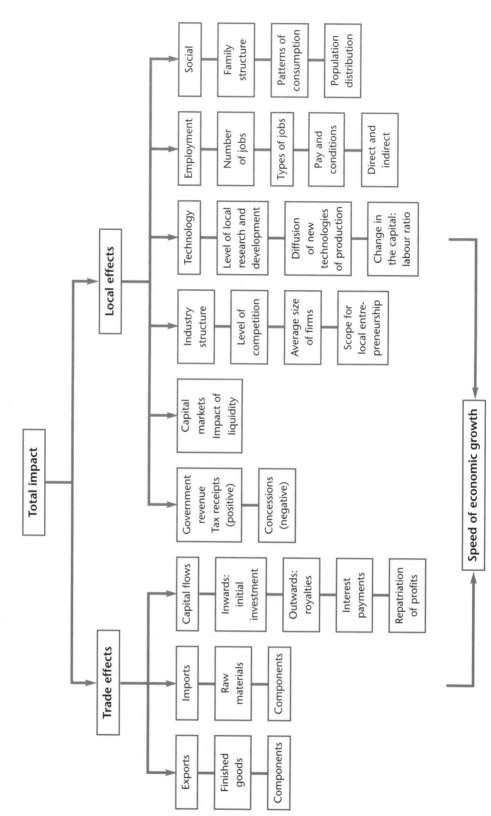

Payments is in surplus and where the reverse is true the account is in deficit. The net value of capital flows in or out of the country – the balance on the capital account – is then added to the balance of trade to give the overall Balance of Payments figure.

The Balance of Payments effect of a multinational moving into a country can be measured by using the following simple formula:

Change in balance of trade + change in capital account
= Change in balance of payment

Or, $\triangle X + \triangle M + \triangle C = \triangle B$

Where $\triangle$ = Change in the value of the relevant variable between time t and time t–1

X = Exports   C = Capital account
M = Imports   B = Balance of Payments

The formula is simple but identifying the values input is a potential nightmare. Two of the largest uncertainties surrounding the estimation are:

■ Should items be valued at cost or market value?
■ Over what time scale should the change be measured?

The net effects may be vastly different if the relevant time scale is changed from, say two to ten years. Using carefully chosen statistics, one can probably prove that a multinational company is either hugely damaging or hugely beneficial to an economy, whilst the reality may be neither.

Local effects

Government revenue

National government payments or receipts may be affected by investments from MNCs on two levels. Firstly, the companies may demand improvements in infrastructure, or rate and tax rebates before they are prepared to invest into a country. On the other hand, when the MNC is profitable, it will be required to pay money in taxes to the host government. It must be remembered, however, that the amount of taxes paid is often subject to internal manipulation by the MNC, through control of the transfer prices used to move goods from one international location to another within the company. Most multinationals will seek to switch their tax liability from high tax countries to low tax countries wherever possible, via changes in the transfer prices. In this way, the net gains to tax revenues in host countries tends to be minimal.

Capital markets

The impact of inward investment upon the local capital markets is very dependent upon the extent to which the foreign investor uses the local markets as a source of funds. Where extensive use is made, the scale of the funds raised may work to reduce the liquidity (number of capital providers versus users) in the market. If, for example, a foreign company makes a debt issue which absorbs a large proportion of the new issue capital available in an economy, then for any remaining local firms that wish to raise funds, the cost of capital can be expected to rise, because of a shortage of supply. The funds' flow into or out of an economy will, via the balance of payments, affect the interest rates in the local area. If the balance of payments is pushed into deficit by large imports for an MNC, then the currency will tend to drop in value, and interest rates rise as a way of protecting the currency from further collapse. Consequently, even when a multinational does not have a direct effect on the local capital markets, it may have an indirect effect through its influence over interest rates.

Industry structure

There is evidence to suggest that when multinational companies move into an economy, they lead to greater consolidation in the related industry sector, because of the greater level of competition that they pose. When foreign direct investment occurs, the average size of firms in the local industry tends to rise, and the scope for local entrepreneurship is reduced because the barriers to entry into the industry are now higher.

The UK furniture industry is an example of one where these effects can be observed. The industry has traditionally been very fragmented, and dominated by relatively small manufacturers working at a local level. The investment by IKEA in large retail outlets across the UK has led to a substantial reduction in the ability of the local firms to compete, not least on the grounds of higher costs. Consequently, the number of furniture manufacturers in the UK has been falling, whilst simultaneously IKEA has been taking a larger share of the UK market.

Industry structure may also be affected by the extent to which a foreign investor is prepared to use local suppliers, but the range of use of local content amongst TNCs varies widely. For example in Mexico, the level of Mexican content in the output of the mesqualidora plants that supply the North American markets in very low. In contrast, in parts of Western Europe the level of local content in production is relatively high.

Technology

The technological effects of investments by a multinational company can, not surprisingly, be both negative or positive. On the positive side, MNCs may be subject to legislation which demands a minimal level of local input into a product and, in producing the local input to high international specifications, higher levels of technological expertise are diffused into the local economy. On the negative side, the technology used by inward investors may, because it originates in the developed economies, be capital rather than labour intensive. As such, it may be 'inappropriate' to the economy of the host if labour is an abundant and cheap resource. Consequently, many MNCs are accused of damaging economies through the encouragement of use of inappropriate technology. MNCs are also frequently criticised because there is a tendency to retain the research and development functions back at HQ, transferring only the new production technologies. The result is that the 'know-how' relating to the creation of technological innovations remains at home, and is not transferred to the host nation. This is particularly important because in some theories of economic growth, technological know-how is fundamental to rapid development.

Employment

Figures published by UNCTAD suggest that MNCs employ only around 3 per cent of the world's labour force but a high proportion of the non-agricultural employees in both developed and developing countries, and so their employment impact is important to consider. Transnational corporations can create employment both directly and indirectly when they invest in an overseas affiliate, and the level of net employment created can have an important influence on the rate of economic development. Whichever way the employment is created, the absolute number of jobs created (net), the type of jobs involved, and the pay and working conditions may vary, and in so doing alter the impact of the multinational on the local economy.

An ILO workshop report published in 1998[2], suggests that the new network-based system of organisation of multinationals poses specific challenges for local employment opportunities in host countries. The report cites the growth of networks, such as those used by Nike Corporation and Benetton, which operate first and second tier supplier systems. First tier suppliers earn a higher added value and are more technically oriented, whilst the second tier provide low skill, low value services to the big multinationals, and historically the less developed nations have been a good source of second tier suppliers. The way to improve the employment benefits from inward investment is for companies to strive to become first tier suppliers, but when such suppliers are big, as in the case of the Brazilian and Indian auto industry, the local prospects for improved status are poor.

The problem of inward investment that creates low grade local jobs is not confined to the developing nations, and the idea of trying to upgrade skills and supplier status holds good across the globe. In the New York garment industry, for example, the Garment Industry Development Corporation, a confederation made up of employers, city representatives and employees, works to help suppliers to build competences and so upgrade their position in the global garment network.

One of the major criticisms of MNCs and host countries is that they have been responsible for the creation of jobs, but that the jobs are generally low level and so represent an exploitation of labour. Evidence from the ILO indicates that by 1996 such companies had been responsible for the creation of a substantial amount of employment within Export Processing Zones in developing countries, but that the jobs consisted primarily of low skilled, low value assembly work. At the same time, Export Processing Zones were criticised by the ILO for their weak labour standards, hostility to trade unions and subordination of young female workers. At the same time, however, there is conflicting evidence that MNCs are being unfairly criticised, and that foreign affiliates generally offer higher rates of pay and better working conditions than local firms. UNCTAD cites the nations of Peru, Thailand, Malaysia and Indonesia as cases where multinationals pay rates that are above local levels. The cases where poor rates of

* www.ilo.org is a very useful website which provides much information on employment issues raised by globalisation, such as forced labour, child labour, working conditions etc.

pay and conditions are prevalent have been shown to relate to companies acting as subcontractors to MNCs rather than the MNCs themselves, and as a result the companies have been pressured into setting minimal standards of employment for their subcontractors. This issue has been given a high political profile, especially where child labour has been concerned, and it can be argued that political lobbying has worked to improve the lot of many indirect employees of MNCs in the developing world.

Inward investment can also work to indirectly create employment through its impact on local supply networks and consumption levels. If, for example, a foreign company uses local companies to supply some of its components, then jobs are likely to be created at these local firms. At the same time, the additional employment allows local spending on consumer goods to rise, and this may in turn lead to further job creation through what is called the regional multiplier effect.

Social

In addition to influencing the local economy of a host country, multinationals can also affect the social infrastructure. For example, the use of large numbers of female workers in many of the MNC-owned electronics assembly plants of Southern Asia has led to a change in the perceived role of the woman in the family. In addition, the employment opportunities created in MNCs tend to be in urban areas, and so the relative attractiveness of rural:urban lifestyles is altered by the presence of large foreign investors. The population distribution of some developing countries has been dramatically altered as a result.

Working in combination, these various effects serve to determine the extent to which MNC investment promotes economic growth and development within an economy. Theories of economic growth use both export expansion and/or import substitution as stimulants to growth, and as Figure 11.1 shows, both trade and local effects combine to determine the NET growth impact of MNC investment. The greater the positive Balance of Payments flows, and the stronger the local linkages that create jobs, stimulate entrepreneurship and diffuse new technologies, the greater the growth impact of foreign direct investment, but the converse is also true, and there are many who argue that for the less developed countries in particular, an open door policy to foreign corporate investors is economically dangerous. The specific issues relating to the role of TNCs in developing countries is therefore the subject of the next section of this chapter.

SPECIAL CONSIDERATIONS FOR FDI IN DEVELOPING COUNTRIES

Figure 11.1 is equally applicable to developing as well as developed nations as a tool for determining the impact of MNC investment in the economy, but there are some characteristics of developing nations which raise particular issues about the role of FDI in development. We will look at these using the same headings as in Figure 11.1 and the preceding analysis on host nations.

Trade Effects

One of the problems for many developing nations is that they suffer from a trade gap, which means that they do not earn sufficient foreign exchange from exports and international aid receipts to cover their requirements for foreign exchange to pay for imports. Supporters of multinational investment in such countries argue that they are good for the economy because most MNCs are likely to be exporters.

There is certainly substantial evidence to show that foreign companies do tend to be the highest exporters from the poorer nations, as is the case in the Malaysian electronics sector, but the benefits of the exports are offset by large levels of imported components. The emphasis by foreign investors on establishing low value added, low skilled, high tech assembly centres means that the links into the local economy are minimal and the associated imports are high. The section of the balance of payments relating to capital flows is also important here. Where FDI has been funded by borrowing from the parent, there will be payments back to the home nation of both capital and interest and this method of financing is very common for investing in poorer countries where the capital markets are less developed. Many developing countries use licensing as a means of obtaining access to new technologies, but such an arrangement will also involve capital flows outwards from the host economy. It is perhaps not surprising then that a recent OECD study of nine Asia Pacific nations showed that in all cases they have suffered a worsening of their balance of payments position as a result of FDI.

One possible cause of the problem is low skill levels in the local workforce, and so if training and education levels were improved, then MNCs could shift more complex production facilities to developing countries which would add more value, and given the higher skill levels, the number of local suppliers could be increased. This implies that when trying to ensure that MNCs have a positive trade effect, governments need to think about much broader policy issues as well. In reality, policies on FDI have to be placed in the context of overall strategies relating to how economic growth is to be achieved.

Local Effects

On a general level, there is evidence to suggest that foreign investment works to create what is often called a 'dual economy' in less developed countries. This is particularly the case where countries operate export processing zones, and the area becomes a foreign enclave which operates in a way that is effectively divorced from the rest of the economy. The term dual economy emphasises this separation, and the specific effects are discussed in more detail below.

Government revenue

The impact on government revenue may be positive or negative depending on the relative amount that is paid out to the investor in concessions versus the sums received in taxation. In reality the net effect on government revenue often reflects the relative bargaining power of the two parties. Powerful MNCs may be able to extract significant concessions from host governments, particularly if the host is small. At the same time, the MNC can also use transfer pricing to reduce the tax burden, by selling its exports to final users at prices which ensure that minimal profits accrue to the overseas unit; if there is little profit, then minimal tax is paid. The large developed nations have begun to establish strict rules on transfer pricing to reduce the risk of such profit manipulation, but the smaller developing countries lack the political power to control the MNCs quite so effectively.

Capital Markets

There are two important perspectives on capital market usage by MNCs that are particularly relevant to developing countries. The first relates to the fact that the size and liquidity of local markets is likely to be limited, and so if a large foreign investor raises local funding, it is likely to leave insufficient capital available for local investors. Over the longer term this can have an effect on the supply of local entrepreneurs, which may dry up due to lack of funding.

An alternative viewpoint is that MNCs are very helpful to the capital markets of poor countries because they fill a 'savings gap'. One model of economic growth, the Harrod–Domar model, shows that the speed of economic growth of a country is dependent upon the level of savings and the capital : output ratio*. The model is shown by the following equation:

$G = S/K$

Where G = annual rate of economic growth
  S = savings ratio
  K = capital : output ratio

Suppose that a country wanted to achieve a rate of growth of 5 per cent and the capital output ratio equalled 4, then the equation can be solved for S, so that

$S = G \times K$ or $S = 4 \times 5 = 20\%$

In other words, 20 per cent of the economy's income would need to be saved in order to provide the investment money required to grow at the desired rate of 5 per cent. Even in most developed countries, this level of savings would be difficult to achieve, but in the poorer nations of the world it is likely to be almost impossible.

Foreign direct investors can play a role in filling the savings gap by bringing money into the economy, so that if the investment is funded from the **home** country there is a net addition to the funds available in the **host** country, and so FDI may work to encourage faster rates of economic growth. This will be particularly true when the foreign investor also chooses to re-invest profits in the host nation, and many countries are now seeking to establish regulations which require minimal levels of re-investment as a direct way of increasing the availability of local investment funds. At present however, such re-investment is relatively rare.

---

* The capital : output ratio measures the ratio of the units of capital needed to produce one unit of output. For example, if £100,000 of capital produces £300,000 of output, then the ratio is 3.

This leads to the conclusion that the local effect in terms of the capital markets may be positive or negative depending on whether the FDI is funded from home or from cash raised locally. This will vary on a case by case basis, and so it becomes very difficult to draw any overall conclusions on the impact of FDI on capital markets in developing countries.

Industry structure

The most important consideration here is the effect of large companies on the level of competition and the encouragement of local entrepreneurship. The manufacturing sectors of developing nations are often characterised by large numbers of small producers. If a leading company comes in as a new investor, the level of competition will increase dramatically and many local firms may go out of business. Equally, if investment is via acquisition of local producers, the number of firms in the industry will decline. The change in the size is important from a social as well as an economic perspective, because the small firms will often be the means by which families are self supporting, and in urban areas they cannot revert to farming to earn a livelihood. The potential therefore arises of a large number of urban unemployed, and in societies where social security benefits are non-existent, the result is increased urban poverty. Obviously, this does not mean that one can argue that MNCs are a major cause of urban poverty in the Third World, but it is something to be assessed when looking at net gains/losses in any particular country.

Technology

Perhaps the greatest criticism that is made of FDI in the developing world is that it makes use of production systems that use technologies which do not match the balance of resources in the host country. The reason for this is simple – the technologies are developed in the rich world, where labour is scarce and expensive, and when investing overseas companies want to use the technologies with which they are familiar. Unfortunately, developing nations tend to have lots of cheap labour available, but very little capital, and so the capital-intensive systems that are introduced are thought to be inappropriate. The problem is exacerbated by the poor educational level of local staff who are then forced into the lower levels of the labour force rather than management positions, so that potentially a vicious circle is created whereby local staff never get to learn how to use the new technologies.

Employment and social

The dual economy concept is particularly obvious when it comes to employment issues. It is still the case that the bulk of the population in developing economies is rural-based, and income levels are low. Foreign investment works to create jobs in urban areas, and so it encourages a high level of rural urban migration – the explosive growth of Mexico City is one such example – where people live in shanty towns on the city outskirts in the hope of earning a better living than back in the villages. Evidence suggests that the pay and conditions of workers in MNCs in developing countries is above average for the locality, and so an urban 'elite' is created. These richer individuals then develop a different lifestyle and pattern of consumption to their fellows and a new subculture emerges. There are some writers who see this process as part of economic development and so almost inevitable, but there are others who regard it as ethically questionable, because it represents rich Western nations imposing their ways on cultures and lifestyles that are valid in their own right. At this point, politics and social ethics start to enter into the debate about international business and such debate is well beyond the scope of this book.

POLITICAL INTERVENTION IN RELATION TO CONTROL OF THE POWER OF MNCS

This brings us to the issue of whether governments should start to intervene to limit the power of MNCs and also whether such intervention is feasible. If you think back to Chapter 2 you may recall that some companies have annual revenues in excess of the GDP of many nations. This means that individual governments may be at a disadvantage in terms of their bargaining power relative to such large concerns. Furthermore, governments may also find it difficult to control MNCs simply because of the fact that their operations cross so many boundaries, and actually defining the span of control within the geographic boundaries of one nation may be impossible.

This is not to say that companies can therefore do what they like without fear of redress. Instead, it means that the regulatory regime needs to be broadened to intergovernmental levels. The growth of regional trading blocs is important here, because it means that the level of international cooperation is higher, and governments have a common interest in monitoring the activities of companies within their bloc. Consequently, institutions such as the European Union now have a very important role to play in monitoring and controlling the activities of transnational organisations. It is too early to say whether such international regulation will prove successful, and the growth of e-commerce makes it even more difficult to see what is going on, but in five or ten years' time it is to be expected that the regulators will be able to match the companies in size, if not in power.

SUMMARY

This chapter has looked at the problems of understanding the effect of foreign direct investment at the national level. It has demonstrated that the effects can be classified in terms of trade and local impact, and much depends on the scale of the linkages that are developed between the foreign company and the local economy. Each investment and each host country will be different, and so it is impossible to reach any definite conclusions on the net gains and losses that may result. The problems that relate to FDI in developing countries have strong overlap with those for all other countries but a number of additional questions need to be asked about the suitability of the investment to local needs. In conclusion, the jury is still out on the overall impact of multinational companies, but one thing is certain – the amount of international trade and investment will continue to grow in the foreseeable future.

CONCLUSION

International business, as this book has shown, straddles all of the main functions of business, but also requires an understanding of the cultural, economic and political environment. By its nature it is a discipline that is continually evolving as new ideas, technologies and business practices emerge. In fact it is this element of evolution and change which makes it such an interesting area of study.

Having completed this book, you should have a much broader, and deeper understanding of the type of problems facing international businesses today, and if you have the chance to work overseas then you will see some of the observations of this book at first hand.

Most people end up specialising in their favoured discipline, but the breadth of international business study will always serve to your advantage. You may find that you are aware of ideas that are new to your boss! Anyway, wherever you end up working in the world, good luck.

ESSAY QUESTIONS

1 Apart from regional trading blocs such as NAFTA or the EU, can you suggest any other international bodies that might be in a strong position to implement international regulations to control the activities of multinationals.

2 If social factors cannot be measured in quantitative terms, then is it sensible to take them into account when assessing the impact of multinational companies?

3 Apart from the employment issues raised in the chapter, in what other ways might a home nation be affected by a company's decision to invest extensively overseas (hint: think about the possible displacement of investment)?

4 Are multinationals good for the world but bad for countries?

Case Study: Foreign Direct Investment by MNCs, and economic development in South East Asia

This case focuses on FDI in just four South East Asian countries – Indonesia, Malaysia, the Philippines and Thailand – and looks at the extent to which government policies to promote export-led FDI have enhanced local capabilities and delivered sustainable economic development.

All four countries have for the last decade or more been major recipients of FDI. Government policies have sought to 'manage' the economic role of such investment, by restricting the access of foreign firms to some sectors, whilst actively promoting and encouraging export-oriented FDI, and this particular approach of a mixed attitude to foreign investment has had very specific effects on the economies of the four nations.

Government Policies Toward FDI

The attitude of governments in newly industrialising countries towards FDI can be expected to reflect their broader economic development strategy. Consequently, across most of South East Asia, governments have been keen to encourage inward investment from foreign companies that wish to export most of their output. In contrast, strict limits and in some cases outright prohibition has been imposed upon investors seeking to supply local market needs. Such policies reflect a commitment to export-led growth as the route to economic development which has followed on from import substitution policies pursued in earlier decades.

The difficulty of this approach is that the *net impact* of export-focused FDI on the local economy is dependent more upon its quality than its quantity. There is evidence that policies towards FDI in Indonesia, Malaysia, the Philippines and Thailand have led to some distortions in the economy which have lowered the 'quality' of investments especially where quality is measured in terms of transfers of technology and know-how to the local economy. The interesting question to consider is precisely why such distortions have arisen.

History of FDI in the Region

The four countries that are the subject of this study have, in combination, been the fifth most popular host to FDI from across the world over the period 1990–97 although both the countries of origin, and the sectors targeted by investors, vary from country to country. The only developing country to rank higher than them was China, with the remaining top places going to the USA, UK and France.

Both Thailand and Malaysia are characterised by receiving around two-thirds of their investment from the South Asia region. Electronics is the dominant sector targeted for investment in both nations, but whilst manufacturing investment is very important to Malaysia, it absorbs only one third of total inflows to Thailand, where distribution, finance, construction and property are important areas for foreign investors.

US companies are responsible for the bulk of FDI in the Philippines, perhaps reflecting the history of links between the two countries, and although the value of inward investment is the lowest of all the four nations, it is also well diversified across sectors. In the case of Indonesia, European companies dominate, and most investment is resource-based in either the petroleum sector or the manufacture of chemicals and paper. In fact Indonesia draws in more non-manufacturing investment that Malaysia, Philippines and Thailand taken together.

Regulation of FDI

The regulatory framework governing FDI is common across the four countries in many respects, although there are differences of detail. Common policies include:

1 **Screening of Inward Investments:** usually via an agency or Board of Investment. The agency seeks to ensure that priority is given to investments that meet the defined criteria and further government development strategies.

2 **Equity Restrictions:** these relate to maximum limits on the ownership of equity in local companies. The intention is to ensure foreign companies only hold minority interests, which range from 30% in Malaysia to 49% in Indonesia and Thailand. In order to protect key sectors such as banking, the maximum limits are set even lower.

   It is usually the case that permission for joint ventures and purchase of minority stakes in local firms requires authorisation from a government body other than the BOI.

3 **Land Ownership Limits**

   Failure to acquire ownership rights to the land on which foreign factories are built can substantially increase the political risks of the MNC, as well as limiting its access to local borrowing facilities. Consequently, restricting rights of access of land is a very useful way of controlling the power of MNCs in the local economy. With the exception of favoured companies, Indonesia, Thailand and the Philippines all impose restrictions on the foreign ownership of land. In Malaysia, with the exception of land in export processing zones, government approval is required before foreign investors can be granted title to the land.

4 **Banned Sectors**

   Government regulations may prohibit foreign investment in specific sectors, or impose strict limits on the size of the investment. Thailand, the Philippines and Indonesia all have sectors in which FDI is banned, although the number of sectors involved has been reduced since the 1997–98 Asian crisis.

Overall, the regulations have in all four countries created a regime within which there is aggressive promotion of export-oriented investments, at the expense of local market-oriented investments which are severely circumscribed. The restrictions on some sectors are counterbalanced by concessions to export-oriented firms, in the form of automatic investment approval rights to land ownership and tax holidays. Incentives generally take the form of either tax holidays, as in Malaysia and Thailand, and/or exemption from restrictions, import duties and trade barriers.

Impact of FDI on the Local Economies

Economic theory suggests that host economies may benefit from both trade effects and the creation of linkages between the MNC and local firms, and the effect of FDI in Malaysia, Thailand, Indonesia and the Philippines can be assessed from both of these perspectives.

The net trade effect depends upon the ratio of exports : imports, and thus can vary company to company and sector to sector. FDI in South East Asia has been very important in spearheading export-led growth, and helping the host economies to register some of the world's fastest growth rates during the 1980s. In all four countries, exports as a percentage of GDP have doubled since 1982, but the type of exports has changed as a result of the FDI. Thailand has moved from being one of the world's largest rice exporters, to a country where 80% of exports are now manufactured goods, particularly electronic products. In Malaysia, the MNC-dominated sectors such as electronics are also those which have experienced the fastest export growth.

The positive effects of the rapid export growth is, however, offset by the heavy dependence of the MNCs on imported components. In some sectors, imports represent up to 90 per cent of the value of the exports. For example, in Malaysia 95 per cent of the value of finished data processing exports is made up of imported parts. Similarly, though not quite as extreme, imports account for 60% of the value of electronic goods exported from Thailand. The statistics suggest that the export sectors are effectively foreign enclaves in the host countries, offering little value added and having minimal links into local businesses. The effect of such structural imbalances in the economies was, according to the OECD, one of the factors leading up to the Asian economic crisis of the late 1990s.

Apart from the trade effect of FDI, the linkages into the local economy of best countries needs to be assessed, particularly in relation to the transfer of technology. In developing nations in particular, technology transfer from FDI offers great potential to improve local research and development capabilities, and encourage sustainable development. Unfortunately, evidence to date indicates that none of the four South East Asian economies have gained much from technology transfer. Indonesia has experienced some basic transfer of skills via on the job training, and Thailand has seen the same through training of more senior staff, but the consensus view is that host countries have gained little.

The minimal impact on development can be seen to be a consequence of a number of inter-related factors:

- encouragement of foreign investment in industries requiring components that meet high technical specifications and are too complex for local production

- an emphasis on special treatment for foreign exporters, such as the creation of export processing zones, which create the equivalent of customs barriers to local suppliers

- limited capacity of local workers to assimilate foreign technology and know-how

- positive discouragement of foreign investment targeted at meeting local market needs.

CASE STUDY QUESTIONS

1 Why is the value added so low in some of the key export sectors, such as electronics?

2 What might be the effect of government regulations in requiring a minimum level of local involvement in senior management posts in host countries?

3 Why might FDI which seeks to serve local markets lead to higher levels of technology transfer than export-oriented investment?

4 If export-led growth via FDI has the effects outlined in the case study, does this mean that MNCs should be banned from investing in developing countries?

Source: Based on information contained in 'South East Asia: The Role of Foreign Direct Investment Policies in Development', S. Thomsen, *OECD Working Papers on International Investment 1999/1*.

Index